D1598417

The Suffering of God According to Martin Luther's 'Theologia Crucis'

American University Studies

Series VII
Theology and Religion
Vol. 181

PETER LANG
New York • Washington, D.C./Baltimore • San Francisco
Bern • Frankfurt am Main • Berlin • Vienna • Paris

Dennis Ngien

The Suffering of God
According to Martin Luther's
'Theologia Crucis'

Foreword by
Jürgen Moltmann

PETER LANG
New York • Washington, D.C./Baltimore • San Francisco
Bern • Frankfurt am Main • Berlin • Vienna • Paris

Library of Congress Cataloging-in-Publication Data

Ngien, Dennis.
    The suffering of God according to Martin Luther's theologia crucis / by
Dennis Ngien; foreword by Jürgen Moltmann.
        p.   cm. — (American university studies. Series VII, Theology and
religion; vol. 181)
    Includes bibliographical references and index.
    1. Luther, Martin, 1483–1546—Views on suffering of God.
    2. Suffering of God—History of doctrines—16th century. I. Title.
II. Series.
    BR333.5.S85N45   231—dc20   94-11414
    ISBN 0-8204-2582-6
    ISSN 0740-0462

Die Deutsche Bibliothek-CIP-Einheitsaufnahme

Ngien, Dennis:
The suffering of God according to Martin Luther's theologia crucis / Dennis
Ngien. - New York; Washington, D.C./Baltimore; San Francisco; Bern;
Frankfurt am Main; Berlin; Vienna; Paris: Lang.
    (American university studies: Ser. 7, Theology and religion; Vol. 181)
    ISBN 0-8204-2582-6
NE: American university studies / 07

The paper in this book meets the guidelines for permanence and durability of
the Committee on Production Guidelines for Book Longevity of the
Council on Library Resources.

© 1995 Peter Lang Publishing, Inc., New York

Printed in the United States of America.

*This book is dedicated to my Ceceilia who shares
my labour and my dream.*

Acknowledgements

This study is a slightly revised version of my doctoral dissertation accepted by the University of St. Michael's College through the Toronto School of Theology of the University of Toronto in 1993.

My initial interest in the theology of Martin Luther began in 1986 when I was a student of Dr. William E. Hordern of Lutheran Theological Seminary in Saskatoon, Saskatchewan. An increasing enthusiasm for the subject of divine passibility was spirited and fostered by reading numerous articles and books published on the subject. My concentrated interest in Luther's understanding of divine passibility was recognized by Dr. David Demson of Emmanuel College in the University of Toronto, under whose direction this study is accomplished. I am especially indebted to Dr. Demson whose continued availability, provocative interaction and constructive criticism have helped crystallize my thoughts. My deepest thanks and appreciation are due to those who help me bring this work to completion. These include Drs. Harry McSorley of St. Michael's College, Iain G. Nicol of Knox College, Harold Wells of Emmanuel College (all of Toronto School of Theology), James Nestingen of Luther Northwestern Theological Seminary in St. Paul, Minnesota, Jürgen Moltmann of the University of Tübingen in Germany and Paul Fiddes of Oxford University in England, for their faithful reading of the manuscript. An extra word of thanks must be extended to Dr. Jürgen Moltmann, an internationally renowned theologian, for his magnanimous spirit and willingness to write the Foreword for my book.

Special thanks are extended to hearty friends including Rev. Dr. Ross Ingram, the Senior Pastor of First Alliance Church at Scarborough, Ontario, whose pastoral mentorship continues to help me strike a blend of the mind and the heart; Dr. Robert Bertram, the former professor of Lutheran School of Theology at Chicago, for his insightful dialogue; Drs. Walter Freitag and Roger Nostbakken of Lutheran Theological Seminary for their unfailing encouragement; Norma Lelless who assisted me in German language; Emily and Nelson Cheng for their labour in typing the manuscript, Dina Abramson for formatting it, Cynthia So for compiling the indexes, and Dr. Bruce Gordon of the University of St. Andrews in Scotland for proofreading it. I am also indebted to generous friends who donate towards this scholarly publication; Knox College of the University of Toronto for providing me with Teaching Assistantships during the years of residence (1988-1993); Knox College Caven Library and the University of Toronto Robarts Library, both of which have provided me with maximum flexibility and freedom to utilize their resources.

Most of all, I am grateful for my caring, faithful, patient, and perceptive critic, my beloved wife, Ceceilia, without whom this study would never have been completed.

Finally, I gratefully acknowledge the Peter Lang Publishing, Inc., for granting me permission to quote from the following source: Reiner Jansen, *Studien zu Luthers Trinitätslehre* (1976).

Soli Deo Gloria!

June 15, 1994   Dennis Ngien   Toronto, Ontario, Canada

Contents

Foreword

This is an excellent study of Luther's theology of the cross, and it is more than only that. While the relevant studies of the Luther scholars Paul Althaus and Walter von Loewenich restrict themselves to Luther, Ngien sets Luther's theology of the Cross within a larger context: In Chapter III he develops Luther's Christology as the presupposition for his theology of the Cross; and in Chapter IV, Luther's soteriology as its consequence. In Chapter V he develops the corresponding teaching of the Trinity in Luther's concept of God. So clearly arranged has Luther's theology of the Cross seldom up to now been presented. The author then goes beyond Luther himself, to place him within the context of medieval-Church and also modern discussions of the essential Apathy or the Passion of God and thereby bring Luther's voice within our hearing. That, too, has until now been done only by intimation, rather than systematically and clearly taken in hand. The logic of his Christocentrism is the reason why Luther was able to free the concept of God from the categories of Greek philosophy. This "revolution in the concept of God" is not yet completed, as the new discussions concerning the passibility or impassibility of God show. The author takes us by means of this dissertation one step further. Luther accepted the Old Church's Theopaschitism, but he rejected the Patripassionism that had already in the Old Church been denied. Ngien shows that Theopaschitism was insufficient to represent the theology of the Cross as theology, but rather that we need a new theology of the Trinity. Only a trinitarian theology of the Cross is real Christian theology. For me Chapter V of this study is especially important.

This study deserves to be published. It will fructify the theological discussion and take it a step further. We need more such dissertations, which uncover new contexts and discover new territory.

Jürgen Moltmann
University of Tübingen
Tübingen, Germany

Abbreviations

WA   *Luthers Werke. Kritische Gesamtausgabe* (Schriften). (Weimar: Herman Böhlaus Nachfolger, 1883).

WA BR   *Luthers Werke. Kritische Gesamtausgabe. Briefwechsel.*

WA TR   *Luthers Werke. Kritische Gesamtausgabe. Tischreden.*

LW   *Luthers Works*. American Edition. Edited by Jaroslav Pelikan and Helmut Lehman. Philadelphia and St. Louis: Fortress Press and Concordia Publishing House, 1955-

BOW   *The Bondage of the Will*

Introduction

The Statement of Purpose

The purpose of this book is to examine the manner in which God's passibility is ontologically constitutive of God according to the logic of Luther's foundational theology, that is, the *theologia crucis*. As this study focuses on Luther's "dei-passionism,"[1] the three major inter-related themes and constituents of his *theologia crucis* will form the substances for our discussion: Christology, Soteriology and Trinity. It must be borne in mind that we are dealing with Luther who wrote in the sixteenth century, that is, at the time when the doctrine of the justification by faith had become central to the Christian faith. It will be made clear that by God's "suffering" Luther means the suffering which God undergoes by becoming a "human sinner", and dying on the cross. That is why he says that the Father does not "suffer", only the Son does. But of course the Son, too, is God. That is how Luther affirms Theopaschitism but repudiates Patripassianism as the early Church does. The basis for the assertion that God suffers is found in his soteriology, which belongs to his Christology. The cross is the self-manifestation of divine love *sub contrario*, in the suffering of the righteous One which is to be interpreted according to the *ratio vicaria*, the joyous change of place (*admirabile commercium*) between the sinner and Christ. God as God does not suffer, but God determines to suffer when He constitutes humanity in Himself, bearing our sin and mortality ontically. The greatest marvel lies in the fact that God in Christ receives that which is "alien" to Himself but "proper" to humanity—the suffering of the opposition between God and man. The reformer [Luther] explicitly asserts that God is passible after the incarnation of the Son.However for him God's eternal Son and the incarnate Son are one and the same; therefore, when this truth is pressed to its logical conclusion, as this study seeks to show, it follows that the suffering of Christ in human history is attributable to the eternal Son of God. In addition, his assertion that the immanent Trinity corresponds to the economic Trinity allows this study to take Luther a step further, by affirming ontologically that the suffering of Christ reaches beyond the temporal state of the incarnation into the eternal being of God. The reformer's use of the doctrine of *"communicatio idiomatum"* supports his understanding of God's passibility. He does not concede the suffering of God *in abstracto*, i.e., when the divinity is considered "in itself"; he concedes no more than the suffering of God *in concreto*, i.e., when the divinity is bound to the humanity in Jesus Christ. The two-nature emphasis is for Luther a response to the way in which God alters our definition of what constitutes divinity. Since God defines the Godself in the incarnate deity, God ceases to be God in a Platonic sense that denies suffering and death to the everlasting divine nature. In the Incarnation, which Luther conceives primarily in terms of its redemption, God has fully become Emmanuel and has entered the plight of human suffering. Therefore it is imperative, according to Luther, not to focus on a prior doctrine of God; but rather to cling to the "clothed God" or "revealed God", the God with whom we have to do, and in whom the passibility question is answered.

The Sources of the Study

The primary source for this study is the critical edition of Luther's works, the *Weimar Ausgabe*, most of which has been translated into English. The English translation of Luther's works will be used in the presentation of the research. References from the original language will be made where helpful. The documents covered in this study include various types of Luther's writings. Lectures, treatises, table talk, letters and sermons are included, with emphasis placed upon those materials pertaining to the suffering of God. While Luther has written much on the suffering of the Christian, this study focuses upon those writings which are directly related to the possibility of God.

The Method of the Study and Organization

The method of this book is systematic, not historical. So the dissertation does not proceed chronologically in the presentation of Luther's view of God's suffering. This systematic treatment of God's suffering will be presented in the following chapters:

Chapter One provides a survey of discussions on the suffering of God in early Church history. Rather than offering a comprehensive review of the history of the doctrine of divine impassibility, I have selected representative theological perspectives from the course of Christian history prior to the time of Martin Luther. This historical background attempts to establish the context for Luther's understanding of the suffering of God. It will be argued that the denial of divine passibility occurred because of the influence of Greek metaphysics upon the church's reading of Scripture, and that the platonic principle of divine apathy, in particular, held in its grip what many of the fathers believed may or may not be said of God.

Chapter Two seeks to understand Luther's thought in the context of his late medieval heritage. There are three major currents of thought in late medieval theology which exercised significant influences on Luther's theological development: nominalism, mysticism and Augustinianism. The survey will emphasize certain elements of theological thought against which Luther works out his theology of the cross. It will be made explicit that Luther's *theologia crucis* is the principle that knowledge of God's true identity comes only from our redeemer and more precisely His saving relationship to us in the suffering and cross of Jesus Christ. It opposes what Luther regards as the theology of the medieval church which he calls *theologia gloriae*—that approach which attempts to ascend to God by speculative, ethical or mystical means. In the cross of Christ abides God's definitive "no" to all human efforts to discern God's being and to achieve salvation apart from the incarnate and crucified Christ. Luther's *theologia crucis* is an elucidation of God's salvific ways with sinners and our participation in them by faith.

Chapter Three discusses Luther's Christology in its relation to the passibility motif. For him, the suffering of Christ as God's own suffering lies in the concrete unity of his personal identity. God can be conceived as the subject of Christ's suffering and even death, but in such a way that these assertions were to be explained according to the *communicatio idiomatum*. Luther uses the doctrine of *communicatio idiomatum* in two ways: a communication between the nature and the person and a communication between the two natures themselves. The former usage predominates in his thought. The suffering of Christ is not only predicated of the one indivisible Person of Christ but also of the divine nature. His Chalcedonian Christology and his usage of the *communicatio idiomatum* will form the contents for the discussion.

Chapter Four discusses the reformer's soteriology and divine suffering. That which reveals divine suffering is the work of Christ, which belongs to his Christology. Given that Luther's *theologia crucis* is about God's ways with us, he focused on the *pro nobis* aspect of Christ the person and therefore on the ontological aspect of Christ's person as he understood it. Christology is understood as the question of the being of Christ as it is inferred by faith from Christ's work. Even in Christology, Luther accentuates the significance of the work that Jesus does as our redeemer and saviour. Thus Luther defines God's passibility as God's "becoming sin" for us and dying. God's love is a "suffering" love because and so long as the world is in sin and under God's wrath. God indeed suffers in His divine being when He willingly assumed the form of a servant. "God is most Himself" precisely in the act of His humble obedience in His Son. In Christ's cross and resurrection, the divine "blessing" triumphs over the divine "curse"—that is for those who believe. The revealed God or clothed God fights against the hidden or naked God to conquer God's wrath "in Himself", and therefore God suffers. It is only in Christ where God is revealed, that the antinomy between the divine impassible/naked God and the divine passible/clothed God occurs, and is resolved.

Chapter Five deals with the doctrine of the Trinity. It begins with an account of the doctrine of the Trinity, which Luther had received from the church, with a view to establish a conceptual framework for his understanding of the suffering of God. Just as Luther develops his Christology in view of the doctrine of justification by faith, he also develops his doctrine of the Trinity with the work of the triune God upon us. The distinctiveness of the Father from the Son, according to Luther, allows the Son to suffer and die under the Father's judgement and abandonment. Yet the shared deity of the three persons means no less than God suffers and dies for us in the Son, and no less than God lives in us by His Spirit. That is how Luther affirms Theopaschitism but rejects Patripassianism. The work of the Spirit is affirmed in that it comforts and communicates to us God's "suffering" love, which in Christ's cross and resurrection, has conquered God's "wrath". In this action and in its communication to us by the Spirit, the divine "blessing" has triumphed over the divine "curse". Since Luther's *theologia crucis* is about God's saving relation to us, not about how God might be for Himself in His interior life, the economic Trinity is the conceptual framework from which the reformer begins to conceive of God's suffering in and through the incarnate and crucified Christ. Though Luther distinguishes with the tradition the immanent Trinity from the economic Trinity, because of his insistence on the unity of God, the suffering of christ touches the immanent Trinity as well as the economic Trinity.

Chapter One

Divine Suffering In Early Church History

Rather than offer a systematic review of the history of the doctrine of divine impassibility, chapter one will give brief attention to the historical background for the passibility-impassibility debate. I will select a few examples of theological perspectives in the course of Christian history prior to the time of Martin Luther.[1]

The word "impassibility" means incapable of experiencing pain or emotion; the word "passibility" means capable of experiencing pain or suffering. Christianity's embrace of impassibility stemmed from two Greek metaphysical concepts: apathy *(apatheia)* and sufficiency *(Autarkeia)*.[2] Russell explains:

Apathy means insensibility to passion or feeling. For Aristotle, immateriality and pure reason *(nous)* characterize God's nature; moreover, an immaterial God of pure reason experiences neither passion nor feeling. God's experiencing passion would imply being acted upon from without. For these reasons, Aristotle attributes apathy to God's nature. So divine apathy undergirds the Christian rejection of external passibility within God's nature.[3]

Divine sufficiency also supports the Greek conviction that no external being affects or moves God. Aristotle's self-sufficient God lacks nothing and desires nothing. Satisfying conditions of insufficiency requires that some being affect or move the individual who experiences deficiency. But a completely actual God like Aristotle's has no potential for change. Consequently, Aristotle exempts his self-sufficient God from movement, and he thus describes God's nature as immutable.[4]

Hence there existed an antinomy, as Moltmann points out, between the Greek idea of God's *apatheia* and Christ's *pathos* on the cross: "The platonic axiom of the essential *apatheia* of God sets up an intellectual barrier against the recognition of the suffering of Christ, for a God who is subject to suffering like all other beings cannot be God."[5]

It was mainly the influence of Greek metaphysics that prompted the early Christians to adopt the position of divine impassibility.[6] Greek philosophers such as Plato, Aristotle, Parmenides and the Stoics developed an understanding of God as the Absolute monad, self-sufficient, immutable, impassible and static.[7] These philosophical categories, which continue through the patristic and medieval periods, have been adopted by Christian theologians to describe God, usually leading to a distortion of God's nature as biblically revealed. More specifically, the idea of divine impassibility, which held its grip on what may or may not be said of the Christian God, was, as Bauckham notes,

> a Greek philosophical inheritance in early Christian theology. The great hellenistic Jewish theologian Philo had already prepared the way for this by making *apatheia* a prominent figure of his understanding of the God of Israel, and virtually all the Christian Fathers took it for granted, viewing with suspicion any theological tendency which might threaten the essential impassibility of the divine nature.[8]

I shall survey historically the theopaschite attempt to reconcile the suffering of the passible Son with the impassible nature of God.

Although early theologians such as Ignatius and Irenaeus occasionally link Christ's passion with God's passion, they deny suffering as a legitimate divine attribute.[9] They subscribe to the paradoxical assertion that God could not suffer except in Christ. God is impassible, yet in Christ He suffers. Commenting on Christ in his *Letter to the Romans* (6:3), Ignatius says, "Let me imitate the Passion of my God"; but in his *Letter to Polycarp* (3:2), he depicts God as "above time, the Timeless, the Unseen, the One who became visible for our sakes, who was beyond touch and passion, yet for our sakes became subject to suffering, and endured everything for us."[10] Furthermore in his *Letter to the Ephesians* (7:2), he says: "There is only one physician—of flesh yet spiritual, born yet unbegotten, God incarnate, genuine life in the midst of death, sprung from Mary as well as God, first subject to suffering then beyond it—Jesus Christ our Lord."[11]   The same is true with Irenaeus, who describes Christ as impassible yet capable of suffering in the incarnate state. In his *Against Heresies III, 16.6.*, he writes of Christ who "took up man into Himself, the invisible becoming visible, the incomprehensible being made comprehensible, the impassible becoming capable of suffering, and the Word being made man, thus summing up all things in Himself."[12] For both thinkers, having adhered to the Greek philosophical idea that emotions are not fitting for deity, suffering finds no eternal grounding in the divine nature. No attempt is made to explain the paradox created by the idea of divine impassibility, this idea which occurs nowhere in the New Testament but is introduced into the doctrine of the Incarnation.[13]

An attempt to break through the Greek axiom of divine impassibility was made by the Patripassianism of the second century, with Noetus and Praxeas as its key representatives.[14] Patripassianism erred in its failure to maintain a distinction between the Father and the Son. Noetus believed that "Christ was the Father in person (who) had been born and had suffered and died."[15] Tertullian wrote of Praxeas who believed that "the Father Himself descended into the virgin, that He likewise was born of her, and He Himself suffered, even that He Himself in Jesus Christ."[16] As such, God, the Father, was viewed as the subject of the earthly sufferings of Jesus.[17]

Tertullian's conflict with Patripassian Monarchianism in the third century helped crystallize the impassibility position. Praxeas, for one, taught that the divine person in Christ was the Father, and that while the flesh suffered, the Father suffered in sympathy (*compassio*) with the suffering of the flesh. Tertullian, by contrast, refused to grant any distinction between suffering (*passio*) and sympathy (*compassio*), thereby accusing Praxeas of "crucifying the Father" and "putting the Paraclete to flight."[18] Tertullian argued, "The Father did not suffer with the Son. ... If the Father is impassible, then he cannot suffer with another; if He can suffer with another, then He is possible. ... But the Father is as unable to suffer with another as the Son is unable to suffer in virtue of His divinity."[19] Tertullian, then was the first to assert the impassibility of the divine nature in Christ, accentuating "the stoic exaltation" of *apatheia*.[20]

The Alexandrian theologians such as Clement and Origen were more explicit in their denial of the possibility of the divine in Christ. Clement says that Christ was "entirely incapable of suffering and inaccessible to any emotion, whether of pleasure or pain."[21] Origen, in an early stage, explicitly affirmed divine suffering in his homily on Ezekiel 6:6. The savior, Origen says, "descended to earth in pity for the human race, He suffered our sufferings before He suffered the cross and thought it right to take upon Him our flesh. For if He had not suffered, He would not have come to take part in human life. First did He suffer, then He descended and was seen. What is that passion which He suffered for us? Love is passion."[22] This idea, however, did not play much part in Origen's developed theology. In his homily on Numbers 23.2, he resorted to the use of allegorical exegesis to dismiss divine passibility. Origen's theology of the divine *apatheia* is obvious in the following passage:

> All those passages in scripture in which God is said to lament, rejoice, hate or be happy are written figuratively and in a human way. It is entirely foreign to the divine nature to have passions or the feelings of mutability, since it endures in unchanged and uninterrupted happiness.[23]

According to Mozley, Gregory of Thaumaturgus, one of the Alexandrian theologians, composed the only treatise on divine impassibility before the nineteenth century.[24] The basic argument of Gregory was, as McWilliams puts it, "God cannot experience a conflict between his will and his nature because of the unity of his character."[25] Hallman further clarifies that "only in us can nature and will be contrary. God's will is always joined to God's essence, even if God submits to suffering when God is by nature impassible."[26]

The impassibility doctrine conquered, and was considered as

axiomatic in the early Christian history. In the Arian controversy of the fourth century, for instance, both Arius and Athanasius asserted that it is the human in Christ which suffers. Athanasius retains the Greek idea of divine impassibility: "In nature the Word Himself is impassible, and yet because of the flesh which He put on, these (i.e. all the wants and sufferings which belong to the flesh), are ascribed to Him, since they are proper to the flesh, and the body itself is proper to the Saviour."[27] The paradox of God is discernible in Athanasius' assertion of the *communicatio idiomatum* through which things pertain to the flesh are ascribed to the divine: the impassible One suffers in Christ.[28]   The impassible Logos assumed the passible humanity in order to redeem it. God became human so that humans may partake of God: "Because the impassible Word was in the passible body of Jesus, it destroyed the body's weaknesses in order to do away with them in us and to 'invest us with what was his,' that is, immortality."[29]   Here Athanasius was in full accord with the Alexandrine claim that "What Christ did not assume, he could not redeem." Athanasius wrote: "He took the flesh and became man and in that flesh He suffers for us." He further wrote that "in that flesh,"

> He carries our infirmities, and He Himself bears our sins that it might be shown that He has become man for us. ... And henceforth men no longer remain sinners and dead according to their proper affections, but having risen according to the Word's power, they abide ever immortal and incorruptible.[30]

Like Athanasius, Gregory of Nazianzus accentuated the substantial unity of the divine Logos and fleshly body in Christ. Gregory, even though constrained by Alexandrian Christology to ascribe the sufferings of Jesus to the Logos, can do so only by a paradox that "by the sufferings of Him who could not suffer, we were taken up and saved."[31] Gregory further elaborated on the redemptive suffering of Jesus Christ:

> ... God, who for us was made man and became poor, to raise our flesh... that we might all be made one in Christ... that we might ... bear in ourselves the stamp of God, by whom and for whom we were made...[32]

Gregory's antithesis between "passible in His flesh, (and) impassible in His Godhead" is a result of the union of the two natures in one Person.   This antithesis left the relation between the divine and human natures in Jesus Christ unattended, eventually leading to the Christological debate between Nestorius and Cyril.   This debate subsequently was "settled" by Leo's Tome and the Chalcedonian formula (A.D. 451), and it ultimately ended with the Monophysite and Theopaschite expressions of the fifth and sixth centuries.[33]

Nestorius, unlike Gregory of Nazianzus' emphasis on Mary as the *Theotokos* (God-bearer), insisted upon Mary the mother of Jesus as *Christotokos* (Christ-bearer).[34] Nestorius' argument is not that Mary only bore the human nature, but that she bore the one person of Jesus Christ who is constituted by two natures and two *hypostases*. He rejected *Theotokos* because this title tended to an understanding of God who experiences suffering in the suffering of Jesus Christ. Nestorius' strength lay in his emphasis on the full humanity of Jesus Christ, accentuating the Antiochene tradition. His weakness lay in his disdain for the "hypostatic union", the concept which he felt eliminated the distinctiveness of the two natures.   Thus he preferred the term "conjunction" to the term "union."[35] The result was that Nestorius could not conceive of the divine nature being involved in the suffering of Jesus of Nazareth.[36] As such the two natures of Christ cannot be regarded as an ontological union but merely a moral union,[37] and thus he was condemned as a heretic at the Council of Ephesus (A.D. 431).

On the other hand, Cyril of Alexandria repudiated Nestorius' use of *Christotokos*, which conceived the indwelling of the Logos as a mere accident.[38] In company with Nazianzus, Cyril affirmed the title for Mary as *Theotokos*, insisting that the two natures be substantially united in the person of Christ. Cyril asserted, "God the Logos did not come into a man, but He 'truly' became man, while remaining God."[39] Cyril affirmed in his *The Epistle of Cyril to Nestorius with the XII Anathematisms* that the differences between the two natures of Christ are not abolished by the union, yet in that union they constitute a single *hypostasis*. Cyril wrote: "Confessing

the Word to be made one with the flesh according to the substance... we do not divide the God from the man, nor separate Him
into parts... but we know only one Christ."[40] Though Cyril was
able to maintain the substantial union of the two distinct natures,
he, like Nazianzus, failed to understand the relation of the two
natures in the one being of Christ. Both Nestorius and Cyril affirm
the impassible nature of God and the passible nature of the flesh.[41]
In Cyril's response to Nestorius' "anathema," he asserted:

> ...although according to His own nature Jesus was not subject to suffer-
> ing, yet He suffered for us in the flesh. ..., and although impassible, in
> His crucified body He made His own the sufferings of His own flesh;
> and by the grace of God He tasted death for all.[42]

Like Cyril, Leo affirmed the Word of God who suffered in the flesh
but refused to include suffering in the impassible God. Leo wrote:

> Thus the properties of each nature and substance were preserved entire-
> ly, and came together to form one person. Humility was assumed by
> majesty, weakness by strength, mortality by eternity; and to pay the debt
> that we had incurred, an inviolable nature was united to a nature that
> can suffer. ... The man Jesus Christ ... was able to die in respect of the
> one, unable to die in respect of the other.[43]

Nevertheless the relationship of the divine nature to the human
nature in the one person of Jesus Christ remained an open question, even after Chalcedon.

The Monophysites and the Theopaschites emerged after
Chalcedon. The Monophysites rejected the Chalcedonian emphasis on two distinct natures, fearing that it tended toward the moral
union of Nestorianism.[44] They instead argued forcefully that Jesus
had only one nature (*physis*) after the Incarnation: "His humanity
was absorbed into the divine like a drop of vinegar into the
ocean."[45] The outcome of such an assertion was the affirmation of
divine passibility, and hence the Theopaschite movement was
born out of the Monophysite emphasis on the one person of Jesus
Christ. Here the Monophysite position led to controversy over the
dogma of the Trinity.[46] The Theopaschites provided the

Monophysites with their distinctive formula: *"unus de trinitate carne passus est."*[47]   McGuckin explains:

> Even after the mystery of the Incarnation the Trinity continues to abide because the same God the Word, even with His own flesh, is one of the Trinity.   And this is not because His flesh is of the substance of the Trinity but because it is the flesh of God the Word who is one of the Trinity.[48]

In this formula: "One of the Trinity suffered in the flesh," Leontius clearly draws a distinction between *hypostasis* and *nature*.   He holds that while God the Word suffers in His human nature, He remains impassible in His divine nature.   From the time of the Incarnation, the human nature becomes essentially Christ's.   The flesh of Christ is the flesh of the Logos, the Son of God.   His flesh is life-giving because it is the very own flesh of the Word that gives life to all things.   All that is Christ's belong essentially to the Logos.   His crucifixion is the death of the Logos in the flesh.   Because the Word and the flesh are constituted as one *hypostasis* or particular reality, the Word suffers hypostatically.   In his twelfth anathema against Nestorius, Cyril wrote:

> If anyone does not confess that the Word of God suffered in the flesh, and was crucified in the flesh, and tasted death in the flesh, and became first-born from the dead, and so as God is life and the one who makes alive, let him be anathema.[49]

Divine passibility was explicitly rejected during the Theopaschite controversy of the sixth century.   The repudiation of the Theopaschite position, as Pelikan notes, occurred precisely because the impassibility of God was a basic presupposition of all Christological doctrine.[50]

The impassibility tradition had been upheld by Hilary of Poitiers, Augustine and later by the scholastic theologians, none of whom were able to break away from the language and conception of immutability derived from philosophical and Christian traditions.   Hilary argues for the unchangeability and impassibility of the Logos: "For (Christ) was able to suffer, and yet the Word was not passible. Passibility denotes a nature that is weak; but suffering in itself is the endurance of pains inflicted, and since the Godhead is immutable and yet the Word was made flesh, such pains found in Him a material which they could affect though the person of the Word had no infirmity or passibility. And so when he suffered his nature remained immutable, because like his Father, his person is of an impassible essence."[51] Augustine saw *passio* as "a commotion of the mind contrary to reason" and therefore unfit for God.[52] In Augustine's thought, anthropopathic language was incorporated into the Bible so as to accommodate to the human language and understanding. For instance, when the Bible speaks of divine emotions, Augustine in summary fashion explains them by placing them not in God's nature but in our perception:

> God's repentance is not because of error; his anger has no ardor of a perturbed mind; his mercy does not have the compassionate misery suggested by the Latin term; the jealousy of God has no spite of mind. But the repentance of God refers to things ruled by his power which change expectedly for us; the anger of God is the punishment of sin; the mercy of God is providence, which does not allow those which it has subdued to love with impunity what it prohibits.[53]

Augustine's influence was so strong that he provided the Western Christianity with the framework within which the discussion of the question of divine immutability and impassibility is held. Ever since Augustine, the paradox of a loving and an impassible God abided. Anselm, for one, in order to preserve the Aristotelian idea of divine impassivity, had to deny any real feelings of love and compassion in God Himself, maintaining that although we experienced God as compassionate, there was really no compassion in God Himself.[54] Anselm asked:

> But how art thou compassionate, and at the same time passionless? For if thou art passionless, thou dost not feel sympathy; and if thou dost not feel sympathy, thy heart is not wretched from sympathy with the wretched; but this it is to be compassionate. But if thou art not compassionate, whence cometh so great consolation to the wretched?[55]

Anselm's solution to the paradox of a compassionate and an impassible God is to assert that

> ... thou art compassionate in terms of our experience, but not compassionate in terms of thy being.

> ... Truly, thou art so in terms of our experience, but thou art not so in terms of thine own. For when thou beholdest us in our wretchedness, we experience the feeling of compassion, but thou dost not experience the feeling. Therefore, thou art both compassionate, because thou dost save the wretched, and spare those who sin against thee; and not compassionate, because thou art affected by no sympathy for wretchedness.[56]

Similarly, Thomas Aquinas upheld the impassibility tradition. Mozley writes of Aquinas: "The notion of a *Deus passibilis* is incompatible with the definition of a primary being who must be 'pure action without admixture of any potentiality, because potentiality itself is later action. Now everything which in any way is changed is in some way in a state of potentiality, whence it is obvious that God cannot in any way be changed'."[57] God is *actus purus*, and thus "(t)he passive *potentia* is wholly absent from Him, for *passio* is to be attributed to something only in respect of its deficiencies and imperfections," and cannot exist in God.[58] Aquinas baptizes impassibility into Christian theology by appealing to how Aristotle understands passion and God's nature.[59] John Russell writes:

> As *Actus purus*, however, God's nature involves no potentiality and hence, no change. But passibility entails change. Therefore Thomas, like Aristotle, ascribes impassibility to his immutable God. He underscores that properties like deficiency, being acted upon from without, and imperfection characterize the nature of passive beings (cf. *Summa Theologica* 1.25.1). Contrastingly, God's acting upon other beings pertains to the *actus purus* nature of God. Accordingly, the idea of *Deus passibilis* contradicts Thomas' idea of a self-sufficient, purely actual, and unchanging God.[60]

Theologians of the Reformation, except in the case of Luther, the Socinians and of certain elements among some Anabaptists, did not bring about any breach with the ancient and medieval theologies in respect to the impassibility issue.[61] The reformer John Calvin, for one, obviously assumed the impassibility of God, for he said: "Surely God does not have blood, does not suffer, cannot be touched with hands."[62] "By a very customary figure of speech," Mozley writes of Calvin, "(God) assumes and applies to Himself human passions."[63] The only reformer, who was receptive to the doctrine of *deus passibilis*, according to Mozley, was Martin Luther.[64] For Mozley, the communication of properties in Luther's exposition occurs not between the nature and the person but between the two natures. "The distinction which Cyril in his *Epistola Dogmatica* draws between the proper nature of the Word and the body which the Word had made His own vanishes in Luther's exposition."[65] Luther's doctrine of *communicatio idiomatum* provided the most complete reciprocity between the divine and human natures and the mutual sharing of attributes.[66] If Christ suffered, God also suffered. It will be seen that for Luther the communication occurs not only from the human nature to the person but also in between the natures themselves. And so the suffering of Christ is predicated both of the Person of Christ and the divine nature. God suffered and died by virtue of hypostatic union *via* the *communicatio idiomatum*. More especially, Luther was highly critical of the understanding that the death of the Crucified One was treated as an event which affected only the "true man" but not "the true God." Simply put, Luther did not define the person of Christ by a prior doctrine of God, namely, the Greek idea of divine *apatheia*. The suffering of Jesus as God's own suffering, for Luther, lies in the unity of the personal identity—Jesus, the God-man *in toto*.[67]

To conclude this chapter, I have provided a survey of theopaschite expressions in early church history in order to furnish the historical and theological context for the present task.[68] Chapter two will analyze Luther's *theologia crucis*, which is for him a theology of revelation centered on the incarnate and crucified Christ, not on any *a priori* doctrine of God.

Chapter Two

Luther's *Theologia Crucis:*
Historical Background and Constitutive Principles

Historical Background: Late Medieval Heritage

Before proceeding to enquire about Luther's *theologia crucis,* it is important to indicate his theological background. After Scripture, the main theological influences upon Luther were nominalism, mysticism and Augustinianism. There are many antecedents and theological themes which Luther took up and reworked in new ways in his own unique theology of the cross. In other words, his *theologia crucis* is not a theology developed in isolation. Lortz estimates that "Martin Luther expressed very few views to which we do not find parallels in earlier theologians and reformers. None the less Luther is something new—an original phenomenon of creative quality and power."[1] Pauck explains:

> Just as he (Luther) developed his own exegetical method by way of a critical and a creative dependence upon the Biblical interpreters of former ages and of his own time, so he formed his theological understanding of the Christian gospel by engaging in a searching conversation with other theologians, old and new.

> His lectures on Romans clearly show that his theological outlook was determined, first of all, by the Bible, then by Augustine, and thereafter by the mystics, particularly Bernard of Clairvaux and Tauler but also by Dionysius the Aeropagite, and then by the Scholastics from Peter Lombard and Duns Scotus to the nominalists, especially Ockham, Pierre d' Ailly, and Gabriel Biel. Moreover, he proves himself to be under the theological influence of the major exegetes on whom he relied—from

Ambrose, Jerome and Augustine down to Faber, Reuchlin and Erasmus.[2]

Given the nature of this study, the review will be limited to a few theologians and certain elements of their theological thought against which Luther worked out his theology of the cross.

Nominalism

Although it is hard to delineate clearly the various branches of scholasticism, says Lage, two major theological traditions may be discerned: the "realist" (*reales*) tradition, or *via antiqua*, which included Bonaventure, Aquinas and John Duns Scotus and the *via moderna* "nominalist" (*nominales, termistae*) tradition rooted in the thought of William of Ockham.[3] Both *viae* share many of their basic theological presuppositions. Following Thomas Aquinas, they conceive of grace as "a certain supernatural thing in man coming into existence from God."[4] They agree that grace was conferred by God as a reward for the acts performed—acts which were deemed by God to be *actus meritorius*, deserving of a reward. Having received *infusio gratiae*, the believer is disposed toward the performance of meritorious acts. The believer, in co-operation with God's grace, performs works for which more grace and merit are bestowed as deserving of a reward. "Central to the process of co-operating with grace in order to receive a further infusion of grace and attain progressive righteousness was the performance of works deemed meritorious by God."[5]

While both *viae* accept these concepts—*cooperari*, the *actum meritorium*, the *infusio gratiae* and *habitus*, they differ markedly in their account of the epistemological requirement, that which is required for good works. The *via antiqua*, represented by the Thomistic tradition in this aspect, holds that the good is located in the natural law (*lex naturalis*). Because natural law is established by the one universal and eternal God, the good must therefore possess a universal and eternal character. This *a priori* nature of the good as universal is readily grasped by all rational creatures.[6] On the other hand, William of Ockham denies the idea of the good as universal.

He rejects all universals as mental constructs and metaphysical speculation. For Ockham, God and the good are not to be trapped in universals. The good is whatever God ordains. God has absolute power (*potentia Dei absoluta*), according to which God is free to change the good. If God is free and has the power to change the nature of the good, it follows that humanity as well has the freedom to conform to the changing will of God.[7] Without this freedom of the will, the concepts of *cooperari* and *actus meritorius*, which are so intrinsic to the scholastic methodology, would be put in jeopardy.

Thomas Aquinas and Duns Scotus develop an understanding of the nature of the self as a participant in the natural law as universal reality. Humanity, though corrupted as the image of God, still possess an inherent nature which is not eradicated by the Fall. Humanity possesses an innate understanding of the good which has its root in what is referred to as the *synteresis*: "The *synteresis* is regarded as an autonomously functioning faculty given to humanity in creation which provides the self with both an inborn ability and an inherent disposition toward performing good works."[8] Aquinas and Scotus identify the *synteresis* with the cognitive and intellective functioning of reason or mind, which is constitutive of "a rational soul."[9] As Aquinas states, "the *synteresis* is ... the law of our mind ..., a habit containing the precepts of the natural law, which are the first principles of human actions."[10] The *synteresis* informs the reason and helps to determine human actions— actions which are conformed to the good promulgated by God. The sense of the good is imprinted into the mind by God so as to be known "naturally."[11] The *synteresis rationis*, as it is characteristically understood by the *via antiqua*, not only provides the self with an inherent understanding of the good and God, but also provides the self with an inborn disposition toward doing the good and obeying the moral precepts by means of *rationis*. Ockham, however, rejects the understanding of *synteresis* as a "faculty of mind" with its "fixed disposition" toward the good because such an understanding, according to Ockham, poses a doctrinal threat to a proper understanding of free will.[12] Whereas in Aquinas and Scotus, the *ratio* is an innate connection between the self and God, in Ockham, reason is reduced to the status of an epistemological instrument. Reason is limited and is reliable only in the realm of nature.[13] Instead of seeing reason as an innate contact between the self and God, Ockham argues that humanity's relationship to God is based on voluntarily conforming our will to the will of the Divine.[14] For Ockham, the human condition is not marked by a lack of knowledge of the good, but the failure of the will to perform the good. What is deficient in humanity is the "affective conformity" of human will to the will of God.[15] That which lies at the centre of the moral life is not reason (*ratio*) but the will (*voluntas*). While both *viae* agree on justification by means of meritorious deeds performed in cooperation with *infusio gratiae*, they disagree concerning the prior need of grace for the performance of good works. The *via antiqua* sees justification by God as a necessary prerequisite for the performance of meritorious deeds (*meritum de condigno*). On the other hand the *via moderna*, with its focus on free will, sees an infusion of grace as a reward fitting to good deeds volitionally initiated by the faithful (*meritum de congruo*), even without the aid of grace.

Ockham, like other Scholastics, perceives God as having two differing modes of power—*potentia absoluta* and *potentia ordinata*.[16] The sense of *de potentia absoluta* is that God could do anything which does not violate the law of contradiction. It is that mode of power that God ultimately has and is the source of all theological truth. The *potentia ordinata*, on the other hand, is that mode of power which God chooses to use, thereby allowing Himself to be limited by a free and uncoerced decision of God. For instance, God by His absolute power could have become incarnate in a dog. But by His ordained power, God chose to become incarnate in a man, Jesus Christ. It is the ordained power which William of Ockham says is guided by necessity. McGrath explains:

> The significance of the distinction between the two powers of God lies in the conception of necessity involved: how can God be said to act reliably, without simultaneously asserting that he acts of necessity? The dialectic between the two powers of God allowed the reliability of God's action to be upheld, without implying that God acts of necessity. God is understood to have imposed upon himself, by a free and uncoerced

primordial decision, a certain self-limitation, in that he is faithful to the
order which he himself has established. In that God is faithful to this
ordained order, he may be said to be reliable; in that this order is itself
the contingent consequence of a free decision of God, God cannot be
said to act of absolute necessity, but merely by a conditional necessity
(*necessitas coactionis or necessitas consequentiae*).[17]

It was the *potentia absoluta* formulated by Ockham which gave rise
to the controversy over the doctrine of justification in the late
medieval period. The issue at stake was whether there was a prior
need for the infused *habitus* of created grace in men if men were to
perform a meritorious act. Was infused grace even a necessary
pre-requisite for justification? The Ockhamists denied *infusio gratiae* as the formal cause of justification on the basis of God's
absolute power. Without the sacramental infusion of grace no one
can earn a real merit (*meritum de condigno*). Rather God, in His
ordained power, deems the action of the free will as meritorious,
and thereby rewards the action of human merit. Ockham claims
that a gracious God, if He so wills it in *potentia ordinata*, infuses
grace as a fitting reward (*meritum de congruo*) to the one who "does
what is in him" or "does the best he could do" (*facere quod in se est*).
Oberman identifies in the nominalists two distinct versions of the
formula "*facere quod in se est*": (i) *a facere quod in se est*, when it
relates to human reason, means that a person who thinks the best
can receive divine revelation as a fitting reward; (ii) *a facere quod in
se est*, when it relates to human will, means that a person who does
the best can prepare for a reception of divine grace as a fitting
reward.[18] Both versions of the formula teach that it is possible to
do *meritorious* works apart from the sacramental infusion of divine
grace. Consequently the free will is elevated as the dominant
agent of meritorious deeds, thereby rendering created grace superfluous for the doing of meritorious deeds. Grace is given to the
one who does meritorious deeds, and as one co-operates with
grace one is given justification. Some Nominalists were condemned by the Church in the 14th century.

The *via moderna*, nominalist thought, has a prime representative in Ockham but it is mediated to Luther through the writings
of Gabriel Biel.[19] Biel clearly supported the Ockhamist belief in a

free will. As Biel writes, "A meritorious act is an act freely chosen
by the will and accepted (by God) for the granting of a reward."[20]
"God does not deny grace to one who does his best"; He infallibly
confers grace upon one who chooses to do his best (*Deus infalli-
biliter gratiam dat*).[21] God helps the one who volitionally does his
best to "love God above all else" (*Diligere Deum super omnia*),
despite the mutable nature of the good. Like Ockham, Biel, within the framework of God's absolute power, denies infused grace as
necessary for justification. No one can earn *meritum de condigno* (a
real merit) apart from the sacramental infusion of grace. However,
by "doing one's very best" (*facere quod in se est*) or literally by
"doing what is in oneself," according to Biel, it is possible to earn
meritum de congruo (a half credit) as a fitting reward.[22] God, by His
ordained power, has committed Himself to infuse grace on everyone who does the best one can. Grace is given to the one who performs meritorious deeds, and as one co-operates with grace one is
given justification. This means the sinner has some claim upon
God, on the basis of his natural abilities and good works.

While the locus of morality for Thomists and the *via antiqua* is
the cognitive and intellective function of the *synteresis rationis*, for
Ockhamists, the emphasis is put on the *voluntas*. Biel, on the other
hand, embraced both the *synteresis rationis* of the *via antiqua* and
the *synteresis voluntatis* of the *via moderna*, giving the *synteresis* a
cognitive content and a volitional force. Knowing the good is just
as necessary as willing that the good be done. For Biel, the *synteresis* is not to be understood as "a faculty of the mind" with its
"fixed disposition" which by its very nature compels the self to
perform meritorious deeds. Rather it is understood as an "inextinguishable spark" with a "general inclination" which by its very
nature "directs (the self) in general toward a just and right activity."[23] Contrary to the *via antiqua* that locates *synteresis* in the rational soul, Biel locates *synteresis rationis* and *voluntatis* in the conscience. The conscience provides the self with an advisory capacity, making the self aware of the will of God or the good. The *synteresis* informs the conscience and in turn directs or guides the self
"in general" towards good acts which culminate in a conformity of
reason and will with God.[24] For Biel, as it is for the *via antiqua*, the

synteresis is an anthropological ground for ethical activity—activity which is divinely deemed as meritorious and therefore deserving of a fitting reward. The Christian life consists of the continuous habit of performing good works until enough merit is obtained so that a person receives grace as a first reward and salvation as the final reward for works done in grace. The soteriological implications of Biel's understanding of the *synteresis, cooperari, infusio gratiae* and *habitus* are inextricably bound with Biel's Christology which sees Christ more as *exemplum* than *sacramentum*. Although Biel acknowledges the efficacy of Christ's suffering and sacrifice, Christ's work is incomplete; it is to be completed by humanity's *obedientia activa* in imitation of divine will revealed in the example of Christ. "If we do not add our merits to those of Christ," affirms Biel, "the merits of Christ will not only be insufficient but non-existent."[25]

As noted earlier, Oberman identifies in the nominalist theologians two distinct versions of the formula *"facere quod in se est."* In Oberman's observation, Luther in his early work, the *Commentary on Sentences* (1509 -1510), breaks with the first version—reason as preparatory for a reception of divine revelation as a fitting reward, but appears to hold the second version till 1516—doing one's best as preparatory for a reception of divine grace as a fitting reward. Thus Oberman discerns some semi-Pelagian elements carried over from nominalism in the young Luther.[26] As late as 1515, especially in his early lectures on Psalms and sermons, Luther was still subscribing to the necessity of doing one's best as a predisposition to the reception of divine grace. "Hence, just as the law was a figure and preparation of the people for receiving Christ, so our doing what is in us (*Factio quantum in nobis est*) disposes us to grace."[27] Like Biel, Luther believed that human nature possesses a "residue of former goods"[28] which is inextinguishable. At the beginning of the *Lectures on Romans*, Luther was somewhat inclined toward *synteresis*. This is evident in his remarks on Romans 1:20, where Luther comments: "the theological *synteresis*, is in every man and is incapable of being obscured."[29] In his *scholia* to Psalm 41, Luther writes that the "*synteresis* and desire for the good is inextinguishable in man."[30] The *synteresis*, for Luther, as

for Biel, is "a preservation, a remainder or left-over portion of our
nature in the corruption and faultiness of perdition. It is like a tinder, a seed, and the material of our future revival and the restora-
tion of our nature."[31] It was not until late 1516 (or early 1517) that
Luther broke with the nominalist concepts of merit and grace, and
came to recognize in his famous *Disputatio Contra Scholasticam
Theologiam* (1517) that "*Ex parte autem hominis nihi nisi indispositio,
immo rebellio gratiae gratiam praecedit.*"[32] "This is said in opposition
to Scotus and Gabriel," thereby rejecting the efficacy of the *synteresis*
as providing a point of contact between God and humanity.[33]
His break with the nominalists came about through his awareness
of Augustine's anti-Pelagian thesis, which became available to
Luther in the dispute between Gabriel Biel and Gregory of Rimini
(Augustinian).[34] Luther found in favor of Rimini, referring to him
as "the only scholastic clean on the Pelagian issue."[35] "Gabriel Biel
says everything well," maintains Luther, "except when he talks
about grace, charity, hope, faith, the virtues about which he
Pelagianizes as much as his Scotus."[36] Luther charged Biel for not
taking the radical nature of sin seriously. The theological *synteresis*,
held by Luther in the beginning of his *Lectures on Romans*, is
rejected by him: "this concupiscence (original sin), is always in us,
and therefore the love of God is never in us unless it is begun by
grace."[37] Already in his writing on Romans 3:10 we find Luther's
contradistinction to scholastic anthropology and moral theory:
"We are so entirely inclined to evil that no portion which is
inclined toward good remains in us."[38] Luther believed that his
real opponent was Aristotle: "The ancient fathers ... spoke about
these things differently, according to the method of Scripture. But
the (scholastics) follow the method of Aristotle in his *Ethics*, and he
bases sinfulness and righteousness and likewise the extent of their
actualization on what a person does."[39] This, Luther believes, is
the underlying reason why sin is twisted so that "it applies to
works alone."[40] Thus for Luther, "the whole of Aristotle's *Ethics* is
the worst enemy of grace."[41] In his *Disputation against Scholastic
Theology*, of 1517, Luther rejected many of the basic premises of
Biel and of late medieval nominalism. Any theology that claims
that humanity has the natural ability to initiate or co-operate with

God in its own salvation is not entertained by Luther. Thus, in thesis 14 of the disputation he writes: "Nor is it surprising that the will can conform to erroneous and not to correct precepts." "Indeed, it is peculiar to it that it can only conform to erroneous and not to correct precepts" (thesis 15).[42] The old Scholastic principle of "like" knowing "like" as the *sine qua non* of fellowship with God was renounced by Luther.[43] Although Luther formally accepted the idea of "*synteresis*" out of an external loyalty to the church, he materially rejected it and rendered the human will impotent to achieve union with God.[44] In lieu of the nominalism's semi-Pelagian view of salvation, Luther asserted justification by grace alone through faith. This break with nominalism was a fundamental step in Luther's development of his unique *theologia crucis*. Luther wrote against Pelagianism:

> What others have learned from Scholastic theology is their own affair. As for me, I know and confess that I learned there nothing but ignorance of sin, righteousness, baptism, and of the whole Christian life. I certainly did not learn there what the power of God is, and the work of God, and what faith, hope, and love are .... Indeed, I lost Christ there, but now I found him again in Paul (namely, his Epistle of Romans).[45]

Thus in 1517, Luther wrote triumphantly: "Our theology and St. Augustine are going ahead, and reign in our University (Wittenberg), and it is God's work."[46]

Mysticism

Mysticism and nominalism in Luther's theology must not be treated as mutually exclusive. Oberman writes:

> His (Biel's) treatise on the life of the Brethren (*De Communi vita*) witnesses to the fact that his association with the movement of organized, often mystical piety is not to be understood as a break with scholastic— and in his case primarily nominalism—training, but rather in conjunction with his life as a theologian and a pastor.[47]

Luther linked medieval mysticism's idea of justification to the

scholastic idea of *facere quod in se est*.[48] Both scholasticism and
mysticism, as Saarnivaara argues, held that there was an ineradi-
cable and uncorrupted divine kernel in the human being.[49]
Tauler's idea of the *homo deificatio* was closely connected with the
scholastic idea of *facere quod in se est*. His idea of *Seelengrund*
("ground of the soul") corresponded to the scholastic idea of *synteresis*, *Seelengrund* being the anthropological basis of mystical
union with God.[50] The ground of the soul, for Tauler, was what
Steven Ozment calls a natural "covenant" between God and the
human, a point of contact between the uncreated and the created.[51]
The primary reason Luther honored the mystics was that his
understanding in his early years found a kindred spirit in theirs in
the stress on humility, resignation of self (*gelossenheit*) and conformity to Christ's humiliation and suffering.[52] However as Luther
came to realize that the plight of the human *coram deo* was that one
possessed nothing intrinsically which enabled one to stand before
God so as to deserve salvation, he rejected a mystical "ground of
the soul": "Mystical rapture is not the passageway to God."[53] This
does not mean, however, that Luther was unaffected by mysticism.
With Tauler, Luther wrote against the mystical attempts to penetrate into God's inner darkness outside the vision of Christ's suffering: "We have access to the eternal incomprehensible God only
through the incarnated, crucified one."[54] Union with God, for
Luther, as for Tauler, cannot be achieved independent of Christ.
Although both Tauler and Luther hold that Christ is the ladder to
the Father, unlike Tauler, Luther rejects our capability of climbing
up the ladder to heaven. For Luther the ladder to heaven is one
Christ descended in order to lead a sinful humanity to the Father.
This stance is supported by Luther's commentary on Galatians
4:19:

> "Until Christ be formed in you." Note Paul's careful choice of words ...
> as he ascribes more to the grace of God than to his own works .... Neither
> did he say, "until you are formed in Christ." No, his words are "until
> Christ be formed in you," because the Christian's life is not his own; it is
> Christ's, who lives in him. ...[55]

Conformitas Christi is for Luther the process of "putting on the
image of Christ"; it is not the result of human preparatory activity

but occurs solely by means of God's gracious activity toward us. That is why Luther says God "condemns what men choose and chooses what men condemn. And this judgement has been shown us in the cross of Christ."[56] The way of salvation is a *via contrarii*, and this soteriological perspective is one of the most distinctive theological themes of Luther—namely, the hiddenness of God is a predicate of the revelation of God. God is hidden in His opposite, and God works contrary to human expectations. The *Deus absconditus sub contrario*, His paradoxical work of salvation, will form what Luther later calls *theologia crucis*.

Luther came to understand *humilitas* theology through his reading of the Roman mystics—Bernard of Clairvaux and Jacobus Faber Stapulensis. In contrast to Dionysian mystical theology which gives priority to the mind in its scrutiny of divine truth, Bernard of Clairvaux represents the affective tradition, with its emphasis on the heart. *Caritas* is the basic principle of "likeness" with the Divine, "in which the perfect correspondence of will make of two, one spirit."[57] Bernard insists upon the necessity of love as the basis of *unio mystica*: "Such conformity unites the soul to the Word. Already resembling Him by nature, it begins to do so by will. It loves as it is loved. If it loves God perfectly then it is wed to him. What more sweet than this conformity?"[58] A proper love-union with the Divine is causally dependent on the increase of humility. That is why Bernard writes, "who(ever) wishes to ascend to the lofty mysteries of Divine love, ... he must have a low opinion of himself."[59]

Stapulensis is a mystic with strong nominalist elements. His focus is on both the heart and the will. Stapulensis' exegesis of Scripture was Christocentric. Its purpose is to disclose the paradigmatic figure of Christ hidden in Scripture. Hermeneutically, Stapulensis, following Augustine and Staupitz,[60] rejected the prevalent literal/historical method of exegesis typical of the medieval exegetes. He considered this method to follow "the letter that kills,"[61] unable to provide true knowledge of the hidden or "spiritual" intention of God. In order to understand the "spiritual" meaning of Scripture, Stapulensis believed that the reader must be "animated by the Spirit"—the same spirit which inspires and speaks through the prophets and Apostles.[62] However the "spiritual" meaning of Scripture, according to him, is only unveiled to one who recognizes his ignorance and approaches the Word of God with true humility. Stapulensis writes: "Those who approach God in presumption and pride are rejected, not just by Paul ... but by Him who resists the proud and gives grace to the humble."[63] According to Stapulensis, true humility is not attainable by means of imitating the works of the saints or those stipulated in the Scripture (*imitatio operis*). Rather, it is achieved only by the spirit of humility (*imitatio mentis*) which is characterized by suffering the humiliation of the *descensus ad infernum* in imitation of the paradigmatic event of Jesus Christ.[64] The Christian is justified by being brought to the depths of despair and hell and, brought back, as was the primary exemplar, Jesus Christ. Through the continuing process of *resignatio voluntatis* and the *descensus ad infernum*, the Christian is stripped of his self-will and pride. He becomes more righteous and Christ-like until eventually he is worthy to receive salvation. While Biel stressed an active obedience to God's will by means of the inherent capabilities provided by the *synteresis*, the mystic Stapulensis stressed a passive obedience in relation to the will of God. Imitating Christ means humbly resigning one's will to the suffering and humiliation of the *descensus ad infernum* as God's will for him.

From the tradition of the *humilitas* theology of Bernard and Stapulensis, Luther came to accept the *resignatio voluntatis, descensus ad infernum* and *obedientia passiva*, with the emphasis upon conformity to the suffering, humiliated Christ. This does not mean, however, that Luther did not oppose the soteriological context of suffering, humiliation and self-mortification. Just as Luther applied Augustine's anti-Pelagian thesis against Biel and other scholastics, he applied it to Stapulensis and *humilitas* theology. Suffering conforms us to God's will, but, according to Luther, conformity cannot be initiated or achieved by a sinful humanity. Suffering, if it is self-chosen, is not true suffering. This does not constitute conformity to Christ in a proper sense. To hold that a sinful humanity can by itself initiate the process of salvation denies the humility required for salvation. The self-chosen imitation of the suffering *Christus exemplum*, according to Luther, is another form of works-righteousness. It represents the "wisdom of the flesh," the "blind reason and heathen ways of thinking."[65] In Luther's words:

> (T)he wisdom of the flesh dissipated the conformity of the will with God, so that it does not wish for what it ought to, and that for which the will of God wishes in order to save it. Rather the will seems in itself to be happy and to be saved by that which the man himself chooses. For discord arises between God and man here, it is apparent, in the means and not the ends.[66]

Conformity to the will of God as a requirement of salvation is for Luther causally dependent upon the prerogative of God, not upon human efforts. Only if we humbly accept our true status as *peccator coram Deo* do we recognize who we really are. Conformity to the will of God is achieved only if we condemn and accuse ourselves as incapable of earning salvation on the basis of good works. Luther writes: "He who justifies himself, condemns God ... He who judges himself and confesses his sins ... has said about himself that which God has said about him. And thus he now conforms to God and is true and righteous, for so is God with whom he agrees."[67] Only when one judges himself as a sinner does his judgement agree with God's judgement. "Be a sinner to yourself and you will be righteous before God."[68] The way of salvation offered by God is antithetical to that advocated by the medieval theology. "We ask to be saved and He in order that He may save us first damns."[69] Here Luther takes up the damnation/justification dialectic in relation to the *opus alienum Dei/opus proprium Dei*, the one work of God. In contrast to the mystics, Luther argues that the union with Christ does not come about through the discipline of a complete submission or self-denial.[70] Rather it happens in the *Anfechtungen* which are laid upon men by God himself. *Anfechtung*, the term which Luther borrowed from the German mystic Tauler, was theocentric and therefore must be distinguished from that which is anthropocentric. *Anfechtung* is sometimes translated as "temptation." Its root means "assail," "combat," or "bodily struggle."[71] *Anfechtung*, says Luther, is the attack of God upon a person, "God's embrace."[72] It is God who performs an alien work of leading the sinner to hell in order to bring him back as His proper work of justification. Luther's initial encounter with the dialectic of the alien and proper work was through his reading of Tauler's sermons as he acknowledged in his marginalia.[73] Luther took over Tauler's terminology, giving it a specific content that is in accordance with his *theologia crucis*. The concepts— *Anfechtung, tribulatio, tentatio, compunctio*—reveal a deeper understanding of Luther's *theologia crucis*: it is the *opus alienum* of God because God meets us in suffering as He suffers with us.[74] Luther learned that the *Anfechtung* had stripped him of any soteriological resources or causal power within himself to save himself, and thus he had no claim upon God. The temptations force the believer to a humility, which is "the basic insight of faith."[75] With this Luther modified Tauler's understanding of *conformitas Christi*. Mortification and suffering are seen as paradoxical signs of God's grace. Luther understood the role of God's grace in conforming us to the will of God as two sides of the single reality of God's unmerited grace, seeing both suffering and redemption, death and resurrection, damnation and salvation as the work of grace. Conforming us to the image of the suffering and humiliated Christ is for Luther God's proper work of justification, thereby uniting suffering and grace as the *opus suum Dei*. Luther writes: "God's alien work ... is the suffering of Christ and sufferings in Christ, the crucifixion of the old man and the mortification of Adam. God's proper work however is the resurrection of Christ, justification in the Spirit, and the vivification of the new man, as Romans 4:25 says: Christ died for our sins and was raised for our justification. Thus conformity with the image of the Son includes both these works."[76] We are conformed to Christ by the alien and proper work of God, both of which is for Luther the one work of God's grace.

For Luther "*fides*," not the "affective *synteresis*," is the basis of *homo spiritualis*, replacing suffering as the ground of the personal and mystical union of Christ and the believer although suffering remains as the context in which the life of faith is lived.[77] In lieu of the imitation of Christ, Luther emphasized the pre-eminence of "*fides abstracta*" which means "putting on Christ and having all things in common with Him."[78] This faith "conjoins the soul with Christ like a bride with her bridgeroom," making of the believer and Christ "as one person."[79] Following his break with scholasticism and throughout the course of his career, Luther consistently upheld that *fides abstracta* alone justifies our being and our deeds. All that is required of the believer is to "cling in faith to this man, Christ—that is the sufficient and necessary condition" by which he "receives" in pure passivity Christ's "alien" righteousness.[80]

Nevertheless, in his discussion of the relationship between faith and works, Luther introduced another concept of faith—that is "*fides incarnata*" which he distinguishes from "*fides abstracta*."

> We also distinguish faith in this way, that sometimes faith is understood apart from work and sometimes with the work. For just as a craftsman speaks about his material in different ways ..., so the Holy Spirit speaks about faith in different ways in Scripture: sometimes, if I may speak this way, about an abstract or an absolute faith and sometimes about a concrete, composite, or incarnate faith.[81]

Luther often declared, on the basis of Matt. 7:18, that "the good tree bears the good fruits."[82] Since "faith is followed by works as the body is followed by its shadow,"[83] says Luther, "(it becomes) impossible to separate works from faith, quite as impossible to separate heat and light from fire."[84] For Luther in order for faith to be real it must lead to good works as the external manifestation of an inward faith. He writes of Paul, "it is true that faith alone justifies, without works; but I am speaking about genuine faith, which, after it has justified, will not go to sleep but is active through love."[85] Real faith must be active, seeking its concretization and validation in good works. The fruits "bear testimony" to the tree which produces them.[86] The theological impetus to act is understood as the inherent consequence of Luther's understanding of faith itself—that is faith as *fides incarnata*. At times when criticized by Karlstadt and the Anabaptists for bifurcating the Christian life, Luther asserts *fides* as *fides incarnata*: "(I)f good works do not follow it is certain that this faith in Christ does not dwell in our hearts."[87] This idea of *fides* as *fides incarnata* helped

Luther meet Karlstadt's and the Anabaptists' accusation that he has divorced faith from works.

While at times Luther speaks of abstract faith—"faith without works"—, at other times he even speaks of an antithetical relationship between faith and works. This is evident in his statements: "Faith does not perform work, it believes in Christ"; "all that is kept is faith, which justifies and makes alive."[88] It is from this perspective that Luther repudiates the soteriology of the Anabaptists for suggesting that the believer "must suffer many things... and imitate the example of Christ," arguing instead that faith "learns about Christ and grasps Him without having to bear the cross."[89] Furthermore one cannot possibly say that a confusion arises in Luther's thought when two contradictory assertions co-exist in the one and same statement: "(W)e, too say that faith without works (absolute faith) is worthless and useless. The 'papists' and 'fanatics' take this to mean faith without works does not justify, or that if faith does not have works, it is of no avail, no matter how true it is. That is false. But faith without works (absolute faith)—that is a fantastic idea and mere vanity and a dream of the heart—it is a false faith and does not justify."[90] In the same statement Luther affirms his own *fides incarnata* but repudiates the *fides incarnata* advocated by the "papists" and "fanatics". Here there is no confusion. Luther stresses both *fides abstracta* and *fides incarnata*, the former being the basis for the latter. For Luther faith alone justifies, not faith and works. But the faith which justifies, since it is trust in Christ, issues in good works. What Luther says here is at the heart of all that he says. This is evident in his commentary on Galatians 5:8 of 1535, where Luther writes, "The Anabaptists have nothing in their entire teaching more impressive than the way they emphasize the example of Christ and the bearing of the cross," but, we must distinguish "when Christ is proclaimed as a gift and when as an example. Both forms of proclamation have their proper time; if this is not observed, the proclamation of salvation becomes a curse."[91] "Scripture presents Christ in two ways. First as a gift ... Secondly, ... as an example for us to imitate."[92] Luther further clarifies :

To those who are afraid and have already been terrified by the burden of their sins, Christ the Saviour and the gift should be announced, not Christ the example and lawgiver. But to those who are smug and stubborn the example of Christ should be set forth, lest they use the Gospel as a pretext for the freedom of the flesh and thus becomes smug.[93]

Augustinianism

Gordon Rupp claims that Luther's relationship with the writings of Augustine was "of decisive importance to Luther's theological development."[94] Luther reportedly read and often memorized Augustine's work.[95] Lienhard observes that in the *Dictata super Psalterium*, Luther's first Psalm lectures, he quotes Augustine 270 times.[96] Luther saw Augustine as the one Church father who truly understood Paul. In his letter to John Lang of 1517, Luther says: "Our theology and St. Augustine are progressing well, and with God's help rule at our University (Wittenberg). Aristotle is gradually falling from his throne, and his final doom is only a matter of time... Indeed no one can expect to have any students if he does not want to teach this theology, that is, lecture on the Bible or on St. Augustine or another teacher of esslesiastical eminence."[97] This regard for Augustine is also evident in his *Preface to the Complete Edition of a German Theology*, in 1518, where Luther confessed: "... no book except the Bible and St. Augustine has been drawn to my (Luther's) attention from which I have learned more about God, Christ, man, and all things...."[98] Luther's early acquaintance with Augustine was through his anti-Pelagian writings which Luther utilized in his critique of the scholastics. The early Luther upheld Augustine's position, in opposition to the Pelagians, that the sinner is justified by faith in Christ, through the grace of God alone.[99] Augustine not only provided Luther with his anti-Pelagian thesis, he also provided Luther with a new Christological formulation which enabled him to come to terms with the late medieval Christological emphasis on the *Christus exemplum*. Erwin Iserloh, notes Lienhard, has identified an important influence on Luther of Augustine: that of Christ as *sacramentum et exemplum*, the conceptual pair found in Augustine's *Treatise on the Trinity* (BK. IV, Ch. 111).[100] Luther utilized this concept to exclude the late medieval *imitatio Christi* devotion. Referring specifically to Romans 6:4, Luther comments, "the apostle speaks here of the death and resurrection of Christ inasmuch as they are *sacramentum* and not inasmuch as they are *exemplum*."[101] In his commentary on Hebrews, Luther points out the error of medieval Christology that puts the emphasis on the *Christus exemplum*, to the exclusion of the *Christus sacramentum*. Luther establishes the basis for his own Christology by making the *Christus sacramentum* prior to *Christus exemplum*. He articulates this in his lectures on Hebrews:

> Therefore he who wants to imitate Christ insofar as he is an example must first believe with a firm faith that Christ suffered and died for him as this was a sacrament. Consequently, those who continue to blot out sin first by means of works and labors of penance err greatly, since they begin with the example, when they should begin with the sacrament.[102]

For Luther, therefore, the real significance of Christ for faith does not lie in the imitation of Christ's sufferings but rather in the believer's participation by faith in His suffering as a sacrament for us. The *conformitas Christi* of the believer which Luther interprets in terms of our participation in the suffering of Christ is therefore the work of the Spirit.[103] Luther takes up Augustine's concept of the "joyous exchange" to explain the Christian life.[104] He writes: "When we have put on Christ in the role of our righteousness and our salvation, then we must put on Christ also as the garment of imitation."[105] The *theologia crucis* without an emphasis on the human participation in the cross is itself transformed into a *theologia gloriae*.[106] That Luther stressed faith in Christ's salvific death on the cross must not be taken to mean a complete exclusion of the imitation of the example of Christ. In his 1519 commentary on Galatians 2:20— "with Christ I have been crucified", Luther appeals to Augustine's *sacramentum* and *exemplum* Christology:

> Saint Augustine teaches that the suffering Christ is both a *sacramentum* and an *exemplum*,—a *sacramentum* because it signifies the death of sin in us and grants it to those who believe, an *exemplum* because it also

behooves us to imitate Him in bodily suffering and dying.[107]

The cross of Christ has a two-fold function: an expiatory function and an exemplary function, both of which constitute the one reality of Christ. The exemplary function is derived from the primacy of the expiatory function, but the former has meaning and validity because of the latter. "For the reformer, an orthodoxy which is not also an orthopraxis would be inconceivable."[108] To embrace Jesus Christ, for Luther, is to embrace his cross or "to have fellowship with Christ in his sufferings."

Two other thinkers of *Schola Augustiniana moderna*, Gregory of Rimini and Johannes Von Staupitz, are relevant to our study.[109] Gordon Rupp sees in Gregory of Rimini a shift away from the nominalist idea of *facere quod in se est* towards an increasing emphasis on the role of uncreated grace in our justification. This theological emphasis issued in the "pastoral reform theology" of Johannes von Staupitz, which influenced Luther in his formative years.[110]

In preparing for the Leipzig debate in 1519, Luther considered Rimini the true disciple of Augustine: "... in debating with me (Eck) rejected Gregory of Rimini as one who alone supported my opinion against all other theologians (scholastics)."[111] Along with Rimini, Staupitz holds that *influentia generalis* shared by all creatures does not "dispose the soul for the reception of grace"; rather it accounts for an adequate explanation of natural human actions. In this both part company with Biel and other nominalists who believed that this general divine influence provided the self a point of contact between God and man. In contrast to them, Staupitz believes that apart from the gracious gifts of God the sinner is not able to perform any act which is meritorious. *Facere quod in se est* means for Staupitz that by doing what is in one, one is shown the extent of his own sin and moral impotence, thereby abandoning all hopes of making oneself righteous before God. He therefore rejects "a created habit of grace within the soul" as "the formal cause of justification."[112] God's renewing work, then, begins with *humilitas* in the sinner.[113]

Staupitz is credited with moving Luther away from the mysti-

cal practice of visions and revelations of God toward "the wounds
of the most sweet saviour" as a way out of despair.[114] In particular Staupitz provided Luther with the theme of *passio Christi*,
emphasizing the humility of Christ. He writes :

> On the hill of Calvary He has shown us a model (*vorbilde*) of all sanctity.
> ... He is a model given by God, according to which I would work, suffer
> and die. He is the only model which man can follow, in which every
> good in life, suffering and death is usefully modeled. Therefore, no one
> can do right, suffer correctly, or die rightly, unless it happens in confor-
> mity (*gleichformig*) with the life, suffering and death of Christ.[115]

Staupitz showed that a Christian, through the "joyous exchange"
with the suffering, humiliated Christ, is enabled humbly and voluntarily to bear the cross as Christ willingly suffered and bore the
cross.[116] The cross must be seen as the centre of the Christian life
as it was so in the life of Christ. Luther gave credit to his confessor and vicar in the Augustinian order who truly became his
"father in God": "If I didn't praise Staupitz, I should be a
damnable, ungrateful, papistical ass... for he bore me in Christ. If
Staupitz had not helped me out, I should have been swallowed up
and left in hell."[117] Luther asserted that Staupitz helped him away
from the human attempt to achieve union with God. In August
1531, when Luther was differentiating between law and gospel, he
told of Staupitz's confession of his own despair concerning his
inability to remain pious before God. Following Staupitz, Luther
resolved his own despair by abandoning all efforts at human piety
by clinging to Christ alone.[118] Staupitz led Luther away from speculation concerning the divinity of Christ to knowledge of God
through the humanity of the incarnate Christ.[119] He warned
Luther that "it is hazardous for persons to trust in their own
strength."[120] Throughout his entire life, Luther was indebted to
Staupitz's pastoral and theological counsel regarding his
Anfechtung about predestination:

> Staupitz used to comfort me with these words: "Why do you torture
> yourself with these speculations? Look at the wounds of Christ and the
> blood that was shed for you. From these predestination will shine."

Consequently, one must listen to the Son of God, who was sent into the flesh and appeared to destroy the work of the devil (I John 3:8), and to make you sure of predestination.[121]

Luther said in 1533 that all his Christocentric thinking stemmed from that of his confessor, Staupitz: "However my good Staupitz said, 'One must keep one's eyes fixed on that man who is called Christ.' Staupitz is the one who started (our) teaching (namely, on justification)."[122] For Luther, as it is for his confessor, "Christology is the subject of theology" (*Christus est subjectum theologiae*).[123] Finally Staupitz also provided Luther with the hermeneutical distinction between "letter" and "spirit" for his reading of Scripture. The bare historical narrative of the Biblical text (i.e. letter) must not obscure the hidden meaning of the text intended by the Holy Spirit (i.e. spirit). In his first major theological work, the *Lectures on the Psalms* of 1513-1515, the young Luther applied this hermeneutical distinction:

> For as the years have passed, so has the relationship grown closer between the letter and the Spirit. For what was a sufficient understanding in times past, has now become the letter to us. Thus at the present time, as we have said, the letter itself is more subtle in nature than before. And this is because of the progress of time. For everyone who travels, what he has left behind and forgotten is the letter, and what he is reaching forward to is the Spirit. For what one already possesses is always the letter, by comparison with what has to be achieved... Thus the doctrine of the Trinity, when it was explicitly formulated at the time of Arius, was the Spirit, and only understood by a few; but today it is the letter, because it is something publicly known—unless we add something to it, i.e., a living faith in it. Consequently, we must always pray for understanding in order not to be frozen by the letter that kills.[124]

While the Late Medieval tradition exercised important influences upon Luther, it must not obscure the fact that Luther was first and foremost a "Biblical theologian." Pelikan writes: "It is important to see the title 'Biblical theologian' as an integral part of Luther's sense of calling. It was as a biblical theologian that he took up the polemics. In fact, it was as a biblical theologian that he became the Reformer. And it is as a biblical theologian that he

deserves to be interpreted."[125]   In contrast to the systematic
method of scholastic theology, Ebeling argues that Luther's theological thinking "developed from the outside in the exegetical
method."[126] Luther exhibited a deep-seated skepticism concerning human speculation about God: "Theology is heaven, yes even
the kingdom of heaven; man however is earth and his speculations
are smoke."[127] His commitment to the biblical texts generated for
Luther an unbridgeable gulf between theology and philosophical
speculation.   In September, 1517, a few months prior to the out-
break of the Indulgence Controversy, Luther vehemently attacked
scholastic theology, and particularly its use of Aristotle:

> It is a wrong thing to say that a man cannot become a theologian with-
> out Aristotle. The truth is that a man cannot become a theologian unless
> he becomes one without Aristotle. In short, compared with the study of
> theology, the whole of Aristotle is as darkness is to the light.[128]

What Luther opposed was not Aristotle as such; rather he rejected
the whole attempt in scholastic theology to make Aristotelian philosophy the presupposition of Christian doctrine, to allow philosophical categories or constructs to rule his theological method,
and subsequently reduce the great themes of Scripture—grace,
faith, justification—to scholastic jargon. Although Luther admittedly gained some knowledge from scholasticism,[129] he warned of
the errors inherent in the exegesis of "strange and monstrous theologians such as Thomas Aquinas, Dus Scotus and many others.
They should read the Bible and leave Aristotle."[130]

Luther's fundamental hermeneutical principle is that a biblical
text is to be taken as it stands (*sensus literalis*).[131]   In exegesis,
Luther gives heed more to intratextual analysis of the text than to
later interpretation of it, thereby allowing the text of the Bible to
formulate the issues of theological discussion. Luther interprets
passages in light of the whole of the Biblical material. The key to
his hermeneutic is the cross of Christ: Christ is the center of his biblical hermeneutic.[132] This Christocentric hermeneutic, according
to Terry Thomas, means for Luther that

> his God, ... was the God revealed exclusively in the Bible, which is the

heart of what brought him to express his theology as a theology of the cross. Who God is in himself would take superlative adjectives beyond human speech, and those who seek the absolute, uncovered God are speculative dreamers, theologians of glory. To be a Christian is to humble oneself before God as he has chosen to make himself known -- through the Scriptures. A Christian theologian is a theologian of the cross. "We know God in Scriptures,"... "where He is revealed to us, and we ought to know about this God alone and withstand all adversaries."[133]

The uniqueness of Scriptures lies in the fact they are "the swaddling clothes and the manger in which Christ lies."[134] "Simple and little are the swaddling clothes, but dear is the treasure, Christ, that lies in them."[135] Luther rejected the allegorical method precisely because it obscured the Christological witness of the plain, literal sense of the Scripture.[136] "Allegories do not provide solid proofs in Theology; but like pictures, they adorn and illustrate a subject."[137] That which bears Christ is truly scripture. Luther did not identify the Word of God with words but with Christ,[138] thereby avoiding a dead literalism.[139]

In contrast to the Scholastic's emphasis on "being," the basic category for Luther's exegesis was "deed."[140] While to be concerned at the outset with God's "being" is for Luther to become involved in human speculation, to be concerned at the outset with God's "deed" is to be concerned with God's redemption and revelation. Thus Luther centers his exegesis upon God's "deed" in Christ. He explains:

> ... Begin where Christ began—in the Virgin's womb, in the manger, and at his mother's breasts. For this purpose he came down, was born, lived among men, suffered, was crucified and died, so that in every possible way He might present himself to our sight. He wanted to fix the gaze of our hearts upon himself and thus to prevent us from clambering into heaven and speculating about the Divine majesty.[141]

Luther's commitment to the Bible demands its liberation from the captivity to hellenized or any *a priori* theological formulations. The Bible precedes any a priori notions of divine impassibility or passibility. The language about the passion of God in the Bible must be taken seriously as it was not by the majority of the early church fathers since the time of Clement of Alexandria. The Bible, according to Luther, literally taught the *"gekreuzigte Gott."*[142] His commitment to the Bible does not mean that Luther wants to ignore the early fathers. Rather, he wants to read them differently from the way in which his opponents read them, as Luther himself asserts in his *On the Councils and the Church* (1539):

> I, too, read the Fathers, even before I opposed the pope so decisively. I also read them with greater diligence than those who now quote them so defiantly and haughtily against me; for I know that none of them attempted to read a book of Holy Scripture in school, or to use the writings of the fathers as an aid, as I did. Let them take a book of the Holy Scripture and seek out the glosses of the fathers; then they will share the experience I had when I worked on the letter to the Hebrews with St. Chrysostom's glosses, the letter to Titus and the letter to the Galatians with the help of St. Jerome, Genesis with the help of St. Augustine, the Psalter with all the writers available, and so on.[143]

Theologia Crucis Defined: Its Constitutive Principles

Luther has been primarily seen as a biblical exegete whose vocation was to discover and proclaim the living Gospel of God.[144] Nevertheless a systematic method, in light of the definition given to systematic theology by Joseph Sittler, can be discerned in Luther's theology: "If, then, by system one means that there is in a man's thought a central authority, a pervasive style; namely, a way of bringing every theme and judgement and problem under the rays of the central illumination..."[145] Many Luther scholars have arrived at the same thesis; namely, that the key to Luther's theological method is his theology of the cross.[146] Walter von Loewenich writes:

> ... the theology of the cross is a principle of Luther's entire theology, and it may not be confined to a special period in his theological development. ... Hence, our investigation has to do not with a specific stage of development, but with the demonstration of a theological thinking.[147]

Theologia crucis, then, has to do with theological method, the way one does theology from the ground up and in its entirety, not with one doctrine (such as atonement) set alongside the others. The cross is "not only the subject of theology; it is the distinctive mark of all theology."[148] The theology of the cross is a method by which Luther conceives of the whole content of the Christian faith and the task of Christian theology. More precisely, Luther's *theologia crucis* is a dialectical principle which is linked with his theology of faith: "The correlative to *crux sola* is *sola fide*, as it is through faith, and through faith alone, that the true significance of the cross is perceived."[149]

During the period of his theological education, Luther was very much preoccupied with the search for the kernel of truth; and writing in a letter he expressed the character of that truth: "the only theology which was of any value was that which penetrated the kernel of the nut and the germ of the wheat and the marrow of the bone."[150] Already in the *Heidelberg Disputation* of 1518, a year after the posting of his ninety-five theses, Luther propounds that the only theology of real value is founded in none other than in the crucified Christ.[151] The *Heidelberg Disputation* represented the first opportunity for Luther to debate his ideas during the triennial convention of the Augustinian order in Germany. Johannes von Staupitz, vicar of the order in Germany, exhorted Luther not to become controversial *coram* Pope Leo X by attacking the system of indulgences represented in his *Ninety-five theses* of 1517; Staupitz directed him to present his wider vision of the evangelical faith. This is why the *Heidelberg theses* of April 1518 are vitally crucial in presenting Luther's thought on such themes as righteousness, grace, justification, and in particular the succinct vision of his theology of the cross. These theses set the direction of Luther's thought and the continual task of theology as he understood. it.[152]

In order to delineate the main constitutive elements of Luther's *theologia crucis*, as Joseph Vercruysse notes, we must study the background leading to the *Heidelberg Theses* during 1518.[153] Although the most succinct expression of Luther's theology of the cross is spelled out in the *Heidelberg Theses*, the expression "theology of the cross" is also found in four other texts.

These four texts were written in the Spring of 1518; they are: *Asterisci Lutheri adversus Obeliscos Eckii*, the Lectures on Hebrews, the *Resolutions disputationum de indulgentiarum virtute*, and finally the famous *Heidelberg Disputation*. The fifth one is to be found in the *Operationes in Psalmos*, Luther's second course on the Psalms, held from 1519 to 1521.[154]

We shall look briefly at the three written during 1518 prior to the *Heidelberg Disputation*, to discern the meaning of Luther's *theologia crucis* in his *Heidelberg Theses*. Limiting the examination of the immediate context in which the term "*theologia crucis*" occurs, I shall follow the study done by Fr. Joseph Vercruysse.[155]

The *Asterisci* is Luther's vehement response to Johannes Eck's *Adnotationes in XVIII Propositiones*.[156] The expression *theologia crucis* occurs in his response to Eck's sixth *Obelisk*, which concerns Luther's 16th thesis on indulgences. Luther deals there with the certainty of salvation of the souls in purgatory. Luther writes in unfriendly fashion of Eck: "*Adeo ignarus est Theologiae crucis, ut credat, ideo illis certum esse, an sint salvandi, quia amici Dei sunt et corpore salutis.*"[157] It is, for Luther, debatable to affirm universally this certainty. "Fear in the soul," Luther says, "makes a man by its very nature uncertain; a fear of which I (Luther) say is in the soul because of the deficiency of love."[158] This fear of uncertainty is what Vercruysse called, "the subjective, existential and personal" kind, experienced by those in purgatory, and even by believers.[159] In his 16th thesis against indulgences, Luther asserts: "Hell, purgatory, and heaven seem to differ the same as despair, fear, and assurance of salvation."[160] This profound uncertainty of the soul in purgatory means for Luther that

> ...He cannot boast on his own merits. On the contrary, full of fear, almost despairing and aware of his attachment to his own life and his deficient love for God, he is existentially uncertain about his own salvation. Being ignorant of the *theologia crucis* means thus to ignore the existence of an all-shaking temptation in Christian experience.[161]

Here already we see in this treatise against Eck Luther's anti-scholasticism, one of the constitutive elements of his theology of the cross.

Turning now to Luther's *Lectures on Hebrews*, the expression *theologia crucis* is mentioned only once in his gloss on Hebrews 12:11.[162] Here Luther speaks of a double way of God's operation, a dialectic between "*alienum opus* (alien work) and *proprium opus* (proper work), as expressed in Isaiah 28:21: "*alienum opus eius ab eo, ut operetur opus suum.*" This working of God is completely "hidden" to the world; it is a scandal to the Jews and folly to the Gentiles. God's proper work is only established and revealed through his alien work, and this is only perceived by the believer in faith. By way of summation of his exposition of Luther's commentary on this verse of the twelfth chapter of the letter of Hebrews, Vercryusse writes

> we perceive some of the main features of Luther's theology of the cross. It is an understanding of the two-fold way by which God operates with man. It is through his visible and apparent *opus alienum*, consisting of sorrow and tribulation, and also of judgement, wrath, death, and evil as summed up in the previous marginal gloss, in brief, consisting of the cross, that God brings a man to his real, invisible, true work, the rejoicing and pacifying justification, yet not revealed, but hidden *sub contrario*, within the storm of his *opus alienum*. This is, however, only understood by the believer, ... (whose) whole life ... consists in faith, i.e. in the cross and sufferings.[163]

In the *Resolutions*, Luther uses the expression *theologia crucis* in the context of a long discussion of Thesis 58 which concerns indulgences and the merits of the saints and of Christ.[164] Just as in the *Lectures on Hebrews*, Luther's discussion of the thesis revolves around the connection between God's double work as *opus alienum et opus proprium*.[165] The immediate subject is the merits of the saints and chiefly of Christ, "who through his efficacious intercession with God obtains for us forgiveness for our debts."[166] Luther writes:

> The merits of Christ perform an alien work ... in that they effect the cross, the labor, all kinds of punishment, finally death and hell in the flesh, to the end that the body of sin is destroyed. ... For whoever is baptized in Christ and is renewed shall be prepared for punishments, cross-

es, and deaths. ... Just so must we be conformed to the image and the Son of God.[167]

The theologian of the cross, then, accepts and consents to the paradoxical working of God: God works a strange work in order to work his proper work.[168]

Luther develops his theology of the cross in Thesis 58 as a polemical tool against Aristotle and his heirs, the scholastic theologians who are identified with a *theologia gloriae*. "From this you can see how, ever since the scholastic theology ... began, the theology of the cross has been abrogated, and everything has been completely turned upside up.... A theologian of glory does not recognize, along with the Apostle, the crucified and hidden God."[169] The theologian of glory sees and knows only a glorious God. Beginning with what can be seen in creation, he sees what is invisible in God, and speaks of a God who is present everywhere and is omnipotent. On the contrary, the theologian of the cross

> knows of a crucified and hidden God, concealed not only because he himself is crucified, but also hidden under all the crosses and sufferings of true Christians, displeased with their own security and suspicious of all that is their own, so that Christ is their light, righteousness, truth, wisdom and all good, concealed through *sub contrario*, in a crucified God. Thus he understands the way God works. Through his *opus alienum* of judgement he realizes his *opus proprium* of salvation.[170]

Thesis 58, according to Vercryusse and Rupp, has provided the theological perspective leading to Luther's construction of his *theologia crucis* in the *Heidelberg Disputation*.[171]

It is a grave error to ignore the connections between the section on the *theologia crucis* (theses 19 through 21) and the rest of the disputation because the whole disputation in its structure forms a well articulated unity. The first two theses provide the proper methological approach to our study of the *Heidelberg Disputation*, revealing the centrality of justification by faith in Luther's theology. Thesis one states Luther's understanding of *iustitia Dei*: "The righteousness of God has been manifested without the law" (Rom. 3:31).[172] Thesis two reaffirms what thesis one says about God's righteousness apart from human works.[173] One must not identify the principle of justification by faith with Luther's theology of the cross,[174] although the former is central to the latter. Luther's theology of the cross goes beyond any theological or doctrinal clarification. The doctrine of justification by faith is only the beginning in the development of Luther's theology of the cross. It finds its concreteness there, as McGrath has written: "Who is this God who deals thus with man? Luther's answer to this question can be summarized in one of his more daring phrases: the God who deals with sinful man in this astonishing way is none other than the 'crucified and hidden God' (*Deus crucifixus et absconditus*)—the God of the *theologia crucis*."[175]

Theses three to eleven lay out Luther's attack on human reason and potentiality, insisting that the sinner surrenders every claim to self-righteousness or self-justification. The works of all people are mortal sins, when they are not done in fear of damnation (thesis 7). Every kind of personal preparation for grace by free will is rejected by Luther. Therefore the theology of the cross calls us to abandon the Bielian theology of "*faciendo quod in se est*", but leads us to a life of discipleship under the cross of Christ.[176] Unless a person despairs of "all created things," knowing the vanity of his efforts, unless he confesses himself as nothing before God, knowing God's way of dealing with him through his *opus alienum*, it is impossible for him to hope in God (thesis 11).

The themes of original sin and free will are meant to disclose human futility before God, and human righteousness *Coram Deo* only in relationship to faith in Christ (theses 13 and 14).[177] This perspective on our righteousness *Coram Deo per Christum solum* is constitutive of Luther's *theologia crucis*.[178] Rupp observed a shift that occurred between the *Dictata* and the *Lectures on Romans* in Luther's understanding of original sin.[179] In the *Dictata* where Luther interprets Psalm 42, he points out that the "*synteresis* and desire for the good is inextinguishable in man."[180] At this stage Luther, like Augustine, believes that original sin persists after baptism only in our "weakness in memory, blindness in the intellect, loss or disorder in the will" (Ps. 71:1).[181] Original sin is, therefore, a mere "remnant." The idea of "*synteresis*" held in *Dictata* and

even at the beginning of his *Lectures on Roman* (Rom. 1:20) is rejected by Luther.[182] When he comes to Romans 3:10, Luther moves
beyond Augustine's concept of original sin as a mere "remnant"
and rejects *"synteresis"*: "We are so entirely inclined to evil that no
portion which is inclined toward good remains in us."[183] "This
cursedness is now natural for us, a natural wicked, and a natural
sinfulness. Thus man has no help from his natural powers but he
needs the aid of some power outside of himself."[184] Thus he says
in Romans 4:7, "this concupiscence (original sin), is always in us,
and the love of God is never in us unless it is begun by grace."[185]
Accordingly this background understanding leads us to appreciate
Theses 13 and 14 of the *Heidelberg Disputation*: "Free will after the
Fall exists only in name."[186] For Luther justification, therefore,
must be foreign to us (*aliena*), and it is imputed to us in our relationship *coram Deo* by faith in Christ. This is central to what Luther
sees as the chief purpose of Paul's Epistle of Romans:

> God does not want to redeem us through our own, but through external
> righteousness and wisdom; not through one that comes from us and
> grows in us but through one that comes to us from the outside; not
> through one that originates here on earth, but through one that comes
> from heaven. Therefore, we must be taught a righteousness that comes
> completely from the outside and is foreign. And therefore our own
> righteousness that is born in us must be first plucked up.[187]

Our righteousness is not something *in nobis*, not in the flesh; rather
it is granted to us only by faith in the incarnate Christ. This is
clearly accentuated in Luther's explanation of thesis 26 in the
Heidelberg Disputation: "In such a way is Christ in us by faith. Nay
rather than in us he is one with us. Now Christ is righteous and
fulfills all the commands of God."[188] The perspective of our righteousness *coram Deo* through faith in Christ alone marks an important point of departure for an application of Luther's *theologia crucis*.

Theses 19 to 21 provide us with Luther's profound theology of
the cross, which is in reality a theology of revelation, grounded in
solus Christus. In keeping with his search for a gracious God, the
emphasis in Luther's theology is knowledge of God that is saving.

For Luther, the true saving knowledge of God is to be found in God's self-revelation through Christ and his cross. Referring to Romans 1:20, Luther asserts that he who attempts to see the invisible reality of God, viz., His power, wisdom, righteousness and divinity, through insight into what can be seen in creation, does not deserve to be called a theologian.[189] "He is not worth calling a theologian who seeks to interpret the invisible things of God on the basis of the things that have been created."[190] God does not wish to be known through his *invisibilis* nor through his creation (theses 19-20). This means that such knowledge of God gained thereby is not true knowledge, since it arises out of human speculation. The knowledge of God which the theologian of glory provides through his speculation upon "the invisible things of God" is not the consequence of God's revelation in the cross and sufferings of Christ, and therefore is not salvific. The recognition of the essences or qualities of God as deduced from "created things," says Luther, does not make one worthy or wise. "This is apparent in the example of those who were 'theologians' and still were called fools by the apostle in Rom. 1:22."[191] Luther argues that the wisdom by which man learns to know God in His works is just as good as God's law. But man's sinful condition "misuses the best in the worst manner" (thesis 24), seeking to draw nearer to God through their good works. "(This) sort of wisdom which sees the invisible things of God in known good works simply inflates a man, and renders him both blind and hard."[192] "It is impossible for a person not to be puffed up by his good works unless he has first been deflated and destroyed by suffering and evil until he knows that he is worthless and that his works are not his but God's."[193] The cross, then, is directed against works righteousness and human efforts to do what is morally good so as to merit justification which only faith in Christ makes possible. Luther asserts, "He is not righteous who does much, but he who, without work, believes much in Christ" (thesis 25). This thesis, as Pannenberg notes, "rejects the Aristotelian notion of justice (as) that (which) is acquired by developing an appropriate attitude or habit of action," thereby it repudiates the attitude of anyone that boasts that he is wise and learned in the law (cf. thesis 23).[194]

Thesis 20 spells out the paradoxical nature of the cross as a reality of revelation: God's revelation is indirect and in concealment. In a sermon dated Feb. 24 1517, Luther says: "*Homo abscondit sua ut neget, Deus abscondit sua ut revelet.*"[195] God's revelation is characteristically veiled and hidden, since men are incapable of seeing God directly (i.e. in His "naked" form). If men were to see God's "face," men would die. God is not immediately recognizable as God. Luther makes allusion to Exodus 33:23 to grasp this paradox. What Moses was able to see is not God's "face," but only His *posteriora*, His "rear parts."[196] Thesis 20 asserts that the opposite of the "*invisibilia Dei*" provides genuine revelation, "*sed qui visibilia et posteriora per passiones et crucem consperta intelligit?*"[197] Thesis 21 further clarifies: "He who does not know Christ does not know God hidden in suffering." A true theologian, for Luther, knows about God as He is hidden ("clothed") in the humanity of Christ, rests on His mother's arms and finally dies on the cross. As Luther says in thesis 20, "But he is worth calling a theologian who understands the visible and hinder parts of God to mean the passion and the cross."[198] His invisible nature is understood in terms of His majestic attributes (cf. Rom. 1:20); His visible nature is understood in terms of His humanity, weakness and foolishness (cf. I Cor. 1:25). For Luther, just as God's invisible nature is opposed to His visible nature, knowledge of God from His works (i.e., creation) is also antithetical to knowledge of God from His sufferings (i.e. the cross of Jesus Christ). Luther writes, "Because men misused the knowledge of God through works, God wishes to be recognized in suffering, and to condemn wisdom concerning invisible things by means of wisdom concerning visible things, so that those who did not honor God as manifested in His works should honor God as he is hidden in suffering."[199] It does not profit anyone to know God in His glory and majesty, unless he recognizes Him in "the shame and humility of the cross."[200] The true saving knowledge of God is to be sought in the suffering and crucified Christ: "true theology and recognition of God are in the crucified Christ."[201] In the Jesus of the cross, God becomes visible, thereby constituting the *locus* of God's hiddenness *sub contraria*. What Luther asserts is that the *deus absconditus* is none other than the *deus revelatus* who can be known only in and through the suffering and cross of Christ, the incarnate and crucified God (*deus incarnatus, deus crucifixus*). The theologian of glory "prefers works to suffering, glory to the cross, strength to weakness, (and) wisdom to folly... (It hates) the cross and suffering and loves works and the glory of works."[202]   Because the theologian of glory expects God to be revealed in glory, majesty and strength, he deduces that God cannot be present in the cross of Christ. He rejects the scene of dereliction on the cross as the self-revelation of God. Luther refers to this theologian as an "enemy of the cross" who refuses to accept reality as it is. The theologian of the cross, however, must be radical in his declaration of the reality *in se*. As Luther explains, "The theologian of glory says bad is good and good is bad. The theologian of the cross calls them by their proper name."[203] *Theologia crucis* calls a thing what it is, declaring that it is God incarnate who suffers death, even death on the cross for the sake of humanity's salvation, that only in the shame and humility of the cross can one find the true and gracious God. That God reveals Himself in His opposites means that God reveals Himself in the folly of the world rather than in wisdom, in the weakness of His humanity rather than in strength, in suffering rather than in power, in humility rather than in glory, in shame rather than in majesty. Victory over sin, death and Satan is made possible only through the humiliation of the cross in which God determines Himself. True theology must be concerned with God as He has chosen to reveal Himself, not with some preconceived notions of God. Luther insists, "*CRUX sola est nostra theologia.*"[204] Any human attempts to know God by way of intelligent reflection upon the nature of man's moral sense or the pattern of the created order are rejected by Luther, and are charged with being *theologia gloriae*. For an example, Philip of Bethsaida represents "a theologian of glory" who seeks for God apart from God's self-definition in the crucified Christ (cf. Jn. 14:8-9). On the contrary, the "theologian of the cross" is one who, through faith, discerns the presence of the hidden God in His revelation in Christ—in His passion and cross. In contrast to a speculative knowledge of God gained by reason, true knowledge of God in the *theologia crucis* is available only to the eyes of faith—*Deus crucifixus pro nobis* only in His suffering and weakness on the cross. In this statement Luther's revolutionary idea of God is discerned. To know the crucified Christ is, for Luther, to know God's suffering revealed in the suffering of the cross.[205]

The final feature of Luther's *theologia crucis* is that God is known through suffering and the cross, both of Christ and of the Christian.[206] The cross of Christ and the cross of the Christian must be distinguished from each other, but not separated. The theology of the cross is practical. Loewenich writes:

> The cross of Christ and the cross of the Christian belong together. The meaning of the cross does not disclose itself in contemplative thought but only in suffering experience. The theologian of the cross does not confront the cross of Christ as a spectator, but is himself drawn into this event. He knows that God can be found only in cross and suffering. ... For God himself is "hidden in suffering" and wants us to worship him as such. ... If we are serious about the idea of God and the concept of faith in the theology of the cross, we are faced with the demand of a life under the cross.[207]

McGrath notes that "a fundamental contention of the *theologia crucis* is not merely that God is known through suffering (whether that of Christ or of the individual), but that God makes himself known through suffering."[208] God is active in suffering and *Anfechtungen,* and they are the *opus alienum* of God through which a person may experience God's *opus proprium* (cf. Thesis 16). The paradox involved is seen with reference to the justification of an individual. "God assaults man in order to break him down and thus to justify him."[209] Suffering reveals the futility of self-justification and the need of God's justification. God creates for us the experience of *Anfechtungen* and suffering, through which we live a life under the cross. God's active suffering under the cross "creates the object of his love" (thesis 28). "Through the cross works are dethroned and (the old) Adam, who is especially edified by works, is crucified."[210] So far

from regarding suffering and evil as a nonsensical intrusion into the world (which Luther regards as the opinion of a theologian of glory) the "theologian of the cross" regards such suffering as his most precious treasure, for revealed and yet hidden in precisely such sufferings is none other than the living God, working out the salvation of those whom he loves.[211]

The Christian lives under the active "love of God". This is clearly expounded in the following statements concerning thesis 28:

... the love of God living in man loves sinners, evil men, foolish men, weak men, so that the love of God makes them righteous, good, wise, and strong. In this way it flows forth rather and confers good. Thus sinners are lovely because they are loved: they are not loved because they are lovely. That is why human love shuns sinners and evil men. As Christ said, "I came not to call the righteous but sinners" (Matt. 9:13). And that is what love of the cross means. It is a love born of the cross, which betakes itself not to where it can find something good to enjoy, but where it may confer good to the wicked and the needy.[212]

Having been "reduced to nothing through the cross and suffering," the christian knows that "sinners are attractive because they are loved."[213] The reality of a saving relationship is encountered in the paradoxical act of the incarnate Christ on the cross who works in terms of law and gospel, wrath and mercy, glory and humility, majesty and shame (cf. theses 23-27). This *sub contraria* nature of His acts on the cross, for Luther, creates the object of His love.

In summation, Luther's *theologia crucis* is to be understood as a theology in which God's true identity can be known only in His saving relationship to us in the suffering and cross of Jesus Christ. True theology has to do with a theology of revelation. For Luther, God has spoken, and therefore we are able to speak about Him. God has disclosed Himself, and therefore we know where we can find Him in order to be saved. The theology of the cross opposes the theology of the medieval church which attempts to ascend to God by speculative, ethical or mystical means. It affirms that God deals with sinners, not on the basis of their achievement or work but rather on the basis of their sin. In the cross of Christ lies God's definitive "no" to all human efforts to discern God's being in itself and to achieve salvation apart from the crucified Christ. Abiding in Luther's theology of the cross is a two-fold principle: we per-ceive God's redeeming work in Christ *sub contraria* and we partic-ipate in it by faith.

Chapter Three

Christology and Divine Suffering

The true theologian, for Luther, is the one who beholds not the invisible but the visible of God. God, hidden to sight in the humanity of Jesus, is visible to the eyes of faith, thereby restraining us "from clambering into heaven and speculating about the Divine majesty."[1] The theology of the cross for Luther is concerned with "a definite person" who is "none other than Christ Himself, in whom 'the whole fullness of Deity dwells bodily,' as St. Paul declares in Col. 2:9."[2] Hence Luther asserts, "Christology is the subject of theology," and "all heresies do contend against this dear article of Jesus Christ."[3] It is beyond the scope of this present study to offer a comprehensive account of the development of Luther's Christology.[4] Our discussion will focus on how suffering can be attributed to God. It will be shown that the suffering of Christ as God's own lies in the unity of His personal identity which, for Luther, is enacted in His work of redemption (See Chapter Four). Luther's understanding of the two-nature Christology and his use of the doctrine of *communicatio idiomatum* will form the contents of our present discussion.

The Christological Question: Christ's Identity Observed

Luther contends that his Christology is not founded upon ecclesiastical arguments and decisions, *in se*, but rather upon the biblical representation of Jesus Christ. His understanding of Christ, he claims, follows from his reading of the Bible, where it is clear that Jesus is presented (and presents Himself) as one with the Father. Moreover, Jesus is presented there (and presents Himself there) as both human and divine. Thus Luther could say that the only God he knows is the one who was incarnate in Jesus Christ.[5] He rejects philosophical attempts to explain this mystery. He does not pretend to understand how Jesus could be both God and human, or how the Divine and human nature could be one, but he accepts both because Jesus Christ in the Bible enacts both the divine and a human life. That is, Luther reads the Gospels as presenting the one historical person of Jesus as speaking and acting as God and man. In so speaking and acting as God and as man, Christ reveals both the divine and human natures, and yet He is one and the same person. "First he speaks as God, then as man. So I learn my article that Christ speaks as God and as man.. If Christ were to speak as God all the time, we could not prove that he was a true man; but if he were always to speak as true man, we could never discover he is also God."[6] Holy Scripture, for Luther, is the prior norm for reading the creeds and councils of the church. Luther is not against dogmas of the church as such, but only a theology that derives dogmas from the church untested by the church's norm. Luther writes :

> These then are the four principal Councils and the reasons they were held. The first, in Nicaea, defended the divinity of Christ against Arius; the second, in Constantinople, defended the divinity of the Holy Spirit against Macedonius; the third, in Ephesus, defended the one person of Christ against Nestorius; the fourth, in Chalcedon, defended the two natures in Christ against Eutyches. But no new articles of faith were thereby established, for these four doctrines are formulated far more abundantly and powerfully in St. John's gospel alone, even if the other evangelists and St. Paul and St. Peter had written nothing about it, although they, together with the prophets, also teach and bear convincing witness to all of that.[7]

For Luther the basic Christological question concerning the person of Christ is settled at Chalcedon (A.D. 451).[8] But he interprets it with strong leanings towards the Alexandrian tradition, affirming the substantial unity of the divinity and humanity of Jesus Christ.[9] Luther has little in common, however, with the classical monophysites;[10] his emphasis on the humanity of Christ precludes monophysitism. He accentuates the unity principle, not by an emphasis on the divinity, but rather by an emphasis on the humanity of Christ.[11] For Luther, Christ's humanity is "the holy ladder" (*scala sancta*) to *his* divinity.[12] "God will, and may, be found only through and in this humanity."[13] Here we see Luther's Christological orientation to the humanity of Christ, which is the starting point of his Christology. With this starting point, he rejects the way of a knowledge of God "from above" which he mentioned in his *Heidelberg Disputation*. "For the Scripture begins quite gently, leading us to Christ, as to a human person and then to a Lord, reigning above all things, and then to a God. Thus I came to recognize God. The philosophers and those versed in the knowledge of the world, on the contrary, have tried to begin from above, and so they have been confounded. One must begin from below and rise up." [14] Although Luther begins his theology from "below," emphasizing the full humanity of Jesus, his theology does not stop short of the basic assertion that God was fully present and active in the life, death and resurrection of Jesus. Luther stood firmly on the principle that the *finitum capax infiniti* and thus it is precisely in the finite human person that the infinite God dwelt.[15] "For God has portrayed Himself definitely and clearly enough in the Word. Therefore it is certain that he who bypasses the person of Christ never finds the true God; for ... God is fully in Christ, where He places Himself for us,...."[16] This then leads to Luther's Christological affirmation: "Yet these two natures are so united that there is only one God and one Lord, that Mary suckles God with her breasts, bathes God, rocks him, and carries him; furthermore, that Pilate and Herod crucified and killed God. The two natures are so joined that the true deity and humanity are one."[17]

For Luther, the Christological understanding of the Word is central to his theological thinking. "The Word is always fundamentally Christ, even though he did not explicitly say so."[18] Early in his lectures on Hebrews in 1517, Luther identified the Word of God with Christ.[19] In his lectures on Galatians in 1535, on Genesis in 1535-1545, and in his sermons on John 1 in 1537, he fully articulated, in a manner similar to Augustine, the identification of Christ with the Word as central to the Gospel.[20] The Word of God is the eternal Word in the eternal, inner life of God. From eternity God has a word, a speech, a thought or conversation within Himself in His divine life, through which God created the universe. No one knew the divine will until the Word was made flesh and proclaimed this to us.[21] Through the eternal Word God communicates Himself to us. This Word of God cannot be known apart from Christ, the incarnate, human Word of God. Christ, the eternal Word, was made flesh in order to reveal God Himself to us. This means that Christ is not only the object of faith but also the ground of faith. Scripture bears witness to Christ. As Watson says, "The creaturely words, whether written or spoken, are for him (Luther) rather the vehicle or media of the Divine creative Word, by which God addresses Himself directly and personally to us."[22]   For Luther, therefore, the Word of God as gospel is nothing but "a joyous sermon concerning Christ, our Saviour," wherein faith, created by the proclamation, "unites us with Christ and makes us owners of all the possessions of Christ."[23]

The Word of God as gospel, for Luther, appears throughout the Old Testament "in the form of promises of the coming Christ, but no less in God's gracious dealings with his covenant people for the sake of the coming Christ."[24] The primary substance of the Old Testament, however, "is really the teaching of Laws, the showing up of sin, and the demanding of good."[25] The Old Testament is something written, a book of laws and promises, and the term "Scripture", die Schrift, properly designates the Old Testament alone.[26] The New Testament, on the contrary, is not Schrift, but Botschaft, that which is proclaimed: "the joyous announcement that the promised Christ has at last come, the liberating news that the righteous God, notwithstanding his holy law and just condemnation of sin, freely forgives sinners for Christ's sake through faith alone."[27]   Accordingly, "the gospel should not really be understood as something written, but rather as a spoken Word which brought forth the Scriptures, as Christ and the apostles have done. This is why Christ himself did not write anything but only spoke. He called his teaching not Scripture but gospel, meaning good news or a proclamation that is spread not by pen, but by word of mouth."[28] The Word of God must therefore not be identified with the "letter" of Scripture. The Old Testament Scriptures are precious because, according to Luther, they are "the swaddling clothes and the manger in which Christ lies."[29] The gospel is both hidden and contained in the Old Testament, awaiting to be illumined by the "star of Bethlehem"—namely, "the new light, preaching and the gospel, oral and public preaching."[30] Christ Himself, and his apostles, brought the gospel hidden in Scripture to light, thereby "produc(ing) in speech and hearing what prior to this lay hidden in the letter and in secret vision."[31] The highest responsibility incumbent upon preachers is to do what Christ and the apostles once did, namely, "to extract the living Word from the Old Scripture, and unceasingly inculcate it in the people."[32] "There is no word in the New Testament that does not look back into the Old, in which it was proclaimed before. The New Testament is nothing more than a revelation of the Old. ... The whole New Testament ... flows out of Moses."[33] The New Testament is nothing but "a public sermon and proclamation of the sayings in the Old Testament and fulfilled by Christ."[34] Christ, for Luther, is therefore essentially the subject of both Testaments, giving Scripture its unity. Luther puts it succinctly and hermeneutically: "Christ is the goal of the whole Scripture."[35] Wherever the prophets and psalmists spoke of the Word of God, it was the words of Christ that were spoken through them: "Wherever God's Word is, there is Christ."[36] Christ in the Old Testament prophesies, as Bornkamm says of Luther, is "always present in double measure, as it were, ... as the one who speaks and the one prophesied."[37] This is clearly taught in the Old Testament, for instance, in Genesis 1. "God speaks, and through His speaking Creation occurs... This Word must be God Himself, because he made creatures through this Word; thus this Word is God. He who speaks and the Word are two persons, yet one God.... It says, 'God spoke.' Yet speaking and God are not one and the same thing." "The Son of God Himself," whom John spoke about in John 1:1, 14, "spoke in the first prophesy" (Gen. 3:15).[38] The Word of God in the Old Testament is the anticipated Christ; it is the historical Christ in the New Testament.[39] "Jesus Christ is Jehovah, God and man."[40] Christ is fully present in the Old Testament in the totality of His person as God-man, imparting Himself wherever His promise is

grasped by faith—"there is no God outside of Christ."[41] As James
Preus says of Luther, God's Word as Gospel is always in the form
of "promise," which is to be believed; and faith is always the same
whether in the Old or New Testament, taking the promise seriously.[42]

In his commentary on Psalm 2:3, the reformer stresses the unity
and the distinction of the Father and the Son. Quoting John 10:30,
Luther declares that the Father and the Son are one. Luther interprets Psalm 2:12 as referring to the unity of the two persons, that
the Father and the Son refer to each other.[43] Their unity constitutes
the ontological ground for our knowledge of God. In Christ we are
given access to knowledge of God. Torrance's words elucidate
Luther's: "The fact that God has named himself to us a Father in
and through Jesus Christ his incarnate Son means that we cannot
and may not seek to have knowledge of God or express it in such
a way as to by-pass his self-naming."[44] He who worships the Son
worships the Father. Christ is equal with God, and thus Luther
asserts, in his comments on Psalm 45:11, "honour him, for he is
your Lord." But the Son is distinct from the Father. The Son is not
merely a creature, but is, as Athanasius correctly says, "begotten,
not created."[45] In his comments on Psalm 2:7-8, Luther took issue
with Arius who argued that Christ was not God by nature but one
who was inferior to God and received what He did not have
before. Arius contended that Psalm 2:8 "Ask of me, and I will
make the nations Your heritage and the ends of the earth Your pos-
session" argues against the divinity of Christ. "If," Arius declared
"Christ is God by nature, then He is already Lord of the nations
and of the ends of the earth. But here He entreats as one inferior
to God and receives what He did not have before."[46] Thus Christ,
for Arius, is not God by nature and His divinity is that which is
received by exaltation.[47] Luther argues the contrary, that this
Psalm

> does not speak of the Son of God as He was from eternity. For in this
> capacity He is the Lord of all living creatures; He received nothing, but
> has all. It speaks rather of the King of Zion, that is, of the incarnate Son
> of God, of the man born of the Virgin Mary, beginning His kingdom on

the physical Zion through the Gospel. To this man, who is made humble below the angels, God gives authority over the nations that all
should be subject to Him.... And the Son is ordered to demand this
authority so that He might actually show reverence toward the Father
and His inexpressible humility.[48]

For Luther, Christ is God by nature though He, according to His
office, subjects Himself to the Father. Christ is the firstborn of all
creation (cf. Col. 1:15). Contrary to Augustine, the verb "begotten"
for Luther is a past tense, denoting "the completion of nativity."[49]
"The Son will be born and has been born today, daily and
always."[50] The adverb "today" must be understood as time as it is
to God, not to us (cf. 2 Pet. 3:8). In eternity there is "no time, neither past nor future, but a perpetual today."[51] Luther refers
"today" to the eternal nativity of the Son. The Son of God was
born from eternity, "without a beginning." Luther wrote in his lectures on Galatians (1535): "Thus Christ, according to his divinity, is
a divine and eternal essence or nature, without a beginning."[52]

In addition to Christ's eternal birth, there is a nativity "in
time." Christ's "humanity is a nature created in time."[53] Dorothy
Sayers' remark that only the Christian God has a "date" in human
history,[54] may be heard as an echo of Luther's comment, quoted by
the authors of the Formula of Concord, that "according to our calen-
dar Jesus the Son of Mary is 1543 years old. But from the moment
that the deity and humanity were united in one person this man,
Mary's Son, is and is called the almighty and everlasting God."[55]
The person of Christ, born of the Virgin Mary, is at the same time
true God and true man. "These two natures in Christ are not confused or mixed, and the properties of each nature must be clearly
understood. It is characteristic of the divinity to be eternal and
without a beginning. Nevertheless the two are combined, and
divinity without a beginning is incorporated into the humanity
with a beginning."[56]

Believing that the Chacedonian formula that preserves the distinction of two natures was rooted in the biblical depiction of
Christ, Luther was therefore obliged to distinguish between the
humanity and the divinity.[57] He asserts against Schwenckfeld that

Christ is a "creature" according to His humanity, and He is a "creator" according to His divinity.[58] Writes Luther:

> *Hoc Schwenckfeld non videt, ideo cum audit patres dicere, Christum secundum humanitatem esse creaturam, statim arripit dictum et depravat et abutitur pro se. Etiamsi dicant patres: Christus secundum humanitatem est creatura, hoc potest utcunque tolerai, sed Schwenckfeld scelerate advertit: Ergo Christus simpliciter est creatura. Quare tu nequam non addis: Christus secundum divinitatem est creator?[59]*

Commenting on Psalm 110:1 in 1532, Luther found the two natures of Christ declared in the verse. The first "lord" designates Christ as the true God; the second "lord" designates Christ as a true man, denoting that the Messiah, or Christ, was one who had been promised to the fathers, and especially to king David, from whom He was to descend.[60] This psalm contains a clear and powerful statement about the person of Christ—namely, He is both David's promised Son according to the flesh and God's eternal Son, as well as the eternal king and priest—and about His resurrection, ascension and spiritual kingdom.[61] Luther says of Psalm 110 as a whole that Christ and the apostles after him often cite this psalm in the New Testament because it constitutes the core and foundation of Christian faith. It confirms the article of faith concerning the person of Christ and His kingdom and righteousness. The divinity and humanity of Christ are equally emphasized in Luther's commentary on Psalm 45: "This psalm is one of the most outstanding as a description of Christ's kingdom and particularly, of His person, stating that He is true God and true man."[62] In his comments on Psalm 8 in 1537, Luther ascribes two different titles to the two natures of Christ.[63] The first title "Lord" is ascribed to the divine majesty, not to any creature, and it means "the right, true and eternal God." The other title "Ruler" is attributed to Christ's human nature, for in scripture it is a common name used for princes or head of the household. Since the King is called "Lord, our Ruler," says Luther, it follows that He must be true God and true man at the same time. The unity of the person of Christ is affirmed in that the psalm speaks only of one "Lord" and "Ruler" (cf. Psalm 8:1). Christ is Lord and God according to His eternal and divine nature;

He is Ruler according to His human nature and indeed, became man to be our sovereign Ruler. As the second Person of Godhead, the incarnate Son ascribes all things to the Father as the Originator; in His humanity He begins His kingdom in the earthly Zion through the gospel.[64]

The article of faith concerning Christ's person is also enunciated in Luther's sermons on John in 1538: "For if this foundation stands and is ours by faith—that Christ is both, God's Son and the Virgin's Son, in one Person, though of two different natures, of the divine nature from eternity from the Father, of the human nature through His birth from Mary—then I have all that is necessary."[65] As true God and true man, Christ redeems us from sin, death, and the power of the devil.[66] The brief words of Psalm 2:7 "The Lord has said: 'You are my Son'," Luther interpreted by a sentence of Apostles' Creed: "He was conceived by the Holy Spirit, born of Mary, a virgin mother, suffered under Pontius Pilate, died, was raised again from the dead by His own power, and sits at the right hand of the Father."[67] The Son became man and assumed the role of a servant, condescending to the miserable level of our sinful condition in order to begin His kingdom in us by sharing all human weakness and misery. "For this reason He also had to die."[68] Having broken death and the grave and all enemies in his death and resurrection, Christ now is "seated at the right hand of the Father."

The two doctrines—that Christ is the second person of the triune God, and that Christ is true God and true man—are, of course, integral to each other. But because Luther's dominant emphasis was on the doctrine of justification by faith, his focus was less on the eternal Word of the Trinity and more on the incarnation of the Word. And incarnation is conceived primarily in terms of the act of the redemption.[69] The "personal union," in Luther's theology of incarnation, must not be conceived as "suppositale union," for the two natures are united "personaliter" in the unity of the person.[70] In the theses of the Disputation On the Divinity and Humanity of Christ in 1540, Luther wrote against the "insulsius" discourse of those who said "humanum naturam sustentari seu suppositari a divina natura, seu supposito divino."[71] Luther uses the terms conjungi and con-

juncto to designate the unity of two distinct natures in the One person of Jesus Christ.[72] Philosophic logic cannot express adequately the unity of two natures; in philosophy, God and humanity are two persons,[73] but they constitute the one and same person in theology.

> *Alia est persona humanitatis, alia est persona divinitatis. In Christo autem sunt humanitas et divinitas. Ergo in Christo sunt duae personae. R(esponse by Luther). Est fallacia compositionis et divinionis. In maiore dividitis humanam et divinam naturam, in minore coniungitis. Haec est philosophica solutio, sed nos dicimus theologie. Nego consequentiam, et ratio est, quia humanitas et divinitas in Christo constituunt unam personam. Sed illae duae naturae sunt distinctae in theologia, scilicet secundum naturas, sed non secundum personam. Nam tum sunt indistinctae, sed duae distinctae naturae, sed indistinctae personae. Non sunt duae personae distinctae, sed sunt distinctae indistinctae, id est, sunt distinctae naturae, sed indistinctae personae.*[74]

For Luther, "human being (*homo*)" signifies an existing person in philosophy while in theology it means "a certain divinity in Christ."[75] The syllogism cannot capture the mysteries of faith, especially that of Christ as both God and man—a divine subject. Luther writes:

> "Man" in philosophy according to its own nature does not signify the Son of God or a divine person. This is the very thing that we call the communication of idioms. The syllogism is not admitted into the mysteries of faith and theology. Philosophy constitutes an aberration in the realm of theology.[76]

Furthermore:

> We say that man is God, and we witness to this by the word of God without a syllogism, apart from philosophy; philosophy has nothing to do with our grammar. You should note this because "man" is and should mean something beyond what it means in the tree of Porphyry, even if it is truly said that God was made man, as they and I say. For here it means something greater and more comprehensive.[77]

The communication of properties requires that a term such as

"Christ"—understood as meaning both God and man—carries a "new" content, designating a meaningful unity *in concreto*. Such "newness" must not be admitted into the philosophical context of meaning, for in theology, "the words used in philosophy become new."[78] There abides in Luther a sharp distinction, not between the words of theology and that of philosophy, but in terms of their meanings. As Luther says, "the same thing is not true in the different professions."[79] There is an "identity of words" in both disciplines, but there is a "difference in meaning" of the same proposition. Luther clearly repudiates the equivocation of the "Sorbonne theologians" in the following passage:

> We say: God is man, which is a simple proposition, not two-fold as the Sorbonne has made it. We condemn the latter. Every man is a creature, this is a simple proposition; this is true in philosophy, but in theology it is false, which is proved in the minor premise, that is Christ is man. The Sorbonne compels us to make all words ambiguous. This is to be resisted. It is not to be allowed that in this proposition, that is, God is man, one may unite theology and philosophy because a distinction is made between man and man. The man who uses words univocally speaks consistently, but not the equivocator, and by the fact that they equivocate they destroy their own argument.[80]

The term *homo*, when used in philosophy, indicates the *persona per se subsistentem*; in theology, the term as applied to *Christus* designates the *persona divina, quae suscepit humanam naturam*.[81] For Luther, theology is not directed toward the abstract entity humanity in itself, but toward the concrete reality where "*humanitas quae non est subsistens, se assumpta*" by the divinity.[82] Whereas in philosophy, these two terms *homo* and *humanitas* are one and the same, this is not so in theology. "*Homo hic in concretis significat, quia est persona, sed humanitas non significat.*"[83] *Homo* signifies a person, and therefore must not be confused with *humanitas*, which for Luther means a *natura humana* that has been assumed.[84] Consequently, one cannot say that the Son of God has assumed a *homo*, otherwise there would have been two persons.

The "*hypostatic union*", for Luther, means that the Logos always exists in union with the flesh, thus he resists any attempt to separate the eternal Word from the humanity, as occurs in the case of the *extra-Calvinisticum*.[85] The hypostatic union is an event in history, but from all eternity Christ's divinity must not be conceived apart from His humanity and vice versa.[86] And when scripture "speaks about the divine nature united with the human in one person, then it is speaking of Christ as composite and incarnate,...his whole person."[87] In this way Luther refused to divorce Christ from God as Philip of Bethsaida did, for in Christ "dwells the whole fullness of Deity bodily" (Col 2:9). There is no valid relation with God that is independent of the man Jesus. God wills that our relation with Him is to be grounded in the person of the Logos who exists, not independently from the man Jesus, but always in union with Him. In his opposition to the Enthusiasts, Luther insists on the revelation of God in Jesus Christ :

> We cannot touch or grasp the divine majesty, any more than we would wish to touch or grasp a devouring fire. ... That is why he has presented his flesh to us, in order that we may attach ourselves to it and to a certain extent be able to touch and comprehend it. ... Therefore do not listen to those who say that the flesh avails nothing. Reverse this word and say that God without the flesh avails nothing. For it is on the flesh of Christ from the Virgin's womb that your eyes must be fixed, so that you may take courage and say: "I have known nothing of God, either in heaven nor on earth, apart from the flesh, sleeping in the Virgin's womb" ... For otherwise God is in all ways incomprehensible, it is only in the flesh of Christ that he can be grasped.[88]

In the disputation of 1539, *The Word is Made Flesh*, Luther accentuates the following rule: *"Et bene notandum est et maxime observandum, quod extra Christum non est Deus alius."*[89] Luther, employing the Cappadocian image of iron/fire, explains: "Anyone who touches the heat in the heated iron touches the iron and whoever has touched the skin of Christ has actually touched God."[90] The man Jesus is the revelation of God, and hence the "theology of ascent" is given up by Luther in favor of the "theology of descent"—God came "down-to-earth" in the man Jesus for us so that we may see, hear and touch him.[91]

Because Jesus is the revelation of God, His cross discloses the nature of God. Luther warned against those whom he called "the fluttering spirits who like to speculate about sublime matters, who would like to bore a hole through heaven and peek in to discover what God Himself is and what He does, meanwhile ignoring Christ as superfluous for that purpose."[92] By descending to the world in the human suffering form of Jesus, God is revealed as the one who loves and suffers. More specifically, the God who hides in the suffering of the cross means for Luther that God suffers. This declaration does not arise from speculation, but rather as a conclusion derived from God's revelation in Christ. This conclusion runs contrary to that of the early church fathers, which was recounted in Chapter one. Under the influence of Greek philosophy, they upheld the impassibility of God. The Greek idea of divine apathy controlled what they declared may or may not be said of the deity of Jesus Christ. They concluded that Jesus suffered in His humanity but not in His divinity. The death of the Crucified Christ, therefore, was treated as an event that affected only the "true man" but not the "true God." Luther is particularly critical of such understanding. "Many heretics have arisen ... who have assailed this article of faith and have been offended at the thought that God should suffer. The Godhead, they argued, is an eternal majesty ... God cannot be crucified! But tell him that this person, who is God and man, was crucified."[93] Hence for Luther Christ's humanity is no curtain behind which an impersonal and immobile God hides, but rather it actually expresses God's heart, the innermost essence of God Himself. This understanding constitutes a revolution in the conception of God in the history of the Church. Luther stands as a deipassionist: God is the personal and living One, who is present in the man Jesus, and who in reality shares in the suffering of the humanity.[94] The cross is a "mask" of God, and an "opposite form" in which God's self-positing in His revelation takes place.[95] *Theologia crucis* evinces the epistemological principle wherein like is known by unlike. To the crucified Christ one finds no equivalents, no analogous knowledge of God. God's nature reveals itself in the suffering of the cross in that the "fullness of God's power" is seen not in the pompous, powerful and the proud, but in the shameful, weak and lowly.[96]

Consequently, that God is identified with the crucified Christ not only reverses all human concepts of God but also refuses any understanding of the crucified Christ on the presupposition of concept of God imported from elsewhere. Walter Kasper writes:

> Luther's *theologia crucis* breaks through the whole system of metaphysical theology. He tries consistently to see, not the cross in light of a philosophical concept of God, but God in the light of the cross. ... For Luther, the hidden God is the God hidden in the suffering and the cross. We should not try to penetrate the mysteries of God's majesty, but should be content with the God on the cross. We cannot find God except in Christ; anyone who tries to find him outside of Christ will find the devil.[97]

Communicatio Idiomatum: Theological Language Applied

Luther not only adopted the Chalcedonian formula that preserved the distinction of two natures in Christ, he also made use of the tradition he inherited of the *communicatio idiomatum* as *modus loquendi theologicus*. The *communicatio idiomatum* is, for Luther, an ontological deduction from the cross and the Incarnation. Luther's handling of the doctrine of *communicatio idiomatum* is a bit strange. He refers to it mainly in his disputes with other theologians (for instance, Nestorius and Zwingli). When he engages in constructive theology or biblical interpretation, it seems he does not use it. However, he could use the doctrine because he found it in harmony with his Christological thinking which he believed was rooted in the Bible. Luther found in the language of Paul the notion of the crucifixion of the Son of God.[98] This means for Luther that God's passibility is not established by the *communicatio idiomatum* but this rather is a theological means to realize or articulate that God, in Christ, did suffer and die.[99] Luther does not start from the doctrine of the *communicatio idiomatum*; rather he starts from the identity of the person of Christ in its unity as depicted in the New Testament. Jesus Christ, as one concrete and living person, is the ground from which Luther is operating. More precisely, the declaration of impassibility goes off the track for the simple reason that Christ did suffer and we are not allowed to separate God and man in Christ as the Nestorians did. If Christ is one with God and one with man, he must be so as a whole person so that suffering is not only be predicated of the human nature but also of the entire person. In and through this person God Himself suffered. Therefore the doctrine of the *communicatio idiomatum* is not the starting point for the affirmation of divine passibility, but rather is the means by which Luther develops the conclusion which he has drawn from the Bible.

We may now turn to the question: in what way can suffering be attributed to God? This question hinges on how Luther uses the doctrine of the *communicatio idiomatum*. We must consider whether the communication of attributes applies only to the relation of each nature to the person of Jesus Christ or to the relation between the natures as well. In the early church, the division between the Alexandrians (Cyril, John of Damascus) and the Antichocheans, as Lienhard observes, is clearly seen in the different ways in which they apply the communication of attributes.[100] The Alexandrian theologians conceived of the communication principally only in one direction, that is in terms of the action of the divine nature with respect to the human nature. The motive of the Alexandria's Christological formulations was to establish the "one sole agent of what happens in Christ."[101] On the other hand, the Antiocheans thought of the communication as the communication of the attributes of each of the two natures to the person.[102] The motive of Antioch's formulation was to establish "two agents of what happens in Christ": the divine Logos or Son is divine, and is impassible; the human Jesus is temporal, and is passible.[103]

It seems Luther follows the Antiocheans. Already in his *Church Postil* in 1522, Luther asserted that what is attributed to the one nature of the person is attributed to the whole person. He illustrates by making a comparison: when we speak of the wounded leg of a man, we say: this man is wounded, even though it is not his soul, nor the entire man who is wounded, but only a part of his body, because the body and soul are one (*eyn ding*).[104] The same illustration also appears in his lectures on the First Epistle of John in 1527: "When somebody is hurt in the leg, one says: the dog bit Peter, the whole person is involved. ... Therefore, do not let yourselves be drawn into this scholarly distinction. Indeed, one says of those who crucified the humanity of Christ, that they crucified the 'Lord of glory'."[105] Luther, in his *Confession concerning Christ's Supper* in 1528, argues against Zwingli: "It is correct to say that the Son of God was crucified and died for us. But if someone objects that the deity cannot suffer and die, we reply that this is true, but yet because the deity and the humanity in Christ are one person, therefore, on account of such personal union the Scripture attributes to the deity whatever belongs to the humanity and vice versa."[106] But Luther goes on to clarify:

> You must confess that Christ, or the person, suffered and died. Now that person is true God. Therefore it is correct to say that the Son of God suffered. For although one part of Him (if I may speak in this way), namely, the deity, does not suffer, yet the person which is God does suffer by reason of the other part, that is, the humanity; just as we commonly say that the son of the king is wounded, although only his foot is actually wounded, ... The whole world speaks this way, not only the Scripture. And truly the Son of God is crucified for us, that is, the person who is God. This person, I say, is crucified according to the human nature. Thus we must attribute to the whole person whatever belongs to either of its parts, because both parts comprise the one person. All the ancient doctors speak this way, and likewise the modern theologians, in every language, and so does the Scripture. The ancients called it "Synechdoche" when I say that Christ is dead according to the human nature.[107]

Here suffering is predicated of the person who is God, not of the divine nature. For Zwingli, any conception of the communication is only nominal; it is only a rhetorical figure of speech, a *praedicatio verbalis*. Thus he uses the doctrine of *Alloeosis* to explain the attribution to the two natures of that which by right belongs to only one.[108] Zwingli accuses Luther of confusing the two natures by making them one. He charges that Luther speaks of the union of two natures in such a way that each nature effected a change in the other, bringing about a *tertium quid*, a Christ who is a combination of both natures. Replying to this charge, Luther argues that "we merge the two distinct natures into one person, and say: God is man, and man is God."[109] Christ our Lord is God and man in one person, neither confounding the natures nor dividing the person.[110] Luther, in keeping with the Chalcedonian orthodoxy, stresses the unity of Christ's person in his repudiation of Zwingli who, in his attempt to secure the transcendence of God, advocates that the Son of God does not suffer and die, and that Christ suffers and dies only insofar as he is a man.[111] Luther in turn accuses Zwingli of being a Nestorian for "separating the person of Christ as though there were two persons."[112] Luther cannot accept the separation between the divine and human nature in Zwingli's Christ. Martin Chemnitz declares in favor of Luther's position: "If Zwingli's *alloeosis* stands, then Christ will have to be two persons, one a divine and the other a human person, since Zwingli applies all the texts concerning the passion only to the human nature and completely excludes them from the divine nature."[113] Zwingli's Christ would ultimately mean that God in the salvific act remains unaffected by the flesh of Christ's humanity. This means God Himself is totally removed from the experience of the depths of suffering on earth. Unlike Zwingli, Luther is unwilling to conceive a Christ in whom the divinity does not suffer. He writes against Zwingli: "Beware! Beware, I tell you, of the '*Alloeosis.*' It is the devil's spawn. For in the end it sets up such a Christ that I wouldn't want to be called 'Christian' after him."[114] "For if I have to believe that only the human nature has suffered, Christ is too feeble a savior for me."[115] Luther asserts God's suffering in Christ in his sacramental controversy with Zwingli: "Rather, (the man) is one person with God, so that whatever God is, there also the man is: God also is said to suffer."[116] "If you could show me a place where God was and the man was not, the person would be neatly split, (and) I could promptly then say, 'Here is God who is not man.' ... Don't give me any of that God."[117] For Luther, as Jenson notes, the traditional doctrine that "one must attribute to the whole person what happens to either nature of the person' has as its content that suffering is 'really' communicated to the Logos, also as God, and God's infinite 'energies' really communicated to the man Jesus."[118]

The communication from the natures to the person, as Elert noted, was emphatically stated in Luther's *Schwabach Articles* in 1529: "One should not believe or teach that Jesus Christ suffered for us as a man or as mankind; but because here God and man are not two persons but one indivisible Person, one must hold and teach that God and man or the Son of God truly suffered for us."[119] Although the two natures are distinct, it is yet one person—"God's Son and the Son of Mary are one"—who suffers as Christ. In his sermon on John in 1537, "We learned that the Son of man was hanged and lifted up as the serpent in the wilderness had been lifted up. This applies properly only to His human nature, since God cannot suffer and be crucified. And yet Christ says here that the Son of God was given into death and was crucified."[120] Luther affirmed, in his opposition to Zwingli, that what is predicated of one of the two natures is found in the whole person of Christ. Because God and man are one entire person, Luther says in the 1537 sermon on Col. 1:19-20 : "It must be said that the person of Christ carries (*führe*) the properties of the two natures .... Hence that which appertains individually to one of the two natures must be attributed to the whole person."[121] "Because God and man are one person, one Christ, one Jesus, one Son of God and Mary, and not two persons, not two Christs, not two Jesuses, not two Sons, the result is that the properties of the two natures in Christ must all be, and in the same manner, attributed to the person."[122]

In his comments on John 14 in 1538, Luther explains the same point at great length. We shall summarize his teachings with a few quotations :

> And now since He is believed as one Person, God and man, it is also proper for us to speak of him as each nature requires.   Some words reflect his human, others His divine nature. Therefore we should consider what Christ says according to His human nature and what He says according to His divine nature.   For where this is not observed and properly distinguished, many types of heresy must result, as happened in times gone by ...[123]

> This is done for the sake of the personal union, which we call the "communication of properties."   Thus we can say; "Christ, God's Son (that is, the Person who is true God), was conceived and born of the Virgin Mary, suffered under Pontius Pilate, crucified and dead." ... He does not do this, of course, according to the divine nature.   But since this is done

by one and the same Person, it is correct to say that God's Son is doing
it. Thus St. Paul declares in I COR. 2:8 : "If they had understood it, they
would not have crucified the Lord of glory."[124]

Whatever this Person, Christ, says and does, is said and done by both,
true God and true man, so that all His words and works must always be
attributed to the whole Person and are not divided, as though He were
not true God or not true man.   But this must be done in such a way as
to identify and recognize each nature properly.[125]

God suffers in the person of Jesus Christ, not in His divine nature
but according to His human nature. Yet God and man are so inseparably united in the one Person of Christ that the suffering is true
of the whole person.   This Luther believes is faithful to the language of the Scripture: Christ was crucified according to His
humanity; since this person is God and man, it is proper to say that
God's Son was crucified.   For Luther the aforementioned statements—God suffered or died—are not verbal declarations (*praedicatio verbalis*) as was the case in Zwingli's theology. For our simple
Christian faith proves that the Son of God, who became man, suffered for us, died, and redeemed us with His blood. That God suffers *realiter* is certain in Luther's disputation concerning the passage: *The Word was Made Flesh* in 1539:

For by this fact (*communicatio idiomatum*) the proper attributes of each
nature are attributed to the person of Christ. For even if he is identical
with the Father, nevertheless, because he became incarnate, suffered,
and was crucified, all things were made subject to him by the Father. In
the Person (of Christ) is God and man: inasmuch as God is God, he did
not suffer, because God is not capable of suffering, but inasmuch as he
is man, he suffers. Nevertheless, because God and man in one person
cannot be separated, we are compelled to say the Christ as true God and
true man suffered for us and the whole person is said to have died for
us.[126]

Luther maintains this understanding as late as 1544, that the person of Jesus Christ suffers not in His divinity but only in His
humanity.[127]

The aforesaid indicates that Luther refers to the doctrine of the *communicatio idiomatum,* according to which the properties of the two natures in Christ are communicated to the *concretum* of His person in such a way that it is proper to say: "The Son of God suffered and died."[128] But did Luther go further than the communication of attributes from nature to person? That is, did Luther conceive in the person of Christ the idea of a real communication of attributes between the two natures themselves? The answer is yes. In his sermon on John in 1537, Luther writes: "the two natures dwell in the Lord Christ, and yet He is but one person. These two natures retain their properties, and each also communicates its properties to the other."[129] On this delicate topic of God's suffering and dying, the authors of the *Formula of Concord* quote Luther saying:

> Unless God is in the balance and throws his weight as a counterbalance, we shall sink to the bottom of the scale. ... If it is not true that God died for us, but only a man died, we are lost. But if God's death and God dead lie in the opposite scale, then his side goes down and we go upward like a light or empty pan. Of course, he can also go up again or jump out of his pan. But he could not have sat in the pan unless he became a man like us, so that it could be said: God dead, God's passion, God's blood, God's death. According to his nature God cannot die, but since God and man are united in one person it is correct to talk about God's death when that man dies who is one thing or one person with God.[130]

Here Luther justifies his remarks on the suffering and death of God in Christ on the soteriological grounds. Already in his *Church Postil* in 1522, Luther says if it is true that only the human nature suffers and the divine nature has no part in it, then Christ is of no more use to us than any other saint because His death is merely that of a human being.[131] Christ's achievement would then become a pure model for the faithful, turning Christ into only an exemplar. For Luther, in order to redeem human beings from the power of death, God had to co-suffer and co-die in Christ. That is why Luther makes use of his image of the scale to illustrate that God can go down, can rise and jump out of His pan. God lets Himself be overtaken by death in the suffering and dying of

Christ, and yet He remains the victor over death.[132] With this it becomes clear how closely the two-nature Christology and soteriology are linked in Luther's thinking. For Luther it is a theological axiom that Christ must be affected by suffering even according to His divine nature, otherwise salvation through Christ's suffering and death are inconceivable to him.[133] Luther therefore thinks of the unity of the natures in Christ in such a way that when Christ's human nature suffers, His divine nature suffers along with His human nature *via communicatio idiomatum*. Luther continued this interpretation in his work *On the Councils and the Church*(1539), where he refuted Nestorius' understanding of the *communicatio idiomatum*: "Nestorius' error was not that he believed Christ to be a pure man, or that he made two persons of him; on the contrary, he confesses two natures, the divine and human, in one person— but he will not admit a *communicatio idiomatum*" between the two natures.[134] The axiom of God's impassibility, as Jansen notes, is the motive of Nestorius' theology.[135] "The *idiomata* of the two natures cannot coincide. That is the opinion of Nestorius."[136] Luther writes: "If I say, 'The carpenter Jesus was crucified by the Jews and the same Jesus is the true God,' Nestorius would agree that this is true. But if I say, 'God was crucified by the Jews,' he says, 'No! For crucifixion and death are *idiomata* or attributes not of divine but of human nature."[137] Luther recognized that Nestorius taught in principle nothing other than what Zwingli taught —namely, "that the divinity of Christ could not suffer" or "Christ, in his divinity, was immortal."[138] In this Luther faults Nestorius for lacking "the intelligence to express his thought properly"—"for after he concedes that God and man are united and joined into one person, he can in no way deny that the *idiomata* of the two natures should also be united and joined."[139] Contrary to Nestorius' position, Luther provides his own reading of the Council at Ephesus in AD 431:

> We Christians must ascribe all the *idiomata* of the two natures of Christ, both persons, equally to him. Consequently Christ is God and man in one person because whatever is said of him as man must also be said of him as God, namely, Christ has died, and Christ is God; therefore God died—not the separated God, but God united with humanity. For about the separated God both statements, namely, that Christ is God

and that God died, are false; both are false, for then God is not man. If
it seems strange to Nestorius that God dies, he should think it equally
strange that God becomes man; for thereby the immortal God becomes
that which must die, suffer, and have all human *idiomata*. Otherwise,
what would that man be with whom God personally unites, if he did not
have truly human *idiomata*? It would be a phantom, as the Manicheans
had taught earlier. On the other hand, whatever is said of God must also
be ascribed to the man, namely, God created the world and is almighty;
the man Christ is God, therefore the man Christ created the world and
is almighty. The reason for this that since God and man have become
one person, it follows that this person bears the *idiomata* of both natures.
140

According to Luther, two heresies are "in opposition" to one
another: Eutyches' heresy consists in his refusal to ascribe the
idiomata of the divine nature to the human nature; just as
Nestorius, on the other hand, refuses to ascribe the *idiomata* of the
human nature to the divine in the one Person of Christ.141 Both
parties have "conceded the antecedent" (i.e. Christ is true God and
true man) but "denied the consequent" (i.e. a *communicatio*
between two natures).142 Both parties, Luther argues, separate the
persons, pulling the humanity away from the deity and making
each nature an independent person.143 Consequently only the
man Christ was crucified as was the case in Nestorius' Christology;
only God is to be worshiped as was the case with Eutyches'
Christology. Unlike Nestorius and Eutyches, Luther is able to
envisage *realiter* that God suffers or that man creates. It is important to note the distinction made by Luther between a communication *in abstracto* and a communication *in concreto*: "If I speak
rightly saying that the divinity does not suffer, the humanity does
not create, then I speak of something in the abstract and of a divinity which is separated. But one must not do that. Abstract concepts should not be cut loose, or our faith will become false. But
one believes in a concrete sense (*in concreto*) saying that this man is
God, etc. Then the properties are attributed."144 When the divinity is understood in an abstract manner, i.e., as not united with
humanity in Jesus Christ, Luther says that God does not suffer.
Suffering and death are alien to the divine nature *per se*, and there-

fore cannot be directly attributed to it. But since the divine nature
has taken to itself *in concreto* the human nature, it can be said that
the divine nature shares in Christ the characteristics of the human
nature.[145] Here Luther transcends the Alexandrian Christology by
asserting the idea of a real communication that moves not only
from the divine nature to the human nature but also from the
human nature to the divine nature. The originality of Luther, says
Lienhard, must be recognized in that by affirming a communication of attributes, Luther took over from the Eastern tradition the
idea of *perichoresis*, by which the natures are united as fire and
iron.[146] Luther thus joins with "the current flowing from the
Cappadocians to John of Damascus, by way of Cyril of
Alexandria."[147]

Luther also discusses the conception of the *communicatio
idiomatum*, of the ascription to one nature of properties which
belong to another, on 29 February 1540, in his *Disputation On The
Divinity and Humanity of Christ*, in which the idea of a "new language" occurs, especially in the context of Christology.[148] "The
theses as a whole," says White, "move in a uniform direction, from
language to metalanguage."[149] Thesis one asserts Luther's orthodox Christology: "This is the Catholic faith, that we confess one
Lord, Christ, true God and man."[150] Theses two, three, four, fif-
teen, seventeen and twenty deal with the *communicatio* and "new"
language:

> Thesis 2: From this truth of the twofold substances and the unity of the
> person follows what is called the communication of properties.

> Thesis 3: So that those things, which are human, are correctly predicat-
> ed of God, and on the other hand, those things which are divine are cor-
> rectly predicated of the *homo*.

> Thesis 4: It is true to say this man created the world, and this God suf-
> fered, died and was buried and so on.

> Thesis 15: It is right to teach that in this matter it is the usage of Scripture
> (*usus loquendi*) that rules, as this also maintained by the orthodox
> Fathers.

Thesis 17: Hence in this matter one must beware of etymology, analogy, consequence, and suggesting similar instances.

Thesis 20: It is certainly the case that all words when used of Christ, take on a new meaning in the thing they describe.[151]

Here we see in Luther the communication between the two natures in Christ. For Luther, the chasm between God and man, between Creator and creature, when one looks away from Christ, is even deeper than it is for philosophy.[152] This chasm between God and man is non-existent in Christ. Thesis 20 explains: *"Certum est tamen, omnia vocabula in Christo novam significationem accipere in eadem re significata."*[153] Nagel explains:

The traditional phrases "according to his human nature" and "according to his divine nature" Luther uses so that the distinction of the natures is not lost; but his usage of them has come free of the dualism which sees divine and human, heavenly and earthly, infinite and finite, impassible and passible, as opposites unreconcilable. They are if you look at God separately, and if you look at man separately, but in Christ this separation is gone. In Christ they have a new meaning; the old meaning applies only to them when separated. In speaking of him we may not speak of the divinity separated from the humanity, or of the humanity separated from the divinity. By such separation our Saviour and salvation are undone. *Extra Christum non est Deus alius.*[154]

To quote Luther:

Christ according to this humanity is a creature and Christ according to his divinity is God; they are so utterly conjoined that one person is two natures.[155]

The human nature is not to be spoken of with the divinity excluded from it. The humanity is not a person but a nature. The two natures are distinct..... That person who created in the beginning was made man. This remains the same person. So very close are the humanity and divinity conjoined in Christ, as soul and body in man, that it is not possible to speak concerning the natures as if they were divided from each other... I confess two natures, but they cannot be separated. This makes a unity greater and more sure than the conjunction of soul and body. These are separated, but that conjunction never, for there are united in one person, the immortal divine nature and mortal human nature. That is Christ, the impassible Son of God. God and man is crucified under Pontius Pilate.

Objection: What is immortal cannot become mortal. God is immortal. Therefore he cannot become mortal.

Response: In Philosophy that is true.[156]

Although Luther did not invent the expressions *genus majestaticum* and *genus tapeinoticon*, they can be used to express his thought.[157] The idea of *genus majestaticum* is the communication of the attributes of the divine nature to the human nature. This means human nature in Christ possesses all properties which otherwise pertain to God. In his *Table Talk,* Luther says that whatever happens and befalls this person Christ, "it happens to and befalls to this God and to this man. From whence it comes that these two natures in Christ communicate their attributes and their properties the one to the other; that is to say, that which is the peculiar property of one nature is communicated also to the other. That is why one says justly of the natures that they are attached to one another, intertwined and united."[158] The indissoluble unity of the person makes possible the communication between the two natures— "deity and humanity, are found in one person, and the attributes of each nature are imputed to the other."[159] "Here creation is attributed solely to the divinity, since the humanity does not create". "Nevertheless," says Luther, "it is said correctly that 'the man created,' because the divinity, which alone creates, is incarnate with the humanity, and therefore the humanity participates in the attributes of both predicates."[160] Accordingly Luther could say: "The Infant lying in the lap of His mother created heaven and earth, and is the lord of the angels."[161] Also the divine property of omnipresence (or ubiquity) is communicated to the human nature. Here lies the doctrinal antithesis between Zwingli and Luther over the Lord's Supper. As Pannenberg notes :

For Zwingli the body of the exalted Christ, like every human body, is spatially limited. If he is present at a particular place (*in certo loco*) in heaven, he cannot be at the same time present in Lord's Supper. Luther, on the other hand, ascribed to the exalted humanity of Christ full participation in the attributes of divine being including omnipresence, so that even after the ascension he is present on earth and can communicate his presence in the Lord's Supper.[162]

The word "*homo*" in the context of faith belongs, for Luther, to a "new and theological grammar."[163] "Man is obviously a new man, and as the sophists themselves say, stands for the divinity."[164] The "new" predication finds no analogies. Its newness lies in its ability to transcend the old and legal grammar which prohibits crediting anyone with predicates which he himself has not gained. "Therefore in theology let faith always be the divinity of works diffused throughout the works in the same way that the divinity is throughout the humanity of Christ.[165] In Luther's hermeneutic of deed, the old and legal grammar of reason is subordinated to the grammar of faith which is "new and theological."[166] In theology, attention is directed not toward the abstract entity "humanity", but rather toward the concrete reality where the human nature has been assumed by the divinity. "*Christus homo, id est, persona divina, quae suscepit humanam naturam.*"[167] This means the term *homo*, when used theologically, takes on a "new" meaning, for it signifies the divine person who assumes the human nature. For Luther, philosophy operates in the sphere of law, and can never arrive at the Gospel. Philosophy and theology have diverse subject matter, *diversa, non contraria*.[168] Philosophy lays necessity on God, robbing him of his freedom.[169] But when Christ supplies the content of words, what words say does not have to coincide with our notion; in theology, the living God is free to give their own definition, "without necessity and analogy."[170] This talk of the "new" language is evident in Luther's *Disputation On The Divinity and Humanity of Christ*:

Thesis 21: For "creature", according to the usage of the old language, and so far as the other things are concerned, signifies a thing separate from the divinity.

Thesis 22: According to the usage of the new language, it (creature) signifies a thing joined inseparately to the divinity, in the same person, in
ineffable ways.[171]

Hence Luther speaks of the variance in meaning of terms between
the disciplines of theology and philosophy: "*Creatura est in veteri
lingua id, quod creator creavit et a se separavit, sed haec significatio non
habet locum in creatura Christo.   Ibi creator et creatrua unus et idem
est.*"[172]

The idea of *genus tapeinoticon* is the communication of the
properties of the human nature to the divine nature. According to
the Greek theologians, the movement went only one way, that is,
from the divine nature to the human nature, retaining the impassibility of God. On the contrary, Luther envisages the movement
going also in the other direction, accentuating the participation of
the divine nature in Jesus Christ in human weakness. The *idiomata* of humanity are communicated to the divinity. In the *Table-Talk*
(1541), which was quoted earlier, Luther allows a predication of
the sufferings of our human nature to the divine nature.[173] Since
the two natures are united in Christ, says Luther, "it comes about
that these two natures in Christ share, the one with the other, their
idiomatum and characteristics ... To be born, to suffer, are characteristics of the human nature, of which characteristics the divine
nature also becomes sharer in this Person."[174] Mary is "a right
Mother of God," and thus, birth, suffering, and death can be
ascribed to the divine nature through the *communicatio idiomatum*.
Accordingly Luther asserts that everything which essentially
belongs to the human nature in Christ is communicated, united
and given to the divine nature.[175] "The deity of Christ, because of
the incarnation and of its personal unity with the humanity," says
Althaus of Luther, "enters the uttermost depths of its suffering."[176]
Luther argues as follows :

*Divinitas non doluit in Christus.   Deus est divinitas.   Ergo non doluit in crue,
et per consequens non est passus.*

*Responsio (Lutheri): Est communicatio idiomatum.   Illa, quae Christus passus
est, tribuuntur etiam Deo, quia sunt unum.*[177]

In this disputation of 1540, Luther rejects the opinion that the deity in Christ did not suffer.

> *Quicquid est subiectum morti, non est Deus. Christus est subiectus morti. Ergo Christus non is Deus.*
>
> *R(esponsio): Est communio idiomatum, est et argumentum philosophicum. Scriptura non dicit: Iste homo creavit mundum. Deus est passus. Ergo non est in verbis, sed in sensu, quamvis scriptura has voces non ponit, tamen habet eandem sententiam.*[178]

The content of God-language, for Luther, is Christologically based: "*Ita necesse est, vocabula: homo, humanitas, passus etc. et omnia de Christo dicta nova esse vocabula*" (thesis 23). Luther writes against Nestorius in the same disputation: "'But,' you object, 'God cannot be crucified or suffer.' I reply, 'I know—while He is not yet man.' From eternity He has not suffered, but since He became man, he is passible. From eternity He was not man, but now, conceived by the Holy Spirit and born of the Virgin, He became God and man, one person, and the same things are predicated of God and man."[179] The Ockhamists insisted on the principle *nulla proportio est finiti ad infinitum*, emphasizing the infinite gulf between those mutually exclusives finite and infinite, and correspondingly were unwilling to predicate the same of God and man (*praedicatio disparata*). Here Aristotle and Luther are comrades against the Ockhamists. Luther writes :

> It is not possible to predicate the same of God and man. Ergo etc. Response: This is a philosophical argument. There is no proportion of creature and Creator, of finite and infinite. However, we do not so much make here a proportion as a unity of finite and infinite. If Aristotle were to hear the above argument, it would never make him into a Christian because he does not himself concede the aforesaid proportion because it is the same proportion of finite and infinite.[180]

Philosophy deals with God *in abstracto*, and therefore God cannot be said to suffer. Theology deals with God *in concreto*, and thus God can be said to suffer: "*Crucifigi est unum idioma naturae humanae, sed qui dua naturae sunt in una persona unitae, tribuitur utrique naturae.*"[181] "*Est vera, quia quod clamat homo, clamat etiam Deus, yet crucifigi dominum gloriae est impossibile secundum divinitatem, est autem possibile secundum humanitatem, sed quia est unitas personae, illud crucifigi tribuitur etiam divinitati.*"[182] This understanding provided in his disputation of 1540 had already been put forth in Luther's sermon on John 3 in 1537, where he said "God," when considered separately, "cannot die." "Now that the human nature is united in one Person with the divine, death, exclusively the attribute of the human nature, is also ascribed to the divine. Now we can say: '.. God suffered, God died'."[183] Quoting from his disputation again: "*Quod praedicatur de homine, non potest de Deo, etc. Ergo. R. Est philosophicum. Theologia facit summam unionem.*"[184] "*Est Communicatio idiomatum.*" Jansen writes of Luther :

> *Die Schrift aber bekennt nun einmal, daß Gottes Sohn leidet. Auch wenn diese Aussage zunächst auf die menschliche Natur Christi zu beziehen ist, so ist doch die göttliche Natur mitgemeint. Denn die Schrift verteilt ihre Aussagen über Christus eben nicht fein säuberlich auf beide Naturen, sondern bezieht sie auf die Person. Die Person Christi ist aber—kraft der Enhypostasie der menschlichen Natur Christi in der göttlichen—Gottes Sohn, "wahrhaftiger Gott." Luther denkt also die Einheit der Naturen in Christus so, daß jede Aussage über die eine Natur sofort auch die andere tangiert. Alles, was der menschlichen Natur Christi widerfährt, widerfährt auch der Gottheit und umgekehrt. Wenn die menschliche Natur Christi leidet so leidet auch die göttliche Natur mit.*[185]

In consequence, Luther turns himself resolutely away from the Platonic idea of divine *apatheia*. In Christ, God suffers; but God's suffering, says Luther, is an incomprehensible mystery: "*Est incomprehensibile quod Deus passus est, id quod etiam angeli non satis comprehendunt et admirantur.*"[186]

The above study shows that Luther, most of the time, uses the doctrine of *communicatio idiomatum* in a traditional fashion, ascribing to the person in His concrete existence that which rightly belongs only to the one nature.[187] According to this usage, God suffers in the person of His Son, not in His divine nature but according to His human nature. Luther believes that this teaching is yielded by the Scripture. However, when Luther uses the phrase "according to His nature," he does not use it in a Nestorian sense, to deny that Christ suffered in IIis divine nature. While on the one hand Luther uses the phrase "according to His nature" in accordance with the early fathers, to assert that "each nature, of course, has its own peculiar character," but he on the other hand uses the phrase to indicate that there is a "communion" between the two natures since the Person of Christ cannot be divided: "For the communion of the natures also effects a communication of properties."[188] Thus Luther employs the second usage, ascribing to the one nature that which properly belongs only to the other. The peculiar property of suffering which rightly belongs to the human nature is thus communicated to the divine nature: "God suffers or dies."[189] This usage is taken over in *The Formula of Concord* which quotes Luther favorably saying, "According to His nature God cannot die, but since God and man are united in one person, it is correct to talk about God's death when that man dies who is one reality or one person with God."[190] Here at the risk of being accused of monophysitism and docetism, Luther moves beyond the Chalcedonian understanding of Christology insofar as it is typically interpreted as saying the human nature suffers but the divine nature does not.[191] Luther's statement declares that the second Person of the Trinity suffers death. It may be noted here that when the issue of Deipassianism arises, it has been used in the history of the church to reject the idea of Patripassianism, i.e., the idea that the first Person of the Trinity, the Father, suffers. One could interpret the above passage quoted in *The Formula of Concord* strictly in terms of the second Person of the Trinity, emphasizing that the divine person of the Son suffers, but not that of the Father. The question as to whether Luther is a Patripassianist will be dealt with in chapter five, where his view of the Trinity will be discussed.

In summation, Luther employs the teaching of the early fathers to express his thought. His use of the doctrine of the *communicatio idiomatum* makes a breach with the hellenistic doctrine of divine *apatheia*, thereby allowing more than a mere verbal attribution of the Christ's suffering to the Word. The suffering of the humanity is not only predicated of the Person of Jesus Christ but also of His divine nature. Luther's use of the abstract phrase, "the divinity cannot suffer or die", assures us that he was fully aware of the apathy axiom, which was at work, for instance, in Nestorius' Christology. But this phrase does not hinder the reformer from making the theopaschite declaration that God and suffering coinhere inseparably in the One person of Jesus Christ. As Jansen comments,

> Freilich auch darin steht Luther in der tradition theolopaschitischen Denkens, daß er bekennt, Gott in seiner Natur könne nicht leiden. Wie seine Auseinandersetzung mit Nestorius zeigt, Kennt er das Apathieaxiom, "daß Gott und Sterben sich nicht zusammenreimen." Ebenso gesteht er zu, daß man auf den Einwand der Vernunft "Ja die Gottheit kann nicht leiden noch sterben" antworten soll: "Das ist wahr." Das hindert den Reformator dann freilich nicht, Kräftige theopaschitische Aussagen zu machen, deren Tenor es ist, daß Gott und Sterben in der Person Jesu Christi zusammenkommen und zusammengehören.[192]

The absolute unity of Christ's person means for Luther that "no suffering, no work can apply to Him without our saying that it touches His entire Person."[193] Luther does not envisage a theology that denies God's suffering in Jesus as the suffering of the eternal Son of God.[194] He rejects theologia gloriae because it fails to define the nature of God in terms of His act of self-identification with the crucified Christ. It subjugates the cross to a preconceived metaphysical idea of divine apathy. If God is denied suffering, then, the cross cannot be a revelation of God. Jesus, the God-man, the crucified One, gives to the predicate "God" its substantial content, revealing the true identity of God. The meaning of the word "God" is provided, not by philosophy, but by its reference to the person of Jesus Christ so that Christian theology must necessarily think about God in connection with the crucified Christ.[195] Christian faith must speak of no other God than the incarnate God —the human God or the crucified God. Passibility is required by Luther's theologia crucis, for God was fully and actively present in the historical Christ who was crucified. The hidden God is the crucified God: the eternal God, who hides in the mortal and suffering form of human existence, is, for Luther, the subject of Christ's suffering and even death, but in such a way that these assertions can be explained only according to the *communicatio idiomatum*. The passibility of God is thus required by the concrete unity of the two natures in the one Person of Jesus Christ. God is, and is revealed as, passible in the Incarnation. Indeed, the divine nature is so united with the humanity, that in respect of His humanity the second Person of the Trinity is now approximately "1543 years old" (That is a rough approximation of the Luther quotation in *The Formula of Concord*).[196] In the Incarnation God suffers not only in the humanity of the Son but also as God the eternal Son because "God's Son and Mary's Son is only one Person" or "one Son."[197] Suffering is therefore ontologically constitutive of the being of God or the eternal Son of God. The safeguards of the *extra-Calvinisticum* are thereby discarded, so that God's heavenly divinity is not waived from being tainted with the suffering of humanity.

Finally, it should be noted, that for God to become flesh still may not address the question about divine impassibility. For Luther, at least, what truly defines divine suffering is not so much God's becoming human—that by itself would be no great indignity—as God's "becoming sin for us," suffering and dying. The suffering of Christ as God's own suffering has more to do with His assumed sinnerhood than His assumed manhood, although of course, the latter is the abiding presupposition for the former (this will be taken up in the next chapter). Nagel summarizes this understanding of Luther's concerning Christ as follows :

> Who he is and what he does are all together in his being born, living, doing, suffering, dying, rising and saving. The verbs tell the story, not categories or definitions of human construction, and the story is all of one piece so that the Incarnation, which has more often suffered being drawn into philosophical patterns and categories, is not one way of salvation and Calvary another, nor Easter, nor Ascension. No one of these may be played off against any other. His achieving salvation for man is whole and complete. What he did and what he suffered go together, as do his person and his work. God's involvement shows scant respect for those definitions of God which put him opposite us, most God by negation of terms of the human condition.[198]

Chapter Four

Soteriology and Divine Suffering

In chapter two, it was shown how Luther's *theologia crucis*, the fundamental principle of his thought, focuses on God's redeeming work in Christ and human participation in it by faith. From what God does in Jesus Christ, Luther conceives of who God is—God is *pro nobis*. Since Luther's theology is about God's ways with us, he particularly focuses on the *pro me* aspects of Christ's person.[1] Luther develops his Christology by his soteriology, understanding the person of Jesus in terms of His work of redemption. This is evident in Luther's explanation of the Second Article of the *Small Catechism*, where we witness how quickly he comes to soteriology, because this is at the heart of his Christology.

> I believe that Jesus Christ, true God, begotten of the Father from eternity, and also true man, born of the Virigin, is my Lord, who has redeemed me, a lost and condemned creature, purchased and won me from all sins, from death, and from the power of the devil, not with gold or silver, but with his holy, precious blood and with his innocent suffering and death, that I may be his own, and live under him in his kingdom, and serve him in everlasting righteousness, innocence, and blessedness, even as he is risen from the dead, lives and reigns to all eternity. This is most certainly true.[2]

Luther continued to develop his Christology by way of soteriology in his *Large Catechism* (1528):

> This man became true God, as one eternal, indivisible person of God and man, so that Mary the holy Virgin is real, true mother not only of the man Christ, as the Nestorians teach, but also of the Son of God, as Luke says (I: 35), "The child to be born of you will be called the Son of God", i.e. my Lord and Lord of all, Jesus Christ, the only, true Son by nature of

God and of Mary, true God and true man.

> ... All men along with him (Adam) are born, live, and die altogether in
> sin, and would necessarily be guilty of eternal death if Jesus Christ had
> not come to our aid and taken upon himself this guilt and sin as an inno-
> cent lamb, paid for us as a faithful, merciful Mediator, Saviour, and the
> only Priest and Bishop of our souls.[3]

The Reformer sought to explain what he found to be the heart of
Scripture by saying, *homo peccati reus ac perditus et deus justificans ac
salvator hominis peccatoris*.[4] Accordingly, our discussion of Luther's
theology, in order to be faithful to the way in which Luther himself
does theology, must take careful note of the fact that the basis of his
understanding is to be found in what he takes to be the character
of the relationship between God and us. This basis may be seen in
his lectures on Psalm 51 (1532) where he asserts, "The proper subject of theology is man guilty of sin and condemned, and God the
justifier and Savior of man the sinner. Whatever is asked or discussed in theology outside this subject is error and poison."[5]

The cross is the self-manifestation of God's love *sub contrario* in
the suffering of the righteous One which is to be interpreted
according to the *ratio vicaria*, the joyous change of place (*admirabile
commercium*) between the sinner and Christ. This chapter will con-
centrate on the relation of God's suffering and Christ's redemptive
act, showing that the suffering of Christ lies not so much in His
manhood—which is the abiding presupposition for redemption—
as in His saviourhood. The cross reveals God's passibility in its
redemptive effect; the act of the cross discloses the very depth of
God's being as love. The discussion in this chapter will be developed, then, under three heads : (I) The self-humiliation of Christ is
the work of His whole person; (II) God's essence and act are one:
God's love *pro me* in suffering is ontologically reflective of God's
essential being as love; (III) The distinction between the *deus
absconditus* and *deus revelatus, deus ipse* or *deus nudus* and *deus indutus* uncovers what is to be said about God's suffering.

Christ's Self-humiliation: Person and Work

For Luther, the Incarnation, the unity of two natures in the person of Jesus Christ, is conceived in terms of the central fact of salvation, the passion and death of Christ. As Congar rightly says, "For Luther, the Incarnation is not only inseparable from the redemptive act; the metaphysical mystery of the hypostatic union is considered solely in the act of salvation of which it forms the very reality."[6] As early as 1509, Luther noted in the margin of the *Sentences* of Peter Lombard: "It is not so much a physical or logical determination as a theological one. It is as if someone were to say: 'What is Christ?' to which the logician replies: 'He is a person, etc...', while the theologian says: 'He is the rock, the cornerstone, etc...'."[7] That is to say, while philosophy concerns itself with ontology, theology concerns itself with God's acts, the end of which is our salvation. Thus the real mystery of the Incarnation, for Luther, does not consist in the fact that Christ assumed our human nature but He assumed our sins.[8] Luther explains :

> If we differentiate two sons in Christ (like Apollinaris of Laodicea), then it must follow that there are also two persons; this would nullify our redemption and the forgiveness of sins. No, the two natures must be the one Christ. Otherwise no satisfaction could have been rendered for our sins, and nothing would come for our salvation. If Christ were only man, his suffering would have been useless; for no man's suffering has ever been able to overcome my sin.... Therefore it was necessary for Him to be God, and, in order to suffer, also true man....[9]

Luther was not concerned with the constitution of Christ in the abstract, but rather with the *pro me* aspects of His person. The following example further elucidates this :

> Christ has two natures. What has that to do with me? If he bears the magnificent and consoling name of Christ, it is on account of the ministry and the task which he took upon himself; it is that which gives him his name. That he should by nature be both man and God, that is for him. But that he should have dedicated his ministry and poured out his love to become my saviour and my redeemer, it is in that I find my consolation and well-being. To believe in Christ does not mean that Christ

is a person who is man and God, a fact that helps nobody; it means that
this person is Christ, that is to say, that for us he came forth from God
into the world; it is from this office that he takes his name.[10]

Only when one realizes that Christ was given *pro me, pro nobis* has
one discerned the import of Christ's accomplishment.   Thus the
suffering and the dying of Jesus is not simply something that happens but happens for me.   Luther declares :

Read with great emphasis these words, "me," "for me," and accustom
yourself to accept and to apply to yourself this "me" with certain faith.

The words OUR, US, FOR US, ought to be written in golden letters —
the man who does not believe them is not a Christian.[11]

For Luther, the person of Jesus Christ is the unshakable ground
of the salvation He achieved "for us"—*qualis persona, talia opera.*[12]
Jesus Christ as one indivisible person, divine man as well as incarnate God, has humbled Himself.   "The man who is called Jesus
Christ, the Son of God, has given himself for our sins."[13]   Christ's
humiliation, for Luther is not an "attribute" of the human Jesus in
which Christ as the Son of God participates by virtue of the union
in His Person.   Rather His humiliation is His own direct action as
a whole person, an "altogether pure and innocent person" who is
constituted as "God and man."[14]   Luther accentuates that

You truly have Him only when you believe that this altogether pure and
innocent Person has been granted to you by the Father as your High
Priest and redeemer, yes, as your Slave. Putting off His innocence and
holiness and putting on your sinful person, He bore your sin, death and
curse; He became a sacrifice and a curse for you, in order thus to set you
free from the curse of the law.[15]

The self-humiliation of Jesus Christ was, for Luther, credited not
only to the human nature but also to the divine.   Christ Himself
affirms that it is an active deed of His One indivisible Person, "not
by compulsion but out of His own free will."[16]   "For in My own
Person of humanity and divinity I am blessed, and I am in need of
nothing whatever.   But I shall empty Myself (Phil. 2:7); I shall

assume your clothing and mask; and ... suffer death, in order to set you free from death."[17] This condescension is the condescension of both the innocent Son of God and the innocent Son of Man becoming the Person of the sinful race, and as both suffering and dying on the cross.

The doctrine of *communicatio idiomatum* is used by Luther to indicate how he conceives Christ's Person in terms of His redemptive work, His incarnate deity in terms of His salvific purpose. Although Luther affirms that the work of Christ to conquer sin and death could be done only by Christ's divinity,[18] he further contends that Christ's divinity must not be conceived apart from His humanity so that the act of His divinity was essentially that of His whole person, both human and divine. The unity of Christ's Person is affirmed in the fact of His conquest of sin and death, even though strictly speaking, the act is of His divinity. "The humanity would not have accomplished anything by itself; but the divinity, joined with humanity, did it alone; and the humanity did it on account of the divinity."[19] When Luther speaks of Christ as the whole Person, he speaks of Him as the doer of the divine action, even though "abstractly" speaking, the act is performed only by the deity.[20] In this way what is communicated to Christ's humanity is not merely His divine nature as such but the divine saving deed, as if the deed were performed by the man Jesus. "Thus it is said: The man Jesus led Israel out of Egypt, struck down Pharaoh, and did all the things that belong to God."[21] This means that the *genus maiestaticum* has meaning only in terms of the *genus apotelesmaticum*, affirming the unity of Christ's Person as constitutive of his redemptive mission. "Whatever this person, Christ, says and does, is said and done by both" natures.[22]

If Luther's "very good and true definition of ... the Son of God and of the Virgin" is based on what Christ graciously did, then the question is: in what way has Christ redeemed? What was His redemptive act on our behalf? In particular, what was required for Christ to remove our curse so as to bring to us blessing? "He himself is Lord of the Law; therefore the Law has no jurisdiction over Him and cannot accuse Him, because He is the Son of God. He who was not under the Law subjected Himself voluntarily to the

Law."[23] To be sure, Christ "in his own person" as the Son of God does not commit sins, but by entering into our place he truly takes upon himself all our sins, and therefore makes himself a sinner, "not only adjectivally but substantively."[24] In our stead, Christ is "not acting in his own person now; now he is not the Son of God, born of the virgin, but he is a sinner,"[25] who has and bears the sins of the world "in his body, in order to make satisfaction for them with His own blood."[26] Luther explains:

> When the merciful Father saw that we were being oppressed through the Law, that we were being held under a curse, and that we should not be liberated from it by anything, He sent his Son into the world, heaped all the sins of all men upon him and said to him: "Be Peter the denier, Paul the persecutor, blasphemer and assaulter, David the adulterer, the sinner who ate the apple in Paradise; the thief on the cross. In short the person of all men, the one who has committed the sins of all men. And see to it that You pay and make satisfaction for them." Now the Law comes and says: "I find Him a sinner, who takes upon Himself the sins of all men. I do not see any other sins than those in Him. Therefore let Him die on the cross."[27]

In the case of Christ, the law raged even more fiercely than it does against us accursed and condemned sinners. "It accused him of blasphemy and sedition; it found Him guilty in the sight of God of all the sins of the entire world."[28] It "frightened Him so horribly that He experienced greater anguish than any man has ever experienced. This is amply demonstrated by His bloody sweat, the comfort of the angel, His solemn prayer in the garden (LK. 22: 41-44), and finally by that cry of misery on the cross (Matt. 27:46): 'My God, My God, why hast Thou forsaken Me?'"[29] This "remarkable duel" (*mirabile duellum*) occurred and in it "the law, a creature, came into conflict with the Creator , exceeding its every jurisdiction to vex the Son of God with the same tyranny with which it vexed us, the sons of wrath."[30] Consequent upon His conflict with the Law, Christ

> suffered its extreme fierceness and tyranny. By performing and bearing the Law he conquered it in Himself. And then, when He rose from the

dead, He condemned the Law, our most horrible enemy, and abolished it, so that it can no longer condemn or kill us. Therefore it is Christ's true and proper function to struggle with the Law, sin and death of the entire world, and to struggle in such a way He undergoes them, but, by undergoing them, conquers them and abolishes them in Himself, thus liberating us from the Law and from evil.[31]

"Since Christ has conquered the Law in His own person," says Luther, "it necessarily follows that He is God by nature."[32] If "except for God no one, neither a man nor an angel, is above the Law" and Christ, because He is above the Law, is "God by nature," why does God have to be man?[33] That he is man is clear. "This man is God." The biblical witness attests not only Christ's deity but also His humanity. And the development of the biblical attestation theologically, in *communicatio idiomatum*, requires us to say that because Christ is one "whole person," indivisibly human and divine, the action of His deity is legitimately man's, though "man" here becomes a "new and theological" word.[34] The answer to the question about the necessity of Christ's humanity lies in His redemptive mission. The purpose for which God became man was our redemption and also its revelation. God wills to "present Himself to our sight."

> Therefore begin where Christ begins—in the Virgin's womb, in the manger, and at His mother's breasts. For this purpose he came down, was born, lived among men, suffered, and was crucified, and died, so that in every possible way He might present Himself to our sight. He wanted us to fix the gaze of our hearts upon Himself and thus to prevent us from clambering into heaven and speculating about the Divine majesty.[35]

For Christ to be human, for Luther, is not the same as for Him to be sin. Christ is not a sinner by virtue of his being human, but he, for our sake, was "made to be sin."[36] "For Christ is innocent insofar as his own person is concerned."[37] It was Christ's "whole person," both God and man, "which was righteous and invincible and therefore could not become guilty.[38] Though Christ "himself was made a true man by birth though the female sex," His incarnation in itself is not his accursedness, poverty or His humiliation. Christ Himself says, "For my own person of humanity and divinity I am blessed, and I am in need of nothing whatever, but I shall empty Myself; and I shall assume your clothing and mask."[39] As "an innocent and private person," Christ is "the purest of persons, ... God and man."[40] But for our sake Christ has "slain the hostility in himself" (Eph. 2: 14-15); He has assumed "the mask of the sinner, ... the vestige of death," and thereby was made to be sin who knew no sin so that we become the righteousness of God.[41] There is indeed a real "exchange": Christ must become a sinner and a curse for us. If one were to deny that Christ is a sinner and a curse, one would also deny that he suffered, was crucified, and was buried. "Just as Christ is wrapped up in our flesh and blood, so we must wrap him and know him to be wrapped up in our sins, our curse, our death and everything evil."[42] For Luther this "happy exchange" was the point of the *communicatio idiomatum*.[43] "Whatever sins I, you, and all of us have committed or may commit in the future, they are as much Christ's own as if He Himself had committed them. In short, our sin must be Christ's own, or we shall perish eternally."[44] In a letter to George Spenlein, in 1516, Luther wrote of this concept of the "joyous exchange" :

> Therefore my dear Friar, learn Christ and him crucified. Learn to praise him, and despairing of yourself, say, "Lord Jesus Christ, you are my righteousness, just as I am your sin. You have taken upon yourself what is mine and have given me what is yours. You have taken upon yourself what you were not and have given to me what I was not."[45]

Consequently to "segregate Christ from sins and sinners and set him forth to us only as an example to be imitated" as the "sophists" do, in Luther's view, is to turn Christ into a new law, rendering Him "not only useless to us but also a judge and a tyrant who is angry because of our sins and who damns sinners."[46] In so doing, the "sophists" have deprived us of the most "delightful comfort," that Christ has become a curse for us to set us free from the curse of the law.[47] Christ is first a pure and innocent Person, both as God and man, so that He could assume "upon himself our

sinful person and grant us his innocent and victorious person."[48]
By this fortunate exchange, Christ, "inside our mask," carried our
sin, suffered and died; and for us he became a curse. "But because
He was a divine and eternal Person, it was impossible for death to
hold him. Therefore He arose from death on the third day, and
now He lives eternally; nor can sin, death, and our mask be found
in Him any longer; but there is sheer righteousness, life, and eternal blessings."[49]

The innocence and the victory of Christ cannot be grasped by
a "loving will"; they can only be grasped by "faith".[50] For Luther,
faith is not a leap into a vacuum because faith and Christ belong
together.[51] As he asserts in his *Lectures on Romans* (1515—1516),
"those who approach God through faith and not at the same time
through Christ actually depart from him."[52] Faith alone grasps the
victory of Christ. "If you believe that sin, death, and the curse
have been abolished, they have been abolished, because Christ
conquered and overcame them in Himself; and He wants us to
believe that just as in His Person there is no longer the mask of the
sinner or any vestige of death, so this is no longer in our person,
since He has done everything for us."[53] Although Christ's being
man does not mean He is a sinner, this does not imply for Luther
two chronologically separate stages in Christ's Incarnation.
Assuming flesh and assuming sin must be viewed as one act, with
Christ's divine-human sinlessness as an underlying presupposition of His assumed sinnerhood, the end of which is His achieving
our redemption.

Why did God become Incarnate? Luther answers, on the basis
of his exegesis, because God loved human beings, and therefore,
sought them, suffered and died for them to forgive and free them
from sin.[54] Love and the unity of the two natures are so interwo-
ven that they form a seamless garment. By reason of Christ's love,
He in the unity of his person and work conquers sin. He "did this
because of His great love; for Paul says: 'who loved me' (Gal.
2:20)."[55] The assumption of our sinnerhood "in Himself" means
that Christ is "nothing but sheer, infinite mercy, who gives Himself
for us and becomes our High Priest, that is, the One who interposes Himself as the Mediator between God and us miserable sin-

ners."[56] Christ interposes Himself in the law's path, and suffers the *alienum opus* in order to save us. Luther explains :

> Thus the curse, which is divine wrath against the whole world, has the same conflict with the blessing, that is, with eternal grace and mercy of God in Christ. Therefore the curse clashes with the blessing and wants to damn it and annihilate it. But it cannot. For the blessing is divine and eternal, and therefore the curse must yield to it. For if the blessing in Christ could be conquered, then God himself would be conquered. But this is impossible. Therefore Christ, who is divine power, Righteousness, Blessing, Grace, and Life, conquers and destroys these monsters — sin, death, and the curse — without weapons or battle, in His own body and in Himself as Paul enjoys saying.[57]

The "blessing" is locked in mortal combat with the "curse" in "this one person" (Christ)—this is the secret of the *iucundissimum duellum*.[58] When two such extremely contrary things come together in Christ, for Luther, it must be the divine powers—divine righteousness, life, and blessings—which triumph over the lesser contraries—sin, death, and curse. Bertram further explains :

> But the secret, indeed the prerequisite of the victory is that it occurs "in his body and in himself." Both sets of contraries are really his. If the sin had not been his, as truly as the righteousness was, the law could easily have avoided its blasphemy against him by cursing only the one and not the other. However, "he joined God and man in one person. And being joined in us who were accursed, he became a curse for us; and he concealed his blessing in our sin, death, and the curse, which condemned and killed him."[59]

"For to conquer the sin of the world, death, the curse and the wrath of God in Himself —this is the work, not of any creature but of the divine power."[60] "Therefore when we teach that men are justified through Christ and that Christ is the victory over sin ... we are testifying at the same time that he is God by nature."[61] What predicates our sin of Christ is that same loving will which Christ who "is God by nature" shares with his Father; both the Father and Son are united in their loving or redeeming will so that Christ became the "associate of sinners."[62] "Of his (Christ's) own free will and by the will of the Father he wanted to be the associate of sinners."[63] There is a deep community of "will" between the Father and the Son in the assumption of our sinnerhood in which God suffers. Thus "only by taking hold of Christ, who, by the will of the Father, has given himself in death for our sins," are we "drawn and carried directly to the Father."[64] The "majesty of God" (*Maiestas Dei*) which for Luther corresponds to the hidden God, the intolerable deity of the *De Servo Arbitrio*, becomes for believers the majesty of God who lovingly conquers our sin in the Person of his Son. This work is appropriate only to the Divine majesty and is not within the power of either man or angel—namely that "Christ has abolished sin."[65] "The Divine Majesty did not spare his only Son but gave him up for us all (Rom. 8:32)."[66] The majesty of God, before whom we face only terror and judgement, now, in Christ, encounters the sinners as the majesty of the loving and merciful God. "By divine love sin was laid upon him," thereby predicating our sin of Christ. "The indescribable and inestimable mercy and love of God" is revealed in the fact that "the Supreme Majesty cared so much for me, a condemned sinner and a child of wrath (Eph. 2:3) and of eternal death, that He did not spare His own Son, but gave Him up into a most shameful death."[67] Similarly Luther declares: "Our God, however, has his honour in this that for our sakes he gives himself down to the utmost depth, into flesh and bread, into our mouth, heart and bosom, and more, for our sakes he suffers himself to be dishonourably treated both upon the cross and altar."[68] Accordingly :

> To know Christ aright is to know him as the one who died for me and took upon himself my sin ... There Christ is God and has put himself in my death, in my sin, and so gives me his living favour. There I recognize how he befriends me and the utter love of the Father is too much for any heart. Thus I lay ahold of God where he is most weak, and think, "Yes, this is God, this is his will and his good pleasure, what there Christ has done for me...." Therefore God is to be known alone in Christ.[69]

And Nagel reminds us of how in this the knowledge of Christ, of God, and of our redemption remain intertwined for Luther, so that to abstract an understanding of any apart from this complex is to speak falsely. He writes: "'God's turning with acceptance toward him' came to Luther from the cross when the cross was Christ's alone, uniquely his, and what he did and suffered there has given complete and sure salvation."[70] In Luther's own words :

> The gospel reveals to us what Christ is, in order that we may learn to know him, that he is our Savior who takes away from us our sin and death, and saved us from all calamity, reconciles us with the Father, and makes us, without any work of ours, upright and blessed. He who does not know Christ in this way must fall into error. For even if you know that he is the Son of God, that he died and rose and is seated at the right hand of God, you have not rightly known Christ, and all your knowledge will not help you. It is necessary to believe and to know that he has done all that for you, to help.[71]

The God who is known in Christ is the God who comes in lowliness or humility. The being of Jesus Christ in humility, suffering and dying on the cross is being in self-humiliation and the atonement effected by him is the act of Christ's self-humiliation. Luther, in his Palm Sunday Sermon on Philippians 2(1522), asserts that the Son of God did not cease to be what He was; His deity did not undergo loss for that is the thing most certain to Him.[72] By becoming what He had not previously been, namely, man, the Son remained what He was. Christ, as God-man, was and continued to be the Son of God, even during His appearance in the form of servant. Christ was not committed to being in the form of God (*forma dei*) only, but could at the same time take upon Himself the form of a servant (*forma servi*). "He took upon the form of a servant and yet remained God and in the form of God. That is to say that he was God and all the divine works and words which he accomplished, he did for our good and served us thereby as a servant."[73] Christ "does not take it (*forma dei*) up nor use it to lord himself over us, rather he serves with it."[74] "Not that he could have divested himself of his divinity, putting it to one side, but he put aside the form of divine majesty and did not act like the God he truly was."[75] This divesting is not the result of the incarnation itself. "Even in His humanity He could have exalted Himself over all men and served no-one. ... He had power to avoid ordinary human vicissitudes; as God He could have behaved quite differently. ... He gave up even the respect, repute, and honor due to him by taking upon Himself the servant-form which He assumed to reveal Himself."[76] Christ could have assumed humanity without assuming the servant form. He was under no necessity of bearing the servant form but willed to do so, showing the extent of His love. In this *forma servi*, he came concealing His majesty so that we do not apprehend him in power and glory but in humility and love. Nowhere else but here, in His own act of self-humiliation, is God truly to be found "for me". In saying this Luther affirmed God's suffering. The obedience of Christ is attributed not only to the man Jesus in relation to God but also His deity.[77] Referring again to the afore-mentioned passage, *Enarratio* 53. *capitis* (1544), Luther asks: "How is Christ our Servant?" He replies, according to the humanity. *"Nunc autem, quia divina et humana Natura copulatae sunt in unam personam et Christus revera est Deus et homo, ideo dicitur eciam 'filius Dei' servus noster."*[78] It has been demonstrated before that Luther concedes the suffering of God, not *in abstracto* but *in concreto*. According to Luther, faith is concerned with the concrete. *"Ideo hoc loco de abstracto tacendum est prorsus, quia fides docet hic hullam esse abstractionem, sed concretionem, coniunctionem et copulationem utriusque Naturae."*[79] Thus when we speak of God in the concrete, according to Luther, it is correct to say that the deity suffers and dies. In keeping with the revelatory character which Luther ascribes to the condescension of God, he does not recoil from— what is expressed by the *genus tapeinoticon*—the understanding that the divine nature is capable of suffering. The Son of God is our servant, who so utterly debases Himself that He assumes the burden of the world's sin. If it was not the very God Himself who became sin and suffered for us, what hope of life is left?[80] Atonement occurs when Christ has really entered our place, and died a real death "wrapped in our sins." Particularly important is the manner in which Luther strips the roses from the cross. In the words of Forde :

> Christ feels himself in his conscience to be cursed by God and really and truly enters into eternal damnation from God the Father for us. Christ's

death is not an active suffering according to some available scheme of recompense. There is no such. His death can therefore only be a passive suffering, a "passion" in the strict sense of the word. There is nothing to do under wrath, death, and so on but to suffer it and to die. Christ, clothed in our sin, can only suffer himself to be attacked. The event must be a real one, and the outcome hangs in the balance.[81]

The theologian of the cross must not look away from the horror of Golgotha, seeking to avoid the way things actually are. He must not behave like a theologian of glory who might speculate about things beyond, guessing about how atonement works in heaven.[82] For a theologian of the cross, there is no other way than God gives the Son to die. Thus Luther writes: "Christ teaches..., that we are lost, and sinners have eternal life, only because God had pity, indeed, that it cost him his own beloved child, whom he put into our misery, hell, and death. ... Now if there were any other way to heaven, he would certainly have established it: Hence, there is no other."[83] The theology of glory seeks for God among the glorious things in the highest heaven; the theology of the cross encounters God in the suffering and death of the crucified Jew. The gospel proclaims the God whose being and life cannot be conceived apart from the life, death and resurrection of Jesus of Nazareth.

If Luther's comments on Psalm 8:5 were taken in isolation, "The deity withdrew and hid so that it seems, and anyone who saw it might say, 'This is not God, but a mere man, and a troubled desperate man at that,' " he might be thought to be saying that the deity had left Christ on the cross, and therefore Christ suffered purely as a man.[84] In fact, however, the deity's withdrawal, for Luther, is one that focuses on the withdrawal of God's power so that the deity only appears to have withdrawn. Luther is clear that the deity is not separated from the humanity, for in Christ, deity and humanity are so unified that they form a seamless garment and cannot be divided. The emphasis here is on how Christ emptied Himself of the divine form by assuming the servant form, that is, He did not exercise His divine power, but withdrew it when He suffered.[85] Luther interpreted Psalm 8 Christologically: "Thus the righteous and innocent Man (Christ) must shiver and shake like a poor, condemned sinner and feels God's wrath and judgement against sin in His tender, innocent heart, taste eternal death and damnation for us—in short, He must suffer everything that a condemned sinner has deserved and must suffer eternally."[86] The emphasis here is not on a deity who is impassible but rather on a deity who manifests Himself in lowliness and powerlessness as the *Deus crucifixus* bears and suffers the judgement of sin. Here lies the paradoxical nature of the cross as a reality of revelation: "God shows that he is God precisely in the fact that he is mighty in weakness, glorious in lowliness, living and life-giving in death."[87] So Luther rejects any division of the Person of Christ so that there is a passible man and an impassible God. "These two natures in Christ ought not to be separated but unified as much as possible because the Son of God is God who suffered, was crucified, was dead, and rose again."[88] Jesus Christ did not exercise His deity sometimes and the humanity at other times. His actions are always those of His divinity and humanity. It is still the human and divine Christ who suffers in and through His humble obedience, even obedience unto death on the cross. Hence Luther emphasizes in a sermon on 1516, "Preach one thing: the wisdom of the cross."[89] Though the cross is at the heart of Luther's theology, yet this does not imply that he ignores the whole life of Christ in his focus on the cross. The whole salvific route of Christ from Christmas to Good Friday is a way of temptation and suffering, since it is a way of lowliness. The theology of the cross begins with the Christmas stories and continues through Jesus' life to the crucifixion. Luther sees the crucifixion as the final culmination of the entire life of Christ which was lived under the cross.[90]

God's love, for Luther, is a "suffering" love because and so long as the world is in sin and under God's wrath. And the divine love which suffers the sinful world and the divine wrath, and finally suffers them into defeat, is always concrete, the love of God in Jesus Christ. Thus there simply is no "suffering" divine love apart from the *communicatio idiomatum*. For Luther, what truly reveals God's passiblity is God's "becoming sin" for us, suffering and dying on the cross. The way of Christ's lowliness means that God indeed suffers in His divine being when He willingly assumes the form of a servant. God is most Godlike in the self-humiliation of His own Son, the act of the passion of God in human history, which is at once an act of God's own life.

A question emerges: Does God suffer in eternity? God indeed suffers in Christ; the nature of God is known from His suffering, His self-sacrifice in Christ. Must the suffering of Christ be predicable of God's eternal nature? The answer to this question has already been supplied previously, but only in scarcity. This question will be considered at length in the following section; and will be further discussed in chapter five which deals with Luther's understanding of the Trinity, particularly, the "immanent" Trinity.

Essence and Act: Love

Luther's *theologia crucis* is thinking about the redemptive act performed by God Incarnate. In this act faith apprehends who God is and the way He is *pro me*. Luther argues from God's act to God's essence, thereby accentuating the principle of correspondence (*Entsprechung*) between God's act and God's essence. God truly is what He does. The acts of God are genuine revelation of God's essence. More precisely, it is important to remember that for Luther the action of God is His coming in Christ, and what we can know about God's essence is determined by what we know of God's revelation in Christ. He holds fast to the insight that God wills to be known in Christ alone, and consequently all theological thinking, for Luther, entails working out the implications of that fact. Wherever we try, speculatively, to comprehend the essence of God apart from God's revelatory acts in Christ, as is the case with *theologia gloriae* which Luther was determined to deny, we end up, according to Luther, in heresy, idle gossip and illusion.[91] The only essence of God which we can know, for Luther, is precisely the essence of the incarnate One who reveals Himself in His acts. As Karl-Heinz Mühlen explained: *"Zugänglich ist Gottes Wesen nur, insofern sich Gott in der Offenbarung in Jesus Christus selbst bestimmt hat."*[92] Hence the reformer asserts, "apart from Christ, there is no God or no Godhead, ... the entire Godhead is in him (Christ) in person and in essence on earth."[93] God's revelation in Christ is therefore the revelation of His essence to us. What is true of Jesus Christ is ontologically true of God.

Luther's relationship with nominalism sheds light on his ontology. For the nominalist, William Ockham, a thing is "essentially" what it "does," that is, a thing "as it is in itself" is known through cognition of its acts.[94] Luther's thought resembles Ockham's when he asserts in his *Commentary on the Magnificat* (1521) that God "is" what He "does" :

> How can one know God better than in the works in which He is most Himself? Whoever understands His works correctly cannot fail to know His nature and will, His heart and mind.[95]

Given the correspondence between essence and act, the knowledge of what God has done in Christ discloses truly who God is in Himself. The event of Christ's self-sacrificial love is indeed the essence of God. "God's very being, God's essence, is found in this coming into the human sphere. Who God is is the result of what God does, and what God does is to act humanly and lovingly."[96] Therefore for Luther the identity of God is inseparable from God's operations. Accordingly, Luther prohibits any theology that seeks "the inner nature of God in some remote sphere above and beyond the structure of God's operations in and upon the world."[97] The God-at-work is the God-revealed. If God can be known in His acts, that means He is to be found in the efficacious activity of Jesus Christ. If God is what He does, then the self-manifestation of His love *sub contrario* in the suffering of the righteous One means that God is a God of love *pro me* in Himself—that is, God not only loves me but loves me in His inner life by virtue of Christ's participation in His inner life. The soteriological aspect of God's "suffering" love *pro me* is genuinely reflective of the ontological being of God as "love." By reason of God's essential being as love, "God is most Himself" precisely in the self-sacrifice and self-humiliation in His Son on the cross, achieving for us the atonement. The nature of God's love *pro nobis* is revealed in God's redemptive act in the incarnate and crucified Christ. God's way of being "most Himself" is by being *pro nobis*, bearing and suffering the judgement of sin, and eventually dying on the cross. The love of God is the true condition of God's suffering in and through the Son's act of humiliation. The depth of God's love expresses itself externally in human history; the self-giving and self-sacrificial aspect of God's nature is revealed in the suffering of the cross of Christ. The affirmation that God is love consistently appears throughout the entire corpus of Luther's works.[98]

The passionate God of the Bible is in sharp contrast to the infinitely apathetic deity of metaphysics. For Luther, what makes God God is the depth of His being as "love"; the Godness of God is "nothing but burning love and a glowing oven full of love."[99] Luther said: "If I were to paint a picture of God I would so draw him that there would be nothing else in the depth of his divine nature than that of fire and passion which is called love for people. Correspondingly, love is such a thing that it is neither human nor angelic but rather divine, yes, even God himself."[100] God opens His personal being to us in the human Jesus who suffers and dies on the cross, revealing to us the depth and certainty of His love. "Thus Christ and the fact that he is 'for us' is the greatest gift of God's love. In this gift God gives himself."[101] This means for Luther, in Althaus' words, that

> the knowledge of God's metaphysical attributes is not ultimately decisive for a man who is seeking salvation....: the ultimate decisive factor is knowledge of God's personal nature and activity, "God is truly known not when we are aware of his power or wisdom which are terrible, but only when we know his goodness and love."[102]

Luther speaks of the character of God's deity by saying that it is "God's nature to give, to bestow, to sacrifice himself and to have mercy."[103] He employs passionate language to express God's love for us. He speaks of God's love as the "blood of love."[104] Christ was "consumed by the fire of boundless love which burned in His heart," and presents Himself as the sacrifice on the cross "with fervent intercession, loud cries and hot, anxious tears."[105] The suffering of the cross in history expresses the unconquerable love of God's heart in eternity. The crucified God of the cross drives us beyond history to God in eternity, revealing the nature of God's eternal love. As Luther says in his sermon *Meditation on Christ's Passion* (1519) :

> ... rise beyond Christ's heart to God's heart and you will see that Christ would not have shown this love for you if God in his eternal love had not wanted (willed) this, for Christ's love for you is due to his obedience to God. Thus you will find the divine and kind paternal heart, and, as Christ says, you will be drawn to the Father through him.[106]

In a 1537 sermon on John, Luther correlates the will of Christ and the will of the Father in such as way as to present their common will, which "pictures God as kindly disposed to us."[107] For Luther , the essence of God is given in His Word, and the Word, Christ, is "nothing but sheer, infinite mercy."[108] In a 1538 sermon on John, Luther correlates the divine mercy in Christ with the "Father's heart and intention," affirming that all this (mercy) "must flow from their sheer fatherly and cordial love."[109] That the nature of God is love was already affirmed in Luther's Christmas sermon in his *Kirchenpostile* (1522).[110] Accordingly, Luther's statements about God's "nature," "heart," and "will" as love cannot be only soteriological, but also statements of Luther's doctrine of the being of God. The uncaused character of God's love *pro nobis* flows from the being of God as love. True knowledge revealed in Christ, for Luther, is not only knowledge of God's way towards me, but also a revelation of God's being as love. "All that Christ does and suffers was ordained by the Father's goodwill," making us sure of God as love.[111] Thus Luther asserts that "through the only-begotten Son and through the Gospel one learns to look directly into God's face. And when this happens, then everything in man dies; man must then confess that he is a blind and ignorant sinner who must forthwith appeal to Christ."[112] Luther's idea of divine passibility hinges upon Christ's death on the cross as a witness to the Godness of God as love.

God's self-sacrifice in His Son unveils His atoning will to reconcile humanity unto Himself. For Luther, God's atoning will in Christ has already existed in the heart of God in eternity before the historical work of redemption on the cross. Already there is a cross in God in eternity before the wood is seen on Calvary (Rev. 13:8).

Christ was "slain" "in promise" before the foundation of the world.[113] This coincides with Luther's idea of the "testament" God made with men, in which the death of a testator must of necessity occur (Heb. 9:16).[114] But God cannot die unless He becomes man. The Incarnation and the death of Christ are both ingredients in God's "testament" which bequeathes forgiveness of sins. The Incarnation is soteriologically necessary, as Luther says in *The Bondage of the Will* (1525), "Here, God Incarnate says, 'I would and thou would not,' God Incarnate I repeat, was sent for this purpose, to will, say, do, suffer, and offer to all, all that is necessary for salvation."[115] God had promised to die. He therefore had to become man in His Son so that He might die and validate God's testament;[116] Christ, the testator, must die, making certain that the promised love comes true in the death of the promisor. By remaining true to Himself, "God does not confine Himself to giving us His Son in His Incarnation, but He also delivers Him into death for us" to fulfill what He has promised.[117] The crucified Christ in history reveals God in that He discloses the depth of God's love in history, that is, in the suffering of the cross for atonement. God reveals Himself in His alien work of suffering as an outflow and expression of God's self-sacrificial love which is ontologically constitutive of God's divine being. Christ thereby unveils historically that which is ontologically true of God's being as love. The love of God thus forms the aetiology of Luther's atonement, creating through the act of the incarnate Christ *sub contraria* "the object of His love" as the teleology of his atonement. Luther concludes his *Heidelberg Theses* with the following statements concerning thesis 28:

> ... the love of God living in man loves sinner, evil men, foolish men, weak men, so that the love of God makes them righteousness, good, wise and strong. In this way it flows forth rather and confers good. Thus sinners are lovely because they are loved: they are not loved because they are attractive.[118]

Moved by His love, God in the person of Jesus Christ suffers in His assumption of our "sinnerhood," and through a "happy exchange" suffers His own wrath and His judgement. Luther sees a unique relation between love and wrath, in which one can perceive the motif of God's passibility. Wrath is an essential element of love; therefore Luther himself speaks of God's love as "wrathful love" (*Zornige Liebe*).[119] As Watson writes :

> For the God whose nature is revealed in the Gospel as pure love and grace is no mild sentimentalist ... Love's wrath, however, is neither the evil passion of offended self-esteem, nor the cold severity of violated justice, but the intensely personal reaction of the Father's all-holy will against evil. Wrath represents the purity of the Divine love which, while it freely and fully forgives sin, never pretends that it is not sin and does not matter.[120]

In Luther's own words: "For love's anger (wrath) seeks and wills to sunder the evil that it hates from the good that it loves, in order that the good and its love may be preserved."[121] Here the "pure love" of God expresses itself in a "wrathful" opposition against anything that stands between God and man so that their unity would not be severed. God's true nature is love, and "wrath is truly God's alien work, which He employs contrary to His nature because He is forced into it by the wickedness of man."[122] God's "pure love" compels Him to pour out His "wrath" against "sin" as His *opus alienum* through which God's redeeming love as His *opus proprium* is expressed.[123] God's wrath is most terrifying when the sinner is not punished but allowed to remain sinful. In Luther's words :

> When God speaks, shows His wrath, is angry, punishes, gives us into the hands of our enemies, send plagues, hunger, the sword and other troubles, it is a certain sign that He is gracious to us. If however, He says "I will no longer punish you and be silent, withdraw my wrath from you, and let you go on and do whatever you want as you think best," this is a sign that he has turned away from us. But the world and our reason turn this upside down and think that the opposite is true.[124]

The "wrathful" opposition against "sin" is not generated by some abstractly conceived justice of God, which demands retribution for the broken law; rather it is generated by God's "pure love" which demands a pure, simple and undefiled relationship. At this juncture, God's wrath and God's jealously intersect so that the former is precipitated by the latter.[125] "This jealousy necessarily becomes wrath in response to sin."[126] The unique relation between love and wrath lies in the fact that God's jealousy cannot allow God to stand by idly nor can it allow us to have another lord or object, for precisely such is the nature of sin. When the understanding of "wrath" is connected with the understanding of the "pure love" of God, one can perceive the motif of divine passibility. This constitutes the main thrust of Luther's soteriology in which the love of God in the incarnate and crucified Christ suffers the sinful world and the divine wrath, and eventually suffers them into defeat. This is the way God is "for us."

If God indeed suffers the death of the Son in reconciling the world unto Himself, then there must always be a cross in the heart of God as He relates to a world which exists in enmity to Him. The historical crucifixion finds its roots in God's eternal resolve, for, in Luther's words, "Christ would not have shown this love for you if God in his eternal love had not wanted (or willed) this, for Christ's love for you is due to his obedience to God."[127] The Son was slain "in promise" from eternity, and thus it is appropriate for God the Son to be obedient unto death, to exhibit His deity in the lowliness of the cross in which God is most Godlike. God the Father who wills and God the Son who suffers in the act of His humble obedience are so intrinsically linked that the cross must not be treated as an event of discontinuity in the life of God. Luther explains that God Himself is "immutable and unchanging in his counsel from eternity. He sees and knows all things; but he does not reveal them to the godly except at his own fixed time."[128] This is in accord with what Luther calls "the necessity of consequence,"[129] out of which God acts freely.[130] God's "aseity" consists in the fact that God is totally independent of others, and correspondingly absolutely free. Luther constantly asserts this against Erasmus, particularly in The Bondage of the Will: "... free choice is plainly a divine term, and can be properly applied to none but the Divine Majesty alone; for he alone can do and does (cf. Ps. 115:3) whatever he pleases in heaven and earth."[131] God's creative power and God's sovereign freedom are linked together, and are necessarily acknowledged by faith; for the trustworthiness of God would be undercut if God is not free and omnipotent.[132] Instead God would be subject to the presumptions of the "haughty bigwigs among the nobility and the smark alecks ...(who)... imagine that they run everything as though God could not run everything without them."[133] If God were to be trusted, according to Luther, we must "ascribe to him truthfulness, righteousness, and whatever else ought to be ascribed to the one who is true. The soul consents to all his will...and allows itself to be treated according to God's good pleasure, clinging to God's promises, it does not doubt that he who is true, just, and wise will do, dispose, and provide all things well."[134] This is in accord with the "power of faith" which Luther also accentuates in his *The Large Catechism* (1528) :

> Thus you can easily understand the nature and the scope of this (first) commandment. It requires that man's whole heart and confidence be placed in God alone, and in no one else. To have God, you see, does not mean to lay hands upon him, or put him into a purse, or shut him up in a chest. We lay hold of him when our heart embraces him and clings to him. To cling to him with all our heart is nothing else than to entrust ourselves to him completely. He wishes to turn us away from everything else, and to draw us to himself, because he is the one, eternal good.[135]

If God is to keep his promises, He must be free and omnipotent, and exempted from the rules laid down by human reason or experience. In order for God to be trusted, God must be unchangeable, constant and the one who alone is free and works "all in all." Commenting on Malachi 3:6, "For I the Lord do not change," Luther writes of God: "I (the Lord) do not lie. I do not revoke the promises I have made through so many prophets. So, have no doubt! Your unworthiness will not hold back My Truth. I have promised freely. I will redeem those promises freely."[136] The biblical understanding of the unchangeability of God, which Luther affirms, is understood not in terms of divine perfection of the Greek metaphysics; rather it is understood in terms of the Hebrew's belief in God's faithfulness and trustworthiness to His "covenant" (Hos. 2:18-20).[137] Nothing can change, and resist God's

will. God cannot be affected or changed by anything that the creatures do, otherwise God would not be God. Therefore there is a
sense in which Luther could think of God as "impassible," that
God "is not subject to the passions that characterize human and
creaturely existence."[138] For instance, God Himself determines
Himself to be divinely loving and good, says Luther, and is not
determined in any way by the attitude or condition of those upon
whom goodness and kindness are divinely bestowed. God "glad-
ly waste(s) His kindness on the ungrateful."[139] It is precisely in
this sense, says Luther, that God "proves that he is good by
nature."[140] Luther predicates divine freedom of God in the manner of Richard Creel who says that God cannot be "causally influenced" by others.[141] But this in no way means that God cannot, in
the freedom of his will, be affected by the sufferings of humanity.
Man's deeds, in Luther's view, do not "necessitate" divine *pathos*
but only "occasion" it.[142] It is God's glory to give, to act, and to
love freely. The immutability of God's freedom must be affirmed
along side of the possibility of God's love in order to avoid attributing to God creaturely passion.

Luther says that we are unable to "give anything to God that
was not previously his own."[143] The key to Luther's atonement,
says Forde, lies in the "reversal": "not that something is given to
God, but that God gives something to us."[144] Light is thrown on
this point by its parallel in Luther's understanding of the eucharist,
not as a sacrifice but as a sacrament. He explains :

> We do not presume to give God something in the sacrament, when it is
> he who in it gives us all things. ... We see, then, that the best and great-
> est part of all sacraments and of the man is the word and promises of
> God, without which the sacraments are dead and are nothing at all. I
> accept for myself alone the blessing therein offered by God—and here
> there is no *officium* but *beneficium*, no work or service, but reception and
> benefit alone.[145]

The creatures do not have soteriological resources within themselves. Being dependent upon God's mercy, the creatures partici-
pate in the fullness of God's being.[146] God shares His attributes
with His creatures through Christ; especially His righteousness He

shares with His creatures through Christ whose sufferings were
not for Himself, but for our sins and griefs. He bore what we
should have suffered. "Here (we) see the foundation from which
St. Paul draws countless streams of suffering and merits of Christ,
and he condemns all religions, merits, and endeavors in the world
through which men seek salvation."[147]   Therefore the cross for
Luther is not the justification of God before man, but rather it is the
justification of man before God. Luther's theology of the cross
must not be converted into a speculative theodicy. For Luther does
not have a theodicy, if by a theodicy we mean a defense and justification of God in the face of the dreadful fact of evil and suffering.
Luther has no interest in abstract speculation as to why God per-
mits evil. Luther, in a letter to a man who lost his only son to an
accident, wrote :

> It is characteristic of our human nature to think that what we wish is best
> and what God does is unsatisfactory. But it would not be good if our
> will is always done because we would then become too sure of our-
> selves. It is enough for us that we have a gracious God. Why he per-
> mits this or that evil to befall us should not trouble us at all.[148]

Luther does not allow talk about God which comes too easily, talk
that assumes it is always easy to know what God is doing or
intending. This is precisely the theology of glory that Luther con-
trasted with true theology, that is, the theology of the cross. "That
person does not deserve to be called a theologian who looks upon
the invisible things of God as though they were clearly perceptible
in those things which have actually happened."[149]   In spite of the
fact that our fallen human nature speculates upon the incomprehensible mystery of suffering, God says "no" to our demand for an
account of His governance of the universe. Nevertheless this "no"
does not come from an angry or distant deity who resents our
inquiries; rather it is a "no" of a loving God who points us away
from abstract speculation towards the concrete image of the suffering and crucified Christ. Suffering is neither rejected nor glori-
fied; it is both acknowledged and overcome. The cross is the *locus*
where we witness God's deepest humiliation in His Son, where we
see God's "suffering" love in which God is most Godlike. The pre-

supposition of the saving love that suffers is the affirmation of a
God who has the power to bequeathe life, a God who can stand in
judgement of sin, a God who can hide His power in suffering and
yet be present in it.[150]

God's "boundless love" is revealed in the fact that God wills to
be *pro nobis* in the suffering of the Son on the cross. God is who He
is in the life of the incarnate and crucified Christ. God in Christ
chooses to meet us "who are in anguish, sin and death" as the committed "lover," "the kind of lover who gives Himself for us" in
order to save us.[151] Yet, in dealing with the theme of passion,
Luther radically distinguishes between humanity's and God's so
as to avoid attributing the unbridled and selfish passion of man to
God. As Luther says, "For this ungodly passion (of man) not only
gives no one his own, serves no one, is kind to no one, but snatch-
es everything for itself, looks for its own in everything, even in
God Himself."[152] The divine passion manifested in the cross of
Christ, for Luther, is the suffering endured only for the sake of its
object. God's will to be our "lover" thus makes Him vulnerable to
rejection and suffering. Suffering then, for Luther, is not what God
wills as such; rather it is what God receives as the result of the
divine will to be our "lover," the one who promises to be and
becomes in reality "our High Priest," interposing "Himself as the
mediator between God and us miserable sinners."[153] God's "yes"
to suffering is based on God's essential being as "boundless love,"
the fact of which is revealed to us in the obedience of the Son as we
see it on the cross. God suffers in the Son's obedience, which is an
act of His eternal will or resolve to love; conversely the life and suffering of Jesus are revelatory of God's eternal nature to give
Himself. God's passion is divine action, for He wills to bring upon
Himself the deepest humiliation in the Son and enacts His will:
The suffering that God undergoes in Christ's passion is a divine
act, not out of a deficiency of God's being but out of God's "boundless love."[154] Christ is the gift of God's love, and in this God gives
Himself in order to redeem us. Deity is revealed in the greatest
lowliness and humility. The key to the divine nature is to be recognized precisely in Christ's obedience unto death, the atonement
which He achieved for us through the "happy exchange"

(*admirabile commercium*) in which Christ, our "lover," willfully "took upon Himself our sinful person and gave unto us His innocent and victorious person, wherewith we being clothed, are free from the cruse of the law."[155] The story of Jesus Christ is the story of how deeply God Himself is implicated in our world. God in Christ has entered the sphere of His counterpart, our humanity, and therefore has entered the area of God-forsakenness, condemnation, contradiction, suffering and death.[156] By so doing, God reveals His real nature, His true deity as self-giving. "God is most Himself" in the lowliness of the cross, not in power and majesty. Hence Luther insists that whoever desires to receive justification must cling to the "coverings of the Godhead", the Incarnate God, Jesus Christ who is in the "bosom of the Father" and has unveiled historically the eternal "heart of the Father".[157] This is how to know God aright, to know Him not by His power and wisdom which terrify us, but by His goodness and love; there our salvation and faith then stand unmovably certain. This double way of apprehending God corresponds to Luther's distinction between the *deus absconditus*, the God with whom we have nothing to do, and the *deus revelatus*, the God who has turned towards us with acceptance and forgiveness.[158] The *deus revelatus* is the God with whom we have to do. This will be the concern for the next section.

Deus Absconditus and *Deus Revelatus*:
The Classic Distinction

Luther makes a sharp distinction between the God who hides in His divine essence or naked majesty, the hidden God or the naked God, and the God who hides or clothes Himself in the flesh of Jesus Christ, the revealed God or the clothed God.[159] Luther uses a variety of terms in making this distinction. Gerrish notes that his term *deus nudus* (naked God) corresponds to *deus absconditus* (hidden God), who

is God in himself (*deus ipse*), a strange terrifying and unapproachable abstraction. This being so, it appears that one must take into account, not only a dual relationship of God to the world, but also a concept of

God as *deus absolutus*, out of relation to the world. This God, too, stands
in antithetical relation to the revealed God, for the *deus revelatus* is the
deus indutus—the God who is not naked, but clothed with his Word.[160]

God clothed in the flesh (*deus indutus*) is set against the naked God
(*deus nudus*) and the revealed God (*deus revelatus*) against the hidden God (*deus absconditus*). In addition, Gerhard Forde mentions a
third pair of terms of Luther's distinction of God which sets "the
preached God over against God not preached."[161]

While the three sets of terms are interchangeable, two kinds of
hiddenness are entailed. The first kind of hiddenness is God's hiddenness in His revelation. God wills to be known in the "precise"
hiddenness, that is, in the human form, Jesus Christ.[162] Gerrish
explains, "His wisdom is hidden under folly, his strength under
abject weakness. He gives life through death, righteousness to the
unrighteousness, he saves by judging and damning."[163] This hiddenness makes "room for faith," the object of which is "things not
seen." Luther explains:

> That there may be room for faith, therefore all that is believed must be
> hidden. Yet it is not hidden more deeply than under a contrary appear-
> ance of sight, sense, and experience. Thus, when God quickens, He does
> so by killing; when He justifies, He does so by pronouncing guilty; when
> He carries up to heaven, He does so by bringing down to hell. ... the
> highest degree of faith is to believe that He is merciful, though He saves
> so few and damns so many; to believe that He is just, though of His own
> will He makes us perforce proper subjects for damnation, and seems (in
> Erasmus' words) "to delight in the torments of poor wretches and to be
> a fitter object for hate than for love." If I could by any means understand
> how this same God, who makes a show of wrath and unrighteousness,
> can yet be merciful and just, there would be no need for faith.[164]

The distinctions between law and gospel, wrath and mercy fall
within this kind of hiddenness. The law as the *opus alienum* condemns, and truly condemns, but so that we might be saved. So
law and gospel both belong to *Deus revelatus*.

The second kind of hiddenness has to do with God hidden
"behind and beyond revelation in the mystery which forms the
background of his almighty double-willing and double-working of

salvation or damnation. 'God Himself' is to be found behind and beyond the word and not in it."[165] Luther finds this distinction between the hidden and revealed God in II Thessalonians 2:4:

> And lest anyone should think this a distinction of my own, I am follow-ing Paul, who writes to the Thessalonians concerning the Anti-Christ that he will exalt himself above every God that is preached and wor-shiped (2 Thess. 2:4). This plainly shows that someone can be exalted above God as he is preached and worshiped, that is, above the word and rite through which "God is known to us and has dealings with us; but above God as he is not worshiped and not preached, but as he is in his own nature and majesty, nothing can be exalted, but all things are under his mighty hand."[166]

Luther himself confronts the question of this hiddenness most acutely in his discussion with Erasmus on why, if there is no free-dom of choice, some believe and others do not. The specific text in question is Ezekiel 18:23: "I desire not the death of the sinner, but rather that he should be converted and live."[167] Erasmus con-tended that if God does not desire the death of sinner, human free will must be the cause of it. Luther, however, saw that Erasmus' inference of free will from this text has confused law with gospel, thereby turning "a sweet proclamation of the gospel promise into a terrible statement of law."[168] For Luther, the Word "I desire not the death of the sinner ..." is not to be taken as a general or an abstract statement about God not preached; rather it is "the sweet voice of the gospel, that it is true of the preached God."[169] Luther states:

> But why some are touched by the law and others are not, so that the for-mer accept and the latter despise the offered grace, is another question, and one not dealt with by Ezekiel in this passage (Ezek. 18:23,32). For he is here speaking of the preached and offered mercy of God, not of the hidden and awful will of God by which he ordains by his own counsel which and what sort of persons he wills to be the recipients and partak-ers of his preached and offered mercy. This will is not to be inquired into, but reverently adored, as by far the most awe-inspiring secret of the Divine Majesty, reserved for himself alone and forbidden to us.[170]

Here a "limit" must be observed for any discourse about God, which for Luther breaks into two types:

> We have to argue in one way about God or the will of God as preached, revealed, offered, and worshiped, and in another way about God as he is not preached, not revealed, not offered, not worshiped. To the extent therefore, that God hides himself and wills to be unknown to us, it is no business of ours. For here the saying truly applies, "Things above us are no business of ours."[171]

In his *Commentary on Genesis* (1535 - 1545), Luther reinforces what he asserted in *The Bondage of the Will* (1525):

> With regard to God, insofar as He has not been revealed, there is no faith, no knowledge, and no understanding. And here one must add to the statement that what is above us is none of our concern. For thoughts of this kind, which investigate more sublime matters above or outside the revelation of God, are altogether devilish.[172]

God not preached, revealed, offered or worshiped, according to Luther, poses a limit for proper theological discourse.[173] Such a deity remains God "in his own nature and majesty"; such a God cannot be banished by theological efforts. What are we to do with the absolute God who is not preached? Nothing. We are to leave the absolute God alone and attend to the God clothed and displayed in His Word. Writes Luther:

> God must be left to himself in his own majesty, for in this regard we have nothing to do with him, nor has he willed that he should have anything to do with him. But we have something to do with him insofar as he is clothed and set forth in his Word, through which he offers himself to us and which is the beauty and glory with which the psalmist celebrates him as being clothed. In this regard we say, the good God does not deplore the death of his people which he works in them, but he deplores the death which he finds in his people and desires to remove from them. For it is this that God as he is preached is concerned with, namely that sin and death should be taken away and we should be saved. For "he sent his word and healed them" (Ps. 107:20). But God hidden in his majesty neither deplores nor takes away, but works life, death and all in all. For there he has not bound himself by his word, but

has kept himself free over all things.[174]

The distinction between the hidden God (hidden in the second, absolute, sense) and the revealed God, according to Luther, does not mean two deities but one and the same who "works life, death and all in all." The impenetrability and undefinability of the *deus absconditus* coinheres with Luther's formula *"Deum esse Deum,"* in virtue of which *Gott an sich* is not at our disposal.[175] *Deus ipse* is defined as "hiddenness"; the divine hiddenness belongs to the divine essence. "God is the one who is hidden. This is His peculiar property."[176] By indicating that hiddenness belongs to God's essence, Jenson notes, Luther continues the medieval tradition of identifying God's deity by means of mere negatives such as "invisibility," "intangibility," and "ineffability," and so on.[177] *"Nam quid Deus in natura sei, definire non possumus. Hoc bene possumus definire, quid non est."*[178] According to Luther God "cannot be comprehended in His unveiled majesty" because the true God's majesty is precisely his hiddenness, ungrasped by any but Himself.[179] "God sees that this way of knowing God (in His naked majesty) is impossible for us; for, as Scripture states (I Tim. 6:16), He dwells in unapproachable light."[180] God affirms Himself as the sovereign "subject" of theology, not as the "object" of human subjective activity. But Luther breaks with the tradition by redefining God's hiddenness (in the first, precise, sense) as God's will to "hide Himself" actively in the antithesis of the cross of Christ. This "precise" hiddenness constitutes for Luther the definitiveness of God's self-revelation in Christ wherein God "has made known what we can grasp and understand."[181] Since God's hiddenness is the predicate of God's deity, God's self-revelation in Christ is not an abolition of his hiddenness. Rather, God reveals Himself by precisely hiding so that the hiddenness of God is also a predicate of the revelation of God. Jenson writes: "God reveals himself by hiding yet again, by exercising his very deity, but now hiding under the opposite of all that sheer omnipotence which hides him and is his mere deity, under weakness and forgiveness and death."[182] Luther has God say: "From an unrevealed God I will become a revealed God. Nevertheless I will remain the same God."[183] Luther expressly affirms that, in His Word, the one God has lifted His veil, taking a step out of His absolute hiddenness. He insists that God, who is hidden in His naked majesty and nature does not concern us, because God has come in the person of Jesus Christ, and therefore has been revealed. The naked God does not concern us because, clothed in His Word and with His Word He is offered, worshiped and proclaimed and therefore is accessible. In Jesus, God wills to be known and so there is revelation. God's essence is accessible insofar as God defines His "hiddenness" in His self-revelation in Jesus' crucifixion and resurrection. The God undefined— the *deus absconditus*—has defined Himself "freely" in His Word as the *deus revelatus* or the *deus praedicatus*. God in His own life corresponds to Christ come and crucified. God really is what He has shown Himself to be, according to which the "absolute" hiddenness of God cannot be spoken of as a hiddenness that possibly contradicts the revelation of God. Henceforth Luther summons theology to stay with God's self-revelation in the incarnate and crucified Christ, with God's "precise" hiddenness in the humanity of Christ. Luther states this in his *The Bondage of the Will*:

> Let it occupy itself instead with God incarnate, or as Paul puts it, with Jesus crucified, in whom are all the treasures of wisdom and knowledge, though in a hidden manner (Col. 2:3); for through him it is furnished abundantly with what it ought to know and ought not to know. It is God incarnate, moreover, who is speaking here: "I would ... you would not"—God incarnate, I say, who has been sent into the world for the very purpose of willing, speaking, doing, suffering, and offering to all men everything for salvation.[184]

Furthermore this summon for theology to focus on God's "precise" hiddenness appears also in Luther's *Lectures on Genesis* 26:9, wherein immediately after affirming the identity of *deus absconditus* and *deus revelatus*, he continues by having God say:

> "I will be made flesh, or send my Son. He shall die for your sin and shall rise again from the dead. ... Behold, this is My Son; listen to Him (cf. Matt. 17:5). Look at Him as He lies in the manger and on the lap of His

mother, as He hangs on the cross. Observe what He does and what He says. Therefore you surely take hold of Me."[185]

Thus what is clear here in Luther is that he affirms the identity of God hidden and God revealed. The question as to whether Luther always and consistently affirms their identity is, perhaps, a subject for an entire thesis. What can be said is that at crucial points, such as in the *Theses for the Heidelberg Disputation*, Luther indicates that though we are forbidden to see God's "face," we, like Moses, are permitted to see God's "backparts," a visible piece of the divine mystery. In this way he affirms an integral relationship between the "economic" hiddenness and the "immanent" ineffability.

Luther is conscious that matters divine are necessarily beyond the gaze of sinful mortals. Following Augustine, Luther believes that it is God's will to accommodate Himself to human capacity. "God lowers himself to the level of our weak comprehension and presents himself to us in images, coverings, as it were, in simplicity adapted to a child, that in some measure it may be possible for him to be known by us."[186] Luther warns against any speculative incursion into the majesty of the naked God, and leads us to biblical theology. He observes "this general rule: to avoid as much as possible any questions that carry us to the throne of the Supreme Majesty. It is better and safer to stay at the manger of Christ the man. For there is a great danger in involving oneself in the mazes of the Divine Being."[187] This understanding is furnished in Luther's Christological interpretation of Psalm 51:1, where he declares that the "absolute God" (or "naked God") and the human creatures are the "bitterest of enemies."[188]

> From this absolute God everyone should flee who does not want to perish. ... Human weakness cannot help being crushed by such majesty.... We must take hold of this God, not naked but clothed and revealed in His Word; otherwise despair crushes us. ... The absolute God, is like an iron wall, against which we cannot bump without destroying ourselves. Therefore Satan is busy day and night, making us run to the naked God so that we forget His promises and blessings shown in Christ and think about God and the judgement of God. When this happens, we perish utterly and fall into despair.[189]

Not only does the majesty of the naked God destroy the creature, but also the revealed God is hostile to anyone who refuses to
receive Him as He is preached or offered in the Gospel. Jüngel, in
commenting on Luther's understanding of the *"Entsprechung"*
between the revealed and the hidden God in their apparently contradictory acts, indicates how both the majesty of the hidden God
and the Word of the revealed God teach the *Socratic dictum*: *"Quae
Supra nos, nihil ad nos"*:

> *Der offenbare Gott ist nun aber dem Menschen feind der sein eigener Feind
> geworden ist. Denn wer sich über den gepredigten Gott erhebt, um sich zu dem
> Gott über uns und damit auch schon über diesen zu erheben, der, überhebt sich
> selbst. Er geht an seiner Selbstüberhebung zugrunde. Diesem sich selbst
> zugrunde richtenden Menschen ist der offenbare Gott feind. Und darin zeigt
> sich die Identität von deus absconditus and deus revelatus. Der deus abscondi-
> tus weist von sich weg, so daß der sich zu ihm erhebende Mensch Gottes und
> sein eigener Feind werden muß. Der deus revelatus weist auf sich hin und
> insofern ebenfalls vom deus absconditus weg. Als der Feind des sich selber
> feindlichen Menschen weist er diesen auf seine Offenbarung im Menschen
> Jesus, wo er als inen freundlicher Gott auf den Menschen wartet. Es
> entsprechen sich also verborgener Gott und Offenbarer Gott mitten im schein-
> baren Widerspruch. Beide lehren uns zu verstehen: Quae supra nos, nihil ad
> nos.[190]

Both as the hidden deity and as the revealed deity, the one God
directs us away from Himself when we seek to grasp Him "above"
His human life and cross and resurrection, toward Himself as He
defines Himself for us in the incarnate Word, through whom we
are restored to the Father.[191]   God "wants us to learn of the
revealed Word painstakingly," wherein God hides Himself as a
witness to God's steadfast love.[192] God is hidden from the world
until He is revealed in the cross of Christ. God is revealed to faith
by His act of hiding Himself in the cross. This act of hiding uncovers for faith the hiddenness of "love" which is painful or passible.
The "precise" hiddenness in the cross of Christ is thus for Luther a
predicate of the revelation of God's love.   In Jenson's words:
"(God) defines his hiddenness, and thus he makes it speakable,
and speaks it, as the hiddenness of love."[193] The certainty of faith,

says Luther, lies only in the one "clothed and displayed in His Word; God works to the end that sin and death may be taken away and we may be saved."[194] "Whoever desires to be saved and safe ..., let him simply hold to the form, signs, and the coverings of the Godhead, such as His Word and His works, For in His Word and His works He shows Himself to us."[195] Luther knows of the hubris of human reason, repeatedly wanting to grasp God "above" His human life. He points therefore forcibly to the *Deus incarnatus* and with Him to the definitive revelation of God in the Gospel. He who rises to the "above"/absolute God rises to death or hell. Thus Luther insists that whoever finds God outside of Christ finds the devil.[196] *"Gerade darum und damit hält er am Evangelium fest: Hier und nur hier ist Gott offenbar und er ist hier offenbar als der aus grundloser Barmherzigkeit und unableitbarer Liebe uns wünderbar rechfertigende Herr, dem gegenüber es nur glaubendes Vertrauen und damütigen Gehorsam geben kann."*[197] Whoever wants to find God must shun the Majestic God, God in His naked immediacy and assume the way of the Divine "from below": "Begin from below, from the Incarnate Son. ... Christ will bring you to the Hidden God. ... If you take the revealed God, he will bring you to the Hidden God at the same time."[198] Grasp God in the way Scripture teaches us: start therefore at the point where God Himself starts, namely, in the Virgin's womb, in the manger, at His mother's breasts. Any attempt to execute the opposite movement, according to Luther, will either end in utter ignorance of God or dash us against the terror of the true God's majesty.

The distinction between *deus absconditus* and *deus revelatus* constitutes for Luther a paradox, in virtue of which even in God's "human", or precise, hiddenness God remains the "divinely" unsearchable and unapproachable majesty in whose presence we would be annihilated if we do not take refuge in the love of God that has appeared in Christ. The incarnate Christ is the happening of God's love that suffers God's own wrath so as to create a people no longer living under the divine wrath. God in the person of His Son, Jesus Christ, this flesh and blood God, the *deus revelatus*, in suffering for us overcomes the *deus absconditus* and abolishes the terror of the *deus absconditus* forever. Christ has entered the terri-

fying abyss of the absconding God as He laments in the cry of
dereliction on the cross, "My God, my God, why have you forsak-
en me? (Ps. 22):"[199] The Son's true "image" is seen in His willingness to communicate the essence of God's love by being forsaken.
Christ struggles against the *deus absconditus*, suffers and overcomes the *deus absconditus* for us on the cross: "... *da (Gethsemane)
streydet Gott mit Gott...*"[200] The depth of God's love is disclosed
precisely in this distinction in God wherein God struggles against
Himself for our sake, thereby also revealing Himself as suffering
against Himself, the *deus revelatus* overcoming the *deus absconditus*.
Faith grasps the true essence of God's love within this dimen-
sion.[201] God's "omnipotent love" suffers and conquers His own
wrath when His very Son accepts the forsakenness, "thereby prov-
ing that he is the dearest Son, who gives this to all if we but
believe."[202] So Luther's enquiry into the atonement is "not
whether there is a blood precious enough to pay God or even to
the devil, but whether God has acted decisively to win us. The
question is whether God can actually give Himself in such a way
to save us."[203] The issue of reconciliation is resolved for Luther by
the affirmation that this "incarnate and human God," who is "the
image of the grace of God against sin,"[204] has acted to conquer the
deus absconditus, getting Him off our backs. God incarnate in Jesus
has reconciled two sets of contraries—the divine blessing and
curse, the divine mercy and wrath, eternal life and death. Christ
interposes Himself as the mediator for the sinner who deserves the
divine curse or wrath and yet receives the love of the Father.[205]
Christ confronts the divine curse through the cross so that both the
divine curse and blessing occur "in Himself," and are finally
resolved on the cross, for those who believe. God endures the contradiction of blessing and curse without being destroyed by it, and
finally overcomes it on the cross of Christ. Luther's distinction of
the *absconditus Deus* and the *revelatus Deus* in the doctrine of God
eventuates in a "battle" between them: "God not preached
devours sinners without regret, but the preached God battles to
snatch us away from sin and death."[206] Forde writes of this veri-
table battle:

It is God against God. The abstract God cannot be removed but must be dethroned, overcome, "for you" in concrete actuality. The clothed God must conquer the naked God for you in the living present. Faith is precisely the ever-renewed flight from God to God: from naked and hidden to the God clothed and revealed. Luther insists that we cling to the God at his mother's breasts, the God who hung on the cross and was raised from the tomb in the face of the dangerous attack launched from the side of the hidden God. ... There is just no other way. The question at stake is whether one will believe God in the face of God.[207]

A proper understanding of Luther's formulation of the distinction between God hidden and God revealed presupposes faith in Christ.[208] Faith, in Luther's sense, is a "flight" (*fugere*).[209] It is "not a repose, but movement."[210] Under *Anfechtung* before *deus absconditus*, says Gerrish, "faith really does take into itself something of the meaning of God's hiddenness even though it is not directed against that hiddenness: rather it is a movement away from the Hidden God."[211] The forbidding image of the hidden God "waits on the edge of faith and for this reason, determines (in some measure) the content of faith, which has the character of a turning away from the hidden God" to the revealed God, the God with whom we have to do.[212] The perennial crisis of *anfechtung* before *deus absconditus* is overcome in the crucified Christ, who suffered on our behalf the same *Anfechtung* that we suffer. The haunting specter of the terrifying *deus absconditus* is confirmed, but more crucially conquered in the gospel, "for those who believe" (Rom. 1:16-17). As Forde puts it, "The fact is that the terror of the absolute God reigns until the proclamation that creates faith announces its end and liberates the believer from it."[213] As stated earlier, that which overcomes the absolute hiddenness of God is not faith but the revealed God. It is God who in hiding Himself in Christ overcomes His absolute hiddenness.[214] It is only in Christ where God is revealed, that an enormous antinomy (*magna pugnantia*) between God hidden and God revealed occurs, and is finally resolved. As Luther puts it, in Christ's cross and resurrection, the divine "blessing" triumphs over the divine "curse"—that is, for those who believe. The incarnate/crucified Christ fights against the naked/hidden God to conquer divine wrath "in

Himself," thereby getting the terror and inscrutability of the *deus absconditus* (i.e., the absolute God) off our backs.

The work of God's love works in a two fold way in relation to God's wrath: (1) In relation to us, the work of God's love itself works wrath (God's alien work) in order to move us to dependence upon God's love (God's proper work). (2) In relation to God, God's love moves God to come to us, thus abolishing His distance from us, which would mean wrath for us. Two contraries are resolved: (1) God's blessing and curse in His dealings with us; and (2) God's blessing in coming to us as opposed to the curse of His remaining at a distance from us.

Thus far we have seen in Luther's theology two pairs: immanent/economic and hidden God/revealed God. The two pairs are not parallels. The *deus revelatus* is economic and immanent: since God is known through His works, the God-at-work (economic) is the God-revealed who is none other than the immanent God. The God of the Gospel corresponds to the immanent God whose essence is located in the incarnate Son. The immanent God is towards us in His revealing and gracious activities of the Son and the Holy Spirit. In addition to these two pairs, there is a third pair: law and gospel. Because the absolute hiddenness of God "causes" us to flee from the hidden God's death-causing powers to the revealed God in Jesus Christ, apart from whom there is no salvation, some interpreters have understood the distinction between God hidden and God revealed to be the distinction between law and gospel.[215] However, since the law and the gospel belong to the work (alien and proper) of the *revelatus Deus*, there is here only a parallel, but not an identity. The distinction, then, between law and gospel, according to Luther, must not be equated with the distinction between God hidden and God revealed because law and gospel both belong to *deus revelatus*. Both law and gospel, in Luther's view, really, are instruments for the salvation in Christ, the law being merely the *opus alienum*. The negative aspect of the *deus absconditus* and of the law is not the same. The law condemns, truly condemns, but so that we might be saved. The law is the strange work of the God of the Gospel—that is, *deus revelatus*. The paradox of God's being, for Luther, is that God kills in order to make alive (I Sam. 2:6). The law is not against God's promises but leads to those promises. In Galatians Luther writes of this double activity of God:

> This does not mean that it was the chief purpose of God in giving the Law only to cause death and damnation. ... For the Law is a Word that shows life and drives us toward it. Therefore it was not given only for the sake of death. But this is its chief use and end: to reveal death, in order that the nature and enormity of sin might thus become apparent. It does not reveal death in a way that takes delight in it or that seeks to do nothing but kill us. No, it reveals death in order that men may be terrified and humbled and thus fear. ... Therefore the function of the Law is only to kill, yet in such a way that God may be able to make alive. Thus the Law was not given merely for the sake of death; but because man is proud and supposes that he is wise, righteous, and holy, therefore it is necessary that he be humbled by the Law, in order that this beast, the presumption of righteousness, may be killed, since man cannot live unless it is killed.[216]

Thus for Luther, as for Paul, there is a revelation of God which is anything but saving, namely, the revelation of divine wrath or condemnation. That God is revealed as "wrathful" is evident in Paul: "The wrath of God is revealed against ... the wickedness of those who by their wickedness suppress the truth" (Rom. 1:18ff).[217] The divine wrath consists in the very fact that God lets the wicked "by their wickedness suppress the truth." "God gave them up," and abandoned them to the untruth.[218] The bitter-counter truth of God's wrath has to be revealed, without which we moralize our sin, placing it in the context of our enmity to God and God's enmity to us. The deepest antithesis is not between our sin and God's grace, but God's Law and God's grace. This antithesis, so offensive to moralists, requires revelation. "Thus the wrath of God remains as a reality in the Christian life, in an ongoing tension, side by side with love."[219] Luther does not present us with a confusion when he asserts the identity of the Christian as *simul iustus et peccator*— justified and sinner as the same time.[220] Luther writes in his *Lectures on Romans* (1516), "Now, is he perfectly righteous? No, for he is at the same time both a sinner and a righteous man: a sinner in fact, but a righteous man by the sure imputation and promise of

God that He will continue to deliver him from sin until He has completely cured him."[221] Sin or unbelief continues to abide even in the life of the Christian: "... sin is always present, and the godly feel it. But it is ignored and hidden in the sight of God, because Christ the Mediator stands between; because we take hold of Him by faith, all our sins are no longer."[222] The Law is the revelation of God, for by it sins are not hidden but are exposed, revealing that the sinner "is forced by the fruits of (his) own ungodliness so that (he) will and (does) nothing but evil" (cf. Rom. 1).[223] However, when Christ and faith are present, sins are "ignored and hidden" in Christ. Faith grasps the saving benefits of Christ's suffering *pro nobis*—that is, faith grasps the benefits that flow from the joyous exchange between the sinner and Christ. When man is viewed in light of the absolute demands of divine righteousness, expressed in God's Law, every person—including the Christian—is guilty of sin, and that sin stirs up God's wrath against him. The believer is never beyond Law and Gospel, which are, according to Luther, radically distinct from each other and mutually contradictory but "very closely joined in experience."[224] Paul indicates this when he says that "we who have been terrified by the Law may taste the sweetness of grace, the forgiveness of sins, and deliverance from the Law, sin and death, which are not acquired by works but are grasped by faith alone."[225] We are confined under a custodian, the Law, not forever but until Christ, who is the end of the Law (Rom. 10:4).[226] When faith comes, says Luther, the "theological prison of the Law" comes to an end.[227] "Therefore you are being afflicted by this prison, not to do you harm but to re-create you through the Blessed Offspring. You are being killed by the Law in order to be made alive through Christ."[228] The Law is the strange work of the God of the Gospel: God kills in order to make alive, this being constitutive of *deus revelatus*. The God of the Gospel does not want to kill us so that we remain in death. "I have no pleasure," He speaks through the prophet, "in the death of the sinner" (Ezek. 33:11). But God wants to kill us in such a way that we may be humbled and may acknowledge our need for the mercy of God and the blessing of Christ. The annihilating knowledge of God revealed in the Law is useful, "causally" useful—if and when it drives us into the arms of Christ. God's "yes" to us is hidden in His severe "no".[229] This double or contradictory activity is done by "the same God who works everything in everyone" (I Cor. 12:6).[230] God corresponds to Himself precisely in these two contradictory activities: the *opus alienum* and the *opus proprium*, the former leads to the latter.

Finally, the polarity between the naked/hidden God and the clothed/revealed God is most properly the polarity between impassibility and passibility respectively. Goetz views this polarity as a contradiction.

> (Luther who), in his theology of the cross affirmed the suffering of God, even unto death, (seems) to take back much of what he said in his equally foundational doctrines of predestination and the *Deus absconditus*. When contemplating the purposes of the hidden God, Luther portrayed an inscrutable impassible, divine sovereignty—a portrayal which was even more severe than Calvin's.[231]

Goetz is right to identify the *deus absconditus* as "an inscrutable impassible, divine sovereignty" who devours sinners without regret. But he fails to grasp Luther's emphasis which sets the preached/revealed God against the not preached/hidden God. God as sheer naked/impassible abstraction is an inescapable terror for us, and can only be overcome by the preached/passible God. The mask of the impassible/naked God cannot be removed by human rationalization. Luther's affirmation that God suffers is set in the context of the distinction between God preached and God not preached. The mask of the impassible/naked God is overcome as the believer is grasped by the preached/clothed God who truly suffers. Luther does not seek to overcome the distinction between the revealed God and the hidden God by a *theologoumenon*. It is the revealed God in act who overcomes the hidden God. The antinomous realities must therefore not be rationally dissolved: the tension is between the killing/impassible/naked God and enlivening/passible/clothed God. He who refuses to have the passible/clothed God not only does not have the God of mercy in Christ, but also encounters the inscrutable and impassible/naked God who devours sinners without regret. Faith lays hold of the crucified God (*Deus crucifixus*) who has conquered the impassible/naked God for us in concrete actuality; unbelief, on the contrary, encounters only the impassible/naked God before whom it faces total annihilation or damnation if it does not cleave to the passible/clothed God of mercy.[232] In his commentary on Psalm 51(1532), Luther asserts that "as you believe, so it will happen, because this faith is not taken from your judgement but drawn from the Word of God." When one trusts God, the divine wrath is placated, "according to Christ's saying (Mat. 18:130, 'As you believe, so be it done to you'."[233] In other words, God is indeed wrathful to unbelief; but He is merciful to faith—that is, to those who "grasp Christ to be the object of mercy."[234] God, for Luther, is thus identified as Him to whom one's heart clings and entrusts itself. God—for faith—is "that to which I must look for all that is good."[235] Luther's *theologia crucis* is a theology of Christ. Ian Siggins elucidates Luther's Christological talk about God in his *theologia crucis*: "He who wants to encounter God must encounter Him where He may be grasped as He cannot be grasped in His majesty: in the Incarnate God, who lives in His mother's lap, and in the crucified God. To cling solely to Christ as He goes through death to the Father is the only way to find God."[236] Faith lays hold of the God who truly suffers in Christ and reveals Himself in His suffering as love—love that suffers the divine wrath to triumph over it, that is, for those who believe. The divine imperative for Luther is to cling to the clothed God, the God with whom we have to do. To seek God outside of the clothed God, in Luther's view, is to "run off to a place where there is neither Word, faith, and Spirit or knowledge of God," and eventually end up "in the midst of hell, death, and sin."[237] "This is Jonah's experience"—a frightening one, until "God seeks out and visits Jonah so soon after his sin (thereby giving to Jonah) a strong token of mercy".[238] God's mercy triumphs over God's wrath, and this is revealed to faith: "For all of this takes place in the heart and conscience, where there is no work and no work can enter."[239] Faith means to flee (*fugere*) to God in Christ. This flight coincides with God's activity as *sub contrarie specie*. Reconciliation with God occurs when God ceases to be "against us" (*contra nobis*), but begins to be "for us" (*pro nobis*) when He is received by faith. "The proclamation of the concrete, incarnate word set against the absolute God so as to create faith is the only way out. Faith means precisely to be grasped by the proclamation in the face of the terror of the absolute God, in the face of tribulation (*Anfechtung*), as Luther puts it."[240] In this way the annihilating being of the *deus absconditus* is overcome "for the believer" by the loving God—the one and same God who has reached His intended goal: to create a people no longer under the divine wrath. It is God who overcomes this wrath by suffering it, and eventually suffering it into defeat on the cross of Christ. And faith follows in trust this action of God. The sinner in humility believes that sin no longer exists, and the divine wrath is placated on account of what God has done—the God of mercy has conquered the God of wrath. And this true knowledge constitutes faith and is saving where a creature knows that this conquering action has been done *pro me*. It is only by knowing God in Christ, that is, according to Luther, the only way God wants us to know Him, that the knowledge of God—"this God, this God-man"—is saving knowledge, the saving knowledge of *sola fide*.

Luther claims that he is not speculating when he speaks about God's wrath or God's inscrutability or God's absolute hiddenness, for, he insists, this God is attested by Scripture (e.g. Matt. 22:14). The hiddenness of the *Deus absconditus* lies not in His wrath, which is known, but rather in the basis for this wrath (Why, Luther asks, in responding to Erasmus, does God "save so few and damn so many?"). The question of election is raised by the gospel itself. Why do some and not others receive the benefits of Christ? Luther speaks of how he has stumbled in utter despair over the problem of predestination.

> Doubtless it gives the greatest possible offence to common sense or natural reason, that God, who is proclaimed as being full of mercy and goodness, and so on, should of His own mere will abandon, harden and damn men, as though He delighted in the sins and great eternal torments of such poor wretches. ... And who would not stumble at it? I have stumbled at it more than once, down to the deepest pit of despair, so that I wish I had never been made a man.[241]

The fact of God's election is revealed, but the why of God's non-election is hidden. What is revealed is the basis for God's election, God's love; what is hidden is the reason why God also works non-election. God reserves to Himself His sovereign freedom to determine *quos et quales*. The hidden will is the divine counterpart of human inquiry: Why some and not others? To pursue the question according to unbelief, Luther avers, only runs one against that "concealed (*occulta*) and dreadful will of God, who, by his own design, ordains whom he wills." On the other hand, faith will reverently adore this "most awesome secret of the divine majesty, reserved to himself alone and forbidden to us."[242] Luther warns against unbelief's speculation about God's justice and will, that is, to seek God's will apart from God's acts in Christ. He calls this logical casuistry a "theology of glory" which no longer distinguishes between God hidden and God revealed. About God Himself— *deus ipse* or *deus nudus*—and what He might do in His absolute majesty, we do not know. Who knows what the *deus absconditus* does and why? The question as to why God chooses so few and damns so many is a forbidden question. Augustine's answer to the forbidden question finds its approval in Luther's theology: "God was making hell for those who are inquisitive."[243] The divine hidden will which predetermines everything and works all in all without distinction is above us. We must observe Luther's *Socratic dictum*: "What is above us is none of our business." However, faith knows the clothed God about whom we do know something, because He is the God who is turned towards us with forgiveness. God is known through His acts; His merciful activity thus reveals the divine subject, the divine character and nature, while the depth of God's being remains hidden. As Christians, we should not search out the *deus absconditus*, the God who shows us His absolute wrath who is awe-inspiring and fear-causing, since He might easily drive us to despair. For us, the right access to God is where He allows Himself to be found, in the human form, in Jesus Christ. This is where we find the *deus revelatus*. Through Jesus the Son, we are directed to the Father and guided by the Holy Spirit. Therefore, as Christians, we can know the heart of God as it is revealed in God's merciful act in His Son. This makes possible the certainty of faith—that is, faith in God's redeeming act which is known through the revelation of His glory under the antithesis of the cross of Christ. The precise hiddenness of God in the cross as a predicate of God's revelation and therefore God's love is that which concerns us. The solution to the absolute hiddenness of God, for Luther as for Staupitz, is not theoretical but practical, that is, by way of the proclamation of the gospel apart from which "God and Satan are virtually indistinguishable."[244] When the believer's conscience faces anxiety or terror *coram deus absconditus*, God does not reach him through theological efforts but in the flesh and blood of the crucified Christ who comes as a baby in the manger and whose life culminates on the cross. The only and practically secured basis, says Luther, is to cleave to the *deus indutus*, to "begin from below, from the Incarnate Son," who has overcome the naked God for us if we but believe. Faith clings to the God who promises to save us freely and apart from merits, stripping us of all soteriological resources within us. The unity of the majesty of the "precisely" hidden God and His revelation is to be made known "when the light of Word and faith comes to an end and reality itself and the Divine Majesty are revealed in their own light" eschatologically.[245] "The light of glory will show us hereafter that the God whose judgement here (in matter of His election) is one of incomprehensible righteousness is a God of most perfect and manifest righteousness. In the meantime, we can only believe this," awaiting its realization in *lumen gloriae*,[246] whereforth God's real self will be grasped fully. A full knowledge of God will occur in the light of glory in which there is no "otherwise of God"—that is, such knowledge will not contradict what has been revealed in Christ.[247] Goetz sees only a contradiction in Luther because he sees Luther as only setting side by side *Deus revelatus* and *Deus absconditus*. But Luther has the former battling the latter. The former overcomes the latter. With what result for the understanding of predestination? In the Preface to Romans, Luther explains :

> When you arrive at chapter 8 (of Romans), dominated by the cross and passion of Christ, you will learn the right way of understanding the divine (predestination) in chapters 9, 10 and 11 and the assurance it gives. If we do not feel the weight of the passion, the cross, and the death we cannot cope with the problem of (predestination), without

either hurt to ourselves or secret anger with God.[248]

The absolute hiddenness of God gives way for faith to the precise hiddenness. Neither faith nor unfaith knows the why of God's non-election. But for unfaith, which looks to God's absolute hiddenness, God's non-election is but the spectre of God's wrath, inducing terror and despair. For faith, God's non-election, being the work of the God of the Gospel is a work of God's precisely hidden majesty, which awaiting the eschatological revelation of glory, will be of a piece with grace and will disclose the perfect righteousness of the God of love. In the *lumen gloriae*, there, when "vision" will have replaced "faith,"[249] man will recognize the genuine mercy and perfect justice of God.

Since Luther's prime interest is the doctrine of justification by faith, his attention focused on the revealed God overcoming the hidden God. For Luther, the revealed God is the trinitarian God, who is revealed in Jesus Christ, as Father, Son and Spirit. God the Father is recognized in the incarnate Son and through the Spirit. The point, according to Pannenberg, is that the individual persons of the Trinity must not be confused with the hidden God,[250] although Luther, as noted by Lohse, continues to speak of the majesty and depth of the revealed God in His work and in His existence as the individual persons of the immanent Trinity.[251] Quoting Luther,

> We distinguish therefore between the Holy Spirit in his nature and substance as God and the Holy Spirit as he is given to us. God, in his nature and majesty, is our enemy, because he demands that we fulfill the laws. ... This is also true of the Holy Spirit. When his finger writes the law on Moses' tablets of stone, he appears in his majesty, accuses us of sin, and terrifies our hearts. However, when he comes to us in tongues and other spiritual gifts, he himself is "gift" because he makes us holy and gives us life. Without this "gift" of the Holy Spirit himself, the law condemns our sin, because the law is never "gift," but always is the word of the eternal and almighty God.[252]

These statements will be rightly understood only if placed in the total context of Luther's doctrine of God.[253] We will consider

Luther's doctrine of the Trinity in the next chapter.

Chapter Five

Trinity and Divine Suffering

This study does not concern itself with all aspects of the doctrine of the Trinity about which Luther spoke, but only with those that directly relate to Luther's understanding of God's suffering.[1] However, the structure of Luther's doctrine of the Trinity must be delineated before the question of divine passibility can be answered, so this chapter begins with a description of it. It must be borne in mind that Luther did not think of God without thinking of Him as triune. Luther knew, of course, that from the days of the early church there was a close relation between the Doctrines of the Trinity and the Incarnation.[2] He was certainly aware of the dictum of the Athanasian creed: "whoever wants to be saved should think thus about the Trinity." The doctrine of the Trinity, for Luther, is indispensable to an understanding of the economy of salvation. The distinctiveness of the persons allows Luther to affirm that God suffers in the Son, and yet he rejects Patri-passianism. The Holy Spirit works subjectively to create in us faith in Jesus Christ, through whom we ascend to the Father.

A Description of the Article of the Trinity

It is pertinent to begin with a review of the most important terms of the doctrine of the Trinity, which Luther inherited. Though Luther showed reserve towards the word "*homoousios*," he used it because the meaning given it by the Council of Nicea was borne out by Scripture. Yet he argued that "no new, nonscriptural word" is really required in dogmatic formulations.[3] He was also not entirely pleased with the concept of "*Persona*," but he used it, just as the early Fathers did, because no better term was available.[4]

For the oneness of God the Latin fathers used *substantia* and *essentia* while the Greek fathers used *ousia*. For the threeness of God the Latin fathers used *persona*, which corresponds to what the Greek fathers call *hypostasis*. In a sermon on John 1 in 1537, Luther wrote: "For want of a better term, we have had to use the word 'Person'; the fathers used it too. It conveys no other meaning than that of a *hypostasis*."[5] Furthermore Luther expressed his reservations about the traditional terms of the Trinity because God is the highest unity (*summa concordia*).[6] The terms "*trinitas*," (trinity) and "*Dreifaltigkeit*" (three-foldness) are inadequate and "risky."[7] The term "*gedritts*" (thirds) and "*Dreiheit*" (threeness) are blasphemous because they remind Luther of Tritheism.[8] As Jansen noted: "*Von 'der alten dogmatischen termini' der Trinitätslehre macht Luther 'nur notgedrungen Gebrauch'. Sie vermogen die gemeinte Sache—so wie Luther sie versteht—nicht in jeder Hinsicht adäquat auszudrucken.*"[9] Luther's intensive preoccupation with the old ecclesiastical theology of the Trinity is evident in his *The Three Symbols or Confession of the Belief of Christ* (1538), *On the Councils and Churches* (1539), *On the Last Words of David* (1543).[10]

The doctrine of the Trinity, mysterious as it is, is not an outgrowth of metaphysical speculation but of revelation. For Luther it is an *articulus fidei*, confessed by biblical writers, uninvented but uncovered by later creeds and historians.[11] Luther finds, for instance, that the prologue of John's Gospel and indeed the whole of the Fourth Gospel advocates the doctrine of the Trinity, that is, the knowledge that God is "three distinct persons" yet "one God."[12] Because the Trinity is an article of faith, Luther says: "*Hier Muß die ganze Grammatik neue Worte annehmen, wenn sie über Gott reden will.*"[13] "*Von diesen Dingen der Göttlichen Majestät kann durch Vernunft und Philosophie nichts, durch den Glauben aber alles richtig gesagt und geglaubt werden.*"[14]

Luther offers a long excursus on the doctrine of the Trinity in his work, *Treatise on the Last Words of David*. In it the starting point is Psalm 33:6 wherein three persons are named: the Lord, His Word and His Spirit; and yet David did not acknowledge more than one Creator.[15] "The Lord does not do His own work separately, the Word does not do His own work separately, and the Breath does not do His work separately."[16] In all his trinitarian remarks one may note that Luther neither separates the single Divinity nor mingles the three Persons. Indeed, he follows the premise of the Creed of Athanasius which declares: "This, however is the real Christian faith, that we honor one single God in three Persons and three Persons in one single Godhead."[17] This premise prohibits the assignment of a work to each person in the exclusive sense that the other two persons have nothing to do with it, for then God's unity would be given up and there would be three gods or creators. In order to avoid tritheism, Luther affirmed Augustine's principle that the works of the Trinity in relationship to all that is outside the Trinity remain inseparably one. God acts in full unity with Himself. It follows from this principle, *"opera trinitatis ad extra sunt indivisa"* that all three Persons are one Creator.[18] On the other hand the difference among the three Persons in the Godhead must not be obscured in order to prevent mingling the three Persons into one Person, as Sabellius, the Arians, Macedonians, the Jews and the Moslems do, each in their own way.[19] Luther remains, as Lienhard notes, faithful to the thought of Augustine when he speaks of "immanental" or innertrinitarian relationships within the framework of which the Father, the Son, and the Holy Spirit must be distinguished, while at the same time the persons must not be separated in their "economic" action towards the creature *ad extra*.[20] In God's own life the persons are distinguished but not separated. So, too, in His action with us the persons are distinguished, but not separated. Luther distinguishes the persons by saying,

> ..., when I go beyond and outside of creation or the creature and move into the internal, incomprehensible essence of divine nature, I find that Holy Scripture teaches me—for reason counts for nought in this sphere—the Father is a different and distinct person from the Son in the one indivisible and eternal Godhead. The difference is that He is the Father and does not derive His Godhead from the Son or anyone else. The Son is a Person distinct from the Father in the same, one paternal Godhead. The difference is that He is the Son and that He does not have the Godhead from Himself, nor from anyone else, but the Father, since He was born of the Father from eternity. The Holy Spirit is a Person dis-

tinct from the Father and Son in the same, one Godhead. The difference
is that He is the Holy Spirit, who eternally proceeds both from the Father
and the Son, and who does not have the Godhead from Himself nor
from anyone else but from both the Father and the Son, and all of this
from eternity to eternity.[21]

Luther grounds the real difference between the three Persons not
in their *opera ad extra*, but rather in their *opera ad intra*, the inner-
trinitarian relations.[22] In order to clarify this point, Luther gives a
crude illustration used by the Scholastics, particularly
Bonaventure.

If, for example, three young women would take a dress and clothe one
of them with this dress, then one could say that all three were dressing
her; and yet only one is being attired in the dress and not the other two.
Similarly we must understand here that all three Persons, as one God,
created the one humanity, clothed the Son in this, and united it with His
Person, so that only the Son became man, and not the Father or the Holy
Spirit. In the same way we should think also of the dove which the
Person of the Holy Spirit adopted and of the voice which the Person of
the Father adopted.[23]

Thesis 40 of his *Disputation on The Divinity and Humanity of Christ*
(1540) also affirms the interdependence of the persons of the
Triune God in the Incarnation: "*Eadem ratione haereticum esset vul-
gatum illud: Tota trinitas operata est incarnationem filii, sicut duae puel-
lae tertiam induunt, ipsa simul sese induente.*"[24]

If the differentiation among the three Persons lies in their
immanent-Trinitarian relations with one another, then why are
peculiar and distinctive works assigned externally to each Person
by way of differentiation?[25] God Himself wants to be known by us
as one God in three Persons. So that we know Him as such, He
reveals Himself accordingly in His Word and in Holy Scripture.
"By ourselves we could not ascend into heaven and discover what
God is or how His divine essence is constituted."[26] For this purpose, the triune God must use visible creatures for His revelation,
accommodating Himself to human capacity so that humans may
understand that which is to be revealed. Following Augustine, the
word "creature" for Luther must be viewed in two different ways:

(i) absolutely—how it is in itself a creature or work, *per se*, of God. In that sense "all creatures are God's work," "the single work of all three Persons without distinction." (ii) relatively—how God uses the creature(s) toward us. "Here distinctive images, forms, and revelations of the three distinct Persons come into being."[27] Luther finds this point demonstrated in the story of Jesus' baptism. God employs the "dove" as an image or revelation, of the Holy Spirit. "This is a distinctive image, which does not portray the Father or the Son but only the Holy Spirit. The Father, the Son, and the Holy Spirit want the dove to depict and reveal distinctively only the Person of the Holy Spirit, so that we become certain that "God's one essence is definitely three distinctive Persons from eternity."[28] The same point is made about the humanity of Jesus, which reveals to us the Son alone. Though the form of humanity is the "same creation of all three" Persons, it is the "peculiar and special" form or revelation of the Son alone. "For thus it has pleased God, that is, Father, Son, and Holy Spirit, that the Son should be revealed to and recognized by humankind in this form or figure of humanity as a Person apart from the Father and the Holy Spirit in one eternal essence of divine nature."[29] In like manner the Father is revealed to us in the form of the "voice", a distinctive revelation of Him alone in the one, indivisible divine essence.[30] For Luther, Augustine's theory of the distinction between reality and sign can be applied to the Trinity only in a modified sense: "But here in this sublime subject it means more. For the humanity of Christ is not a mere sign or a mere figure, as the dove and the voice also are not empty figures or images. No, the humanity in which God's Son is distinctively revealed is reality, it is united with God in one Person, which will sit eternally at the right hand of God...."[31] God reveals Himself as Father by the sign of a voice, and He reveals Himself as Spirit by the sign of a dove. But these signs occur in a singular, passing event, while Jesus' humanity is eternally bound to the Son of God. Here it becomes clear how much Luther's view of the Incarnation affects his understanding of the Father and of the Holy Spirit, as he says "the Father is not known except in the Son through the Holy Spirit."[32] The sign of the voice and the sign of the dove are recognized only as they are related to the sign-reality of the incarnation.

The guiding concept for the unity of operations of the Godhead, for Luther, is "appropriations," which appears in his creedal explanations.[33] Father, Son and Holy Spirit are, at the same time, Creator, Redeemer and Sanctifier even though the Trinity functions *ad extra* as one.[34] *Communicatio operationes* is a development of the doctrine of the economic Trinity. But Luther in his use of it never neglects to insist that God is inseparably one *ad extra*. In his commentary on such texts as Genesis 1 and John 1, Luther follows the ascriptive patterns of Augustine and Hilary by associating the articles on the Father, Son, and Holy Spirit with creation, redemption, and sanctification respectively.[35] But he stressed the unity of the works of the Godhead: "Nor is it possible in this manner to divide God subjectively, for the Father is not known except in the Son and through the Holy Spirit. ..."[36] The appropriations therefore function to give the certainty of God's triunity ("*Dreieinigkeit*").[37] We assert the trinity because the *opus indivisum trinitatis* is a three-fold work. This two-fold emphasis on God's unity and threefoldness is found in Luther's interpretation of the Apostle's Creed: "*Das sind gleich als unterschiedliche kleider, das man die personen nicht ineinander menge. Denn wie wol alle ding schaffen und erhalten, für sunde genug thun, sunde vergeben, vom tode auff wecken und ewiges leben schencken wercke sind, die sonst niemand thun kan denn Gott allein, Sind dennoch hie sonderliche wercke einer jeden person zugeeignet, auff das die Christen einen einfeltigen, gewissen verstand hetten, Das nur ein einiger Gott sey, und dennoch drey unterschiedliche personen sind inn einem einigen Göttlichen wesen, wie es die heiligen Veter aus Mose und aus der Propheten und Aposteln schrifften mit vleis zusamen gelesen und wider alle Ketzer erhalten haben.*"[38]

In these remarks on the unity of the trinitarian God Luther seems, according to Bornkamm, to render the distinction of the Persons insignificant.[39] "*Wenn man beachtet, wie Luther hier plötzlich die 'Ordnung der Personen' einführt, so wirkt das zunächst nicht wie ein theologisches Argument, sondern eher 'wie ein Zeichen theologischer Korrektheit'.*"[40] Yet, Luther justifies the "*Ordnung der Personen*" theologically: "For He (Father) is the fountainhead or wellspring (so to say) of the Godhead (Divinity) in the Son and the Holy Spirit, and when the Father is mentioned, the Son cannot be divorced from Him but must simultaneously be named and meant. Likewise the Holy Spirit is named and meant together with the Father and Son, because none of the Persons can be a separate God apart from the others."[41] While Luther emphasized the *homoousio-unity* in the Western tradition more than he emphasized the primacy of the Father in the Eastern tradition, he stopped short of the heresy of modalism: The Son is a Person distinct from the Father. Thus "strictly speaking," in Lienhard's finding, "there is a balance in Luther between the Western tradition with its own insistence on the *homoousios* (Augustine) and the Eastern tradition in its affirmations of the primacy of the Father(Basil)."[42] Where Athanasius stressed the unity of divine nature, the Cappadocians emphasized the threefoldness of the divine *hypostases*, giving primacy to the Father, "the fontal principle in the consubstantial triad." "The Father is He out of whom and toward whom the Son and the Holy Spirit are reckoned, and by the communication of His nature He makes the unity of the Trinity."[43]

Luther expresses his theology of the Trinity in an excursus, *The Three Symbols* in 1538. First of all, he quotes favorably Athanasius, who distinguishes the three Persons: "The Father is of no one, neither born nor made nor created. The Son is of the Father, not made or created but born. The Holy Spirit is of the Father and the Son, not born or created, but proceeding."[44] For the eternal begetting of the Son by the Father, Luther turned to Psalm 2:7, "The Lord said to me, 'You are my son, today I have begotten or borne you'."[45] While the theologians of the Eastern Church designate John 15:26 as the biblical ground for their rejection of the procession of the Holy Spirit from the Father and the Son, Luther tried to justify the *"filioque"* precisely from this biblical reference.[46] John 15:26 in Luther's translation reads: "When the Comforter comes, whom I shall send to you, the Spirit of truth, who proceeds from the Father, he will testify of me." Therefore the Holy Spirit "proceeds" from the Father and is "sent" by the Son. To be "sent" and to "proceed," for Luther, are basically nothing other than two different aspects of the same act so that we can assert at once: the Holy Spirit "proceeds" from both the Father and the Son.[47] Luther continues his argument in the line of Augustine: "Just as the Son is born of the Father and yet does not depart from the Godhead, but on the contrary remains in the same Godhead with the Father and is one God with him so also the Holy Spirit proceeds from the Father and is sent by the Son, and does not depart from the Godhead either, but remains with the Father and the Son in the same Godhead, and is one God with both."[48] For the Son, to be sent is to be referred to His "origin" from the Father; likewise for the Holy Spirit to be sent is to be referred to His procession from the Father and the Son.[49] In this discussion the relation between the Immanent and economic Trinity is brought into view. More precisely, the relation is brought into view, when Luther relates the eternal generation of the Son and the eternal procession of the Holy Spirit on the one hand to the temporal missions of the Son and the Spirit in the world on the other.[50]

For Luther an "eternal immanent birth" of the Son and an "eternal immanent proceeding" of the Spirit constitutes his view of the difference of the Persons in God.[51]   How the connections of their immanental relationships exist in the Godhead cannot be grasped by reason but can only be believed. It is not even to be investigated by the angels, who with joy nevertheless incessantly behold it. For Luther, it is sufficient that we might grasp a certain distinction of the Persons in the Godhead.[52]   Thus Luther finally comes to assert:

> These, then, are the differences between the Persons as given to us in the gospel. Whoever wishes to do so can ponder on it further, but he will find nothing of greater certainty. Therefore we ought to stay with this in all simplicity and be satisfied with it, until we arrive in heaven, where we shall no longer have to hear it or believe it, but clearly see and apprehend it.[53]

As Schwarzwäller writes of Luther: "*Die Erkenntnis der inner trinitärischen Bezüge gehört sensu strictiore ausschließlich in die Vollendung.*"[54]

One question above all emerges now: How was Luther able to speak about the "immanent" Trinity? Here he reasoned a *posteri-*

ori from biblically-witnessed salvation history in the world back to God's eternal essence.[55] If Christ is born physically in our history, yet is the Son of God, He is born eternally in God. If God the Father is the Creator of the world, then God's origin must be in Himself, from whom the Son and the Holy Spirit obtain their essence. God's historical revelation in three Persons mirrors God in His eternal essence. Statements on the immanent Trinity could therefore be derived through inferring the essence of the Father, the Son and the Holy Spirit from the way they are revealed to us. These statements maintain that God is "beforehand in eternity," as the one that He reveals Himself to be.[56] Torrance's words reflect Luther's: God "has opened up himself to our knowledge in his own being as Father, Son and Holy Spirit for what he has revealed of himself to us through Christ and in the Spirit he is in himself."[57] Here Luther does not affirm a recent notion that the immanent Trinity is the economic Trinity.[58] For Luther, we know the Trinity only because we see God acting in Jesus and the Holy Spirit (economic Trinity). From this, the immanent Trinity could be deduced. Luther interprets the economic Trinity as the self-manifestation of the immanent Trinity.[59] In other words, statements on the immanent Trinity are nothing other than the theological premises for the economic Trinity.[60] In order to show the relation between the economic and immanent Trinity, Luther asserted emphatically that there is one Son and one Spirit, yet of two different "births" or "proceedings". The Son, who is born in the world, and the Spirit who proceeds into the world are born and proceeded "beforehand" in God's eternal essence. Luther wrote of such trinitarian apriorism:

> Therefore it was indeed fitting that the middle Person was physically born and became a Son, the same who was born beforehand in eternity and is Son, and that it was not the Father or the Holy Spirit who was thus physically born and became as Son... The Holy Spirit proceeds physically, the same who proceeds in eternity and is neither born nor Son. And thus the Father remains of himself, so that all three Persons are in majesty, and yet in such a manner that the Son has his Godhead from the Father through his eternal immanent birth (and not the other way round), and that the Holy Spirit has his Godhead from the Father

and the Son through his eternal immanent proceeding. The Son shows
his eternal birth through his physical birth, and the Holy Spirit shows
his eternal proceeding through his physical proceeding. Each of them
has an external likeness or image of his internal essence.[61]

Luther interprets John 15:26 both immanent-trinitarianly and eco-
nomic-trinitarianly so that the knowledge of God the Father to
which we can ascend through the Son and in the Spirit is a knowledge of God as He eternally is in Himself as Father, Son and the
Holy Spirit.[62] This means that before God created, redeemed and
poured forth His Spirit to sanctify, He already existed eternally as
Father, Son and the Holy Spirit. The *opera trinitatis ad extra* and the
opera trinitatis ad intra thus can be distinguished, but cannot be separated. God *in se* and God *pro nobis* cannot be separated. Though
he distinguishes with the tradition the immanent Trinity from the
economic trinity, he insists on their unity by affirming that God is
"beforehand in eternity". So what we encounter in revelation in
the economic Trinity, for Luther, corresponds to what God is in
eternity, the immanent Trinity. Nevertheless the weight of Luther's
theology concentrates on the discussion of the economic Trinity,
from which the immanent Trinity can be deduced. Luther conceives of God according to His work or God as He wishes to be
known in the Incarnate Son. His evangelical emphasis reinforces
the way he must travel: to consider God primarily in terms of His
saving work in His people or in terms of faith's experience of God's
salvific activity. "Or, to put it medievally, God in his *operationes ad
extra*, in his *potentia ordinata*."[63]

There appears in Luther a lively penetration of the article on
the Trinity by his doctrine of justification by faith. While Luther on
the one hand says that the article on the Trinity is "the highest article in faith—the article on which all the others hang" ("*der höchst
artikel ym glauben, darynnen die andern alle hangen*"),[64] on the other
hand, he says of the "main article (of the creeds), the one concerning Jesus Christ," that "all the others attach themselves to it and
firmly support it" ("*dem fallen alle artickell zu und stehen jm fest
bey*").[65] "*So dient auch dieser Artikel von der Gottheit Christi dazu, daß
alle andern Artikels des Glaubens dadurch erhalten werden.*"[66] From

this we can conclude, as Elert does, that Luther "recognized more and more the Christological approach to the doctrine of the Trinity as the only one that was compatible with his theology."[67] Furthermore Christology and Trinity must not be neatly separated for both are related in the Reformer's soteriology. This is evident in the exposition of the three articles in the Creed of his *Large Catechism* (1538) where Luther explains :

> Here in the Creed you have the entire essence of God, his will and his work exquisitely depicted... In these three articles God has revealed and opened to us the most profound depths of his fatherly heart, his sheer unutterable love. He created us for this purpose, to redeem and sanctify us. Moreover, having bestowed upon us everything in heaven and on earth, he has given us his Son and his Holy Spirit, through whom he brings us to himself.... We could never come to recognize the Father's Favor and grace were it not for the Lord Christ, who is a mirror of the Father's heart. Apart from him we see nothing but an angry and terrible Judge. But neither could we know anything of Christ, had it not been revealed by the Holy Spirit.[68]

Here in the doctrine of the Trinity we meet the same structure as in Christology: just as Luther develops his Christology in terms of justification, he develops his doctrine of the Trinity in terms of the work of the triune God in us.[69] This interpretation of the Trinity in soteriological terms gives full expression to God's love, revealing God's ways with us. What is established here is that God alone is the one who acts, who is as Father, Son and Spirit the *justificans ac salvator hominis peccatoris*.[70] Hence in keeping with the dominant emphasis of soteriology, Luther not only sticks to his own rule—to view God primarily in terms of His saving activity towards us, but he also refrains from speculation about the characteristics of the immanent Trinity.[71] God is in Himself what He does in us, the former being the premise for the latter.

Theopaschitism vis-a-vis Patripassianism

The essential idea of the school of modalism was that there is one God-head, designated as Father, Son and Spirit. These terms do not stand for real distinctions, but are successive revelations of the same person. Father, Son and Spirit are identical. The modalistic solution to the mystery of threeness and oneness was, then, not three distinct persons, but one person with three different names or roles which are appropriate and applicable at different times.[72] Modalism safeguards the *"monarchia"* (unicity) of God by teaching that God *"simpliciter"* (i.e., Father) was incarnated in the Son.[73] It follows from this that the Father suffered along with Christ, since He was present in and identical with the Son. This idea, labeled "patripassianism," was condemned as a heresy. Praxeas' concession that the Father suffered only with the Son did not impress Tertullian:

> (Our heretics) indeed, fearing to incur direct blasphemy against the Father, hope to diminish it by this expedient: they grant us so far that the Father and Son are two; adding that, since it is the Son who indeed suffers, the Father is only his fellow-sufferer. But how absurd are they even in this conceit! For what is the meaning 'fellow-suffering', but the endurance of suffering along with another? Now if the Father is incapable of suffering, he is incapable of suffering in company with another; otherwise, if He can suffer with another, He is of course capable of suffering.[74]

The main reason for the rejection of patripassianism was not so much its conflict with the hellenistic conception of divine impassibility as with the biblical revelation.[75] The distinguishing characteristic of patripassianism, Sarot notes correctly (i.e., in terms of the history of dogma), does not lie in its denial of the impassibility of God but in its refusal to make a distinction between the Father and the Son.[76] Patripassianism erred in its failure to endorse the trinitarian distinctions between the Father and the Son. However the writings of the patripassianists must be understood for the purpose of this study in the context of the question: how does one reconcile belief in the incarnation, which is integrally related to the nature of God, with belief in an impassible God? Because the axiom of divine impassibility was assumed by Tertullian, he rejected the idea that the Father "fellow-suffered" on the cross. Hence the new term coined by Moltmann, "patricompassianism," does not meet Tertullian's objection, and cannot be used to distinguish itself from "patripassianism".[77] Strictly speaking, "patricompassianism," for Tertullian, is identical to "patripassianism," both of which fail to distinguish the trinitarian persons sufficiently.[78]

How does Luther avoid the heresy of "patripassianism," a variation of modalism? First Luther maintained a unity of the Godhead with "distinctions," arguing against Sabellius who juggles the three persons into one person.[79] Luther, in speaking about the economy of salvation, refuses to distinguish the persons with respect to God's works ad extra so that what is done by one person must be ascribed to all three persons "without distinction." Luther explained:

> When we confess in the children's Creed: "I believe in God the Father Almighty, Creator of heaven and earth", we do not mean to imply that only the Person of the Father is the almighty Creator and Father. No, the Son is likewise almighty, Creator, and Father. And yet there are not three almighty creators and fathers but only one almighty Creator and Father of heaven and earth and of us all. Similarly, the Father is our saviour and Redeemer, the Son is our Saviour and Redeemer, and the Holy Spirit is our Saviour and Redeemer, and yet there are not three saviours and redeemers, but only one Saviour and Redeemer.[80]

Just as God acts in full unity with Himself *ad extra*, so the worship of the Trinity from the outside is indivisible. "For there is one Divine essence of all three persons and we or the creature do to each person of the Godhead what we do to the one God and all three persons without distinction. In relation to us, He is one God."[81] Nevertheless "within himself," says Luther, "he is distinctive in three Persons."[82] The unity of Godhead "with distinction" is to be maintained as seriously as the unity of God's acts *ad extra* "without distinction."

Second we must ask how Luther understands the doctrine of the Incarnation. Is the whole Trinity incarnate? To this Luther replies no. The divine nature, for Luther, designates one person of the Trinity or the whole Trinity (*tota divinitas*). Thesis IX and X of his *Promotionsthesen für George Major* read:

Thesis IX. Ut quaelibet person sit ipsa tota divinitas, ac is nulla esset alia.

Thesis X. Et tamen verum est, Nullam personam esse solam, quasi alia non sit, divinitatem.[83]

When dealing with the doctrine of the Trinity, we cannot say that the divine nature in itself becomes incarnate; rather we say it is the divine nature in the person of the Son which becomes incarnate, that is, one person alone. Likewise we cannot say that the divine nature "suffers" or "dies." But we can say that the divine nature of the Son, one person of the Trinity, *quando capitur pro persona* "suffers" or "dies". Luther explained this in his *Disputation On The Divinity and Humanity of Christ* (1540):

> *Nam et nos dicimus, unum Deum esse et non plures, sed illa unitas substantiae et essentiae habet tres distinctas personas, sicut Christi natura unita est in una persona. Cum ergo dicitur: Divinitas est mortua, tunc includitur, quod etiam pater et Spiritus sanctus sint mortui. Sed hoc non est verum, quia tantum una persona divinitas, sed filius est natus, mortuus et passus, etc. Ideo natura divina, quando capitur pro persona, est nata, passa, mortua, etc., hoc est verum. Est ergo distinguendum. Si intelligis divinam naturam pro tota divinitas seu unitate, tunc argumentatum est falsum, quia solus Christus non est tota trinitas, sed tantum una persona trinitatis. Ergo tantum est unus Deus. Hic praedicamus, quomodo fieri possit, ut illae tres personae sint unus Deus et essentia una. Sed incomprehensibilia esse credimus, si comprehendi possint, non opus esset credere.*[84]

Lienhard observes that Luther begins with the divinity of Christ and then moves to the three persons of the Trinity.[85] Siggins explains :

> Because the Son is one undivided essence with the Father and the Spirit, where we hear one person speak, we hear the entire Deity. So when we grasp the Son of God we grasp the Father too: the whole Trinity is known in the Person of Jesus Christ: "Since Christ, who is one undivided person, God and man, speaks to us, we are sure that God the Father and God the Spirit — that it is the whole divine Majesty — is also present and speaking. So God is entirely comprehended in this one person, and you need not nor dare search elsewhere."[86]

When Luther says "the whole Trinity is found in this Man," he does not intend modalism; rather all the divinity (*tota divinitas*) is present in the Son taken in isolation, but the Son alone is not the only person, as if there were no other. Thesis X of his *Promotionsthesen für Georg Major* reads: "*Et tamen verum est, Nullam personam esse solam, quasi alia non sit, divinitatem.*"[87] The unity of the Trinity, for Luther, goes beyond what we meet at the level of the creatures or that of mathematics. Thesis VII reads: "*Haec unitas trinitas (ut sic dicamus) est magis una, quam ullius creaturae, etiam mathematicae unitas.*"[88] Here Luther employs a "new" language to explain the mystery of the unity of the Trinity. This grammar assumes new utterances, since it wishes to speak about God. Numerical order ceases to be one, two, three: "*Cessat etiam numeri ordo: unus, dua, tres.*"[89] Within creation it is indeed valid; but here there is no order with respect to number, place, and time. Thus we must establish another form of speaking than that which has to do with creation. Here there is no order, but "coeternity," "co-equality," "image," "nature," must thus be employed in a new way. Thesis VI explains this: "*Ac is hic aliquid diceretur improprie, tamen res ipsa defendenda est per scripturas contra Diabolum.*"[90] In his disputation on *The Word was Made Flesh* (1539), Luther replies to argument 16 of Dr. Jonas: "There is a distinction of unity and trinity in theology. But such a distinction is in philosophy. Therefore there is, in theology, some necessary mathematical philosophy."[91] After asserting, in reply, that "the Trinity in theology is vastly different from the way it is accepted in mathematics,"[92] Luther then concludes: "We say that mathematics should remain in its own sphere and domain. We are not concerned with disputing about trinity and unity, because mathematics cannot concede that trinity is unity. ... Even if it is not true in nature, it can very well be true in God, and it is."[93] Then it is possible to say that which is trinitarian can be one thing; in God there is both unity and trinity.[94]

The unity of the divine nature means that each person is in Himself truly God: the Father is wholly God, the Son is wholly God, and the Spirit is wholly God. But there is only one God, yet three distinct persons. The unity of the Trinity is taken as seriously as the distinction of the persons. Only the person of the Son became incarnate and was crucified; neither God the Father nor God the Spirit became incarnate and was crucified. For Luther a distinction must be made between the divine nature in itself which does not suffer nor die and the divine nature of the Son which suffers or dies in His concrete unity with the human nature. It is incorrect, says Luther, to assert that the Divinity is Dead, implying that even the Father and the Spirit suffer dying.[95] Luther declares in his *Confession Concerning Christ's Supper* (1528):

> I believe and know that Scripture teaches us that the second person in the Godhead, viz. the Son alone became true man, was conceived by the Holy Spirit without the co-operation of man, and was born of the pure, holy Virgin Mary as of a real natural mother, ...; so that neither the Father nor the Holy Spirit became man, as certain heretics (Noetus, Praxeas) have taught.[96]

"For thus it has pleased God, that is, Father, Son and Holy Spirit, that the Son should be revealed to and recognized by humankind in this form or figure of humanity as a person distinct from the Father and the Holy Spirit in one eternal essence of divine nature."[97] Only God the Son, was born, suffered, and therefore He alone was on the cross. Thus it does not make any sense to speak of God in a simple untrinitarian manner as was the case in the modalistic form of patripassianism.[98] That the triune God and the crucified Jesus belong together drives Christian theology to be serious about the trinitarian distinctions of persons in the Godhead. Because the Person of the Father is distinct from the Person of the Son, says Luther, "we should not say that the Father suffered for us" on the cross.[99] The Son is the being of God, going out of the Godself, becoming incarnate, assuming the servant form and becoming obedient unto death on the cross. "For this Person (Christ) is both true God and true man, one Divine Being with the Father, one God, and therefore one voice or one word or one work. Therefore we can and must say: 'God was crucified and died for me'."[100] To say that the Father suffers on the cross is, for Luther, to follow the rules of the *Mathematica*; but our new language is effective *contra Diabolum*. Patripassianism occurs precisely because it fails to distinguish between God the Father and God the Son, holding that in the suffering of Jesus, God *simplicter*, and not God the Son, was involved.[101] By rejecting the unity of Godhead without distinction, and by affirming the Incarnation of the Son alone, Luther has repudiated the modalistic form of theopaschitism. However this does not mean that Luther repudiates the passibility of God. We have seen before that the theopaschite formula is not a theo-logical formula but is a *Christo*-logical formula.[102] For Luther, "*theos*" does not mean "God *simpliciter*," or the Divinity , but "God incarnate, the incarnate Logos" *in concreto*. Luther did not assert that God *simpliciter* "*passus est*" or that the Divinity "*passus est*." For Luther, though the divinity "by itself" cannot be said to suffer, it suffers when it is incarnate with the humanity. The divine nature of the Son is incarnate, and therefore can be said to suffer.

As was discussed in chapter three, Luther affirmed that "According to his nature God cannot die, but since God and man are united in one person, it is correct to talk about God's death when that man dies who is one reality or one person with God."[103] Christ is God and man in one person. Therefore, whatever is said of Him as man, must also be said of Him as God namely that Christ died, and Christ is God, therefore God dies—"not the separated God, but rather God united with humanity."[104] Here it can be argued that Luther seems to contrast God in Christ with the "separated God'. If one proceeds, however, from this contrast, we may ask who the latter is. The "separated God" is, for Luther, actually God who is the origin of the Incarnation—namely, the "Person" of the Father. As has been noted in the previous section, the Father, according to Luther, is the "origin" of the Divinity, from whom the Son and the Spirit derive their divinity. He is also, in that sense, the origin of the Incarnation. We have already seen in his interpretation of the three names, that where Luther speaks of the Trinitarian Person of the Father he often says simply "God". In this sense the statement "God in His nature cannot suffer" could be understood: as the Father, He cannot suffer, for as the Father He is the source of all life, that proves Himself to be the victor over death.[105] The question of God's passibility therefore casts a new light on Luther's theology of the Trinity. While God as the Son is exposed to the suffering and dying of Jesus, still God as the Father remains the One from whom suffering and death can claim nothing. Luther conceives the theology of the Trinity in such a way that it includes the Incarnation and Passion of God in Christ, not as an addendum but as ontologically constitutive of God. With this the reformer distinguishes himself clearly from Modalism. In the words of Jansen:

> Denn für ihn ist Menschwerdung und Leiden, Tod und Auferstehung Jesu Christi im Sein Gottes selbst begründet. Die Lehre von der Trinität als einer Differenzierung im Sein Gottes ermöglicht es dem Reformator, die Inkarnation und die Passion Gottes in Jesus Christus lehren zu können. Gerade darin ist Luther weit vom metaphysischen Monotheismus entfernt, der die Unvergänglichkeit, Unveränderlichkeit, Unteilbarkeit, Leidensunfähigkeit und Unsterblichkeit Gottes lehrt.[106]

The suffering of Christ as God's own suffering lies in the concrete unity of His personal identity—the "God-man" in toto. In concreto, the incarnate Son suffers in the act of his self-humiliation. By "suffering," Luther does not mean "anguishing," but rather the kind of suffering which God "does" by assuming our "sinnerhood" in His incarnate Son.[107] That is why Luther says the Father does not "suffer" in the sense of the firsthand "cross-bearing" of our sin and dying, only the Son does. For Luther only the incarnate Son, in whom the entire Deity dwells, suffers on the cross, not the Father. Only one person of the Trinity suffered death. In this way Luther affirms theopaschitism but rejects patripassianism, a variation of modalism.

Luther, like the orthodox Christology, rejects the patripassianists who extend the suffering of Jesus' death to the Father because it collapses the distinction between the Father and the Son. The reformer reacted to this modalistic theopaschitism by predicating the suffering of death only of the Son. Luther in no way is threatened by the Sabellian problem. The question remains to be answered: Does Luther divorce the suffering of Christ from the Father? Can the Father of Jesus Christ suffer? For Luther Christ suffered in his person; and this person (hypostasis), God's Son, is of one being (homoousios) with the Father. If God is in Christ, then whatever God the Son suffers becomes the suffering of God by the union of the persons of the Trinity. "For in him the whole fullness of deity dwells bodily" (Col. 2:9). In this manner the Father, though He does not suffer dying as the Son does on the cross, suffers through divine unity with the Son. "The Father and the Son are one" (cf. John 14).[108] The concept of *perichoresis* was already assumed by Luther as he said in his sermon on John 14 (1538): "Believe Me that I am in My Father and the Father is in me."[109] Since the Father and the Son mutually coinhere in one another, it is appropriate to talk also here about a marvelous exchange. For Luther it is important that whatever could be said about the Son could also be said about the Father, since the two, as Scripture says, are one. The suffering of Christ as the eternal Son is therefore also that of the Father because of their divine unity. In God's own life the Father and the Son are distinguished but not separated. So, too, in His action towards us they are distinguished (the Son, not the Father, dies), but not separated (the Father wills the death of the Son and knows—suffers—the death of the Son). Modalistic forms of the theopaschite doctrines are rejected by Luther. But a qualified understanding of "patripassianism" is attributable to Luther's theology, that is, by the principle of *perichoresis*: the Father suffers in and through the divine unity with the Son, and is therefore no apathetic being whose essence is unaffected by the pain and suffering of creation. This is in accordance with Luther's *theologia crucis* in which the triune God is one with the crucified Jesus. That God is identified with the crucified Jesus compels theology to speak of God in a trinitarian way, affirming not only the distinctions in God as Father, Son, and Holy Spirit but also their unity. This will be further considered in the final section where the relation between the immanent Trinity and economic Trinity with respect of divine suffering will be discussed.

The Work of the Holy Spirit

Contrary to Montanus, a second century prophet, who claimed to be the Incarnation of the Holy Spirit, Luther used the term incarnation only of the Son.[110] The unity of humanity and deity in the

Person of Jesus is the single work of the one God without distinction, *opera ad extra sunt indivisa*. But only the Son assumed the humanity, Luther tells us in traditional fashion, although he employs the ungainly figure from Bonaventure of the three girls of whom only one put on a dress, with the help of the other two. Luther also speaks in a more formal way, saying that the person of Christ, who "had been from the beginning, was sent by the Lord and the Holy Spirit."[111] He, by saying that "Christ was sent by the Father and the Holy Spirit," avoids any ontological subordination of the Spirit.[112] The Spirit did not assume the humanity nor did the Spirit assume the servant form and thereby "suffer" in the assumption of our "sinnerhood." The Trinity is the "subject" of Christ's act of self-humiliation, in which God truly suffers death, yet suffers death only in the incarnate Son.[113] If the Spirit does not suffer in the sense that the Son does, then what is the role of the Spirit in relation to the cross?

It would be out of keeping with Luther's theology if one were a theologian of the cross when interpreting the person and work of Christ, but when interpreting the work of the Holy Spirit one turned oneself into a theologian of glory. This would be to forget that the theology of the cross applies just as completely to God the Holy Spirit as it does to God the Son.[114] The Holy Spirit's work is not to reveal God apart from the crucified Christ. It is not His office to fill our hearts with other glory than the glory of the cross. His work is hidden and veiled to human beings. The Spirit is the one who creates faith in Christ. Faith, a gift of the Spirit, is justifying faith—faith in the crucified Christ, which believes against reason and against all appearances. Luther's understanding of the Holy Spirit emerges in clear fashion in his response to the charismatic challenges to his understanding of the doctrine of salvation, and so this response will be the focus of concentration in this section.[115]

The central question put by Luther in his inquiry about Karlstadt is "What makes a person a Christian?" "My sincere counsel and warning is that you be circumspect and hold to the single question, what makes a person a Christian? Do not on any account allow any other question or other art enjoy equal importance. When anyone proposes anything ask him at once, 'Friend will this make one a Christian or not?' "[116] Luther denies that a person can do anything to gain salvation.[117] Not even faith is constitutive to making a person Christian. "Always something is lacking in faith. However long our life, always there is not enough to learn in regard to faith."[118] For Luther, what makes a person Christian is the Person, Jesus Christ, who died for us in His assumption of our sinnerhood and was resurrected from the dead for our salvation. We are related to God through Jesus Christ, and are to trust in Him alone for salvation and not in the inner or mystical life nor in our outward behaviour. So, says Luther,

> my brother, cling firmly to the order of God. According to it the putting to death of the old man, wherein we follow the example of Christ, as Peter says (I Pet. 2:21), does not come first, as this devil (Karlstadt) urges, but comes last. No one can mortify the flesh, bear the cross, and follow the example of Christ before he is a Christian and has Christ through faith in his heart as an eternal creature. You can't put the old nature to death, as these prophets do, through works, but through the hearing of the gospel. Before all other works and acts you hear the Word of God, through which the Spirit convinces the world of its sin (John: 8). When we acknowledge our sin, we hear the grace of Christ. In this Word the Sprit comes and gives faith where and to whom he wills. Then you proceed to the mortification and the cross and the works of love. Whoever wants to propose to you another order, you can be sure, is of the devil. Such is the spirit of this Karlstadt.[119]

The work of the Holy Spirit is to create faith or trust in Christ, by hearing (*ex auditu*) the Word which in proclamation comes from outside of us (*extra nos*). Luther's quarrel with Karlstadt, Müntzer and others is that they invert this order. "Dr. Karlstadt and these spirits replace the highest with the lowest, the best with the least, the first with the last. Yet he would be considered the greatest spirit of all, he who has devoured the Holy Spirit feathers and all."[120] God who comes by way of the cross, for Luther, deals with us in a two-fold manner: first "outwardly," then "inwardly."[121]

> Outwardly he deals with through the oral word of the gospel and through material signs, that is baptism and the sacrament of the altar.

Inwardly he deals with us through the Holy Spirit, faith, and other gifts. But whatever their measure or order the outward factors should and must precede. The inward experience follows and is effected by the outward. God has determined to give the inward to no one except through the outward. For he wants to give no one the Spirit or faith outside of the outward Word and sign instituted by him, as he says in Luke 16:29, "Let them hear Moses and the prophets." Accordingly Paul can call baptism a "washing of regeneration" wherein God "richly pours out the Holy Spirit" (Titus 3:5). And the oral gospel is "the power of God for salvation to every one who has faith" (Rom. 1:16).[122]

The "order" of salvation in Luther's theology begins with the Word addressing us *extra nos* through proclamation of what Christ has done *pro nobis*, followed by the Word being heard and believed, and we thereby are saved by calling upon God. This order is constituted by the "whole root and origin of salvation" which "lies in God who sends."[123] As Luther says: "For these four points are so interrelated that the one follows upon the other, and the last is the cause and antecedent of all the others, that is, it is impossible for them to hear unless they are preached to; and from this, that it is impossible for them to believe if they do not hear; and then it is impossible for them to call upon God if they do not believe; and finally it is impossible for them to be saved if they do not call upon God."[124] While preaching is indispensable to the engendering of faith, it is the work of the Spirit to "give" faith in the heart.[125] Here we see Luther's view differs from Augustine's. Jansen notes: "*Augustin möchte aber folgendes betonen: Der uns als Gabe gegebene Geist, welcher in uns die Liebe zu Gott weckt, ist kein anderer als Gott selbst. Luther hat die Grundstruktur dieses augustinischen Gedankens übernommen, sie aber anders ausgefüllt. An Stelle der Liebe tritt bei Luther der Glaube als Wirkung des heiligen Geistes.*"[126] The work of the Holy Spirit is related to the Word and the community of the Word, as Luther expressly says:

The creation is past and redemption is accomplished, but the Holy Spirit carries his work unceasingly until the last day. For this purpose he has appointed a community on earth, through which he speaks and does all his work. For he has not yet gathered together all his Christian people, nor has he completed the granting of forgiveness. Therefore we believe in him who daily brings us into this community through the Word, and imparts, increases, and strengthens faith through the same Word and the forgiveness of sins.[127]

The same idea also appears in his Gospel sermon preached on a Pentecost Sunday in 1522:

> It is a faithful saying that Christ has accomplished everything, has removed sin and overcome every enemy, so that through him we are lords over all things. But the treasure lies yet in one pile; it is not yet distributed nor invested. Consequently, if we are to possess it, the Holy Spirit must come and teach our hearts to believe and say: I, too, am one of those who are to have this treasure.[128]

The work of the Holy Spirit thus is to communicate to us the Gospel that, in Christ's cross and resurrection, the divine blessing has conquered the divine curse. "The work (of redemption) is finished and completed, Christ has acquired and won the treasure for us by his sufferings, death, and resurrection, etc."[129]

> But if the work remained hidden and no one knew of it, it would have been all in vain, lost. In order that this treasure might not be buried but put to use and enjoyed, God has caused the Word to be published and proclaimed, in which he has given the Holy Spirit to offer and apply to us this treasure of salvation. Therefore to sanctify is nothing else than to bring us to the Lord Christ to receive this blessing, which we could not obtain by ourselves.[130]

The Reformer knows of no influence of the Holy Spirit which is not "Christ-centered."[131] The Holy Spirit is the "mediator of the real presence of Christ in faith."[132] Thus he who spurns knowing the Father in the Son loses all knowledge of God. It is by the Holy Spirit that we are led to see God in the flesh, in whom the Father is mirrored: "*Von Christo aber Kundten wir auch nichts wissen, wo es night durch den Heiligen geist offenbaret were.*"[133] The God who came to us in Christ is the same God who comes as the Holy Spirit.[134] More fully:

> Although the whole world has sought painstakingly to learn what God

is and what he thinks and does, yet it has never succeeded in the least. But here you have everything in richest measure. In these three articles God himself has revealed and opened to us the most profound depths of his fatherly heart, his sheer, unutterable love. He created us for this very purpose, to redeem and sanctify us. Moreover... we could never come to recognize the Father's favor and grace were it not for the lord Christ, who is the mirror of the Father's heart. Apart from him we know nothing but an angry and terrible Judge. But neither could we know anything of Christ, had it not been revealed by the Holy Spirit.[134]

The Holy Spirit is a "real and divine sphere of revelation in which the risen Christ alone is present, (not as) an idea (but as) a redemptive reality."[135] "By this Holy Spirit, as a living, eternal, divine gift and endowment, all believers are adorned with faith and other spiritual gifts, raised from the dead, freed from sin, and made joyful and confident, free and secure in their conscience."[136] The Spirit confers in our hearts the assurance that God wills to be our Father, forgive our sin, and bequeathe eternal life on us. The Spirit comes to us, says Luther, in order to "inculcate the sufferings of Christ for the benefit of our salvation."[137] Luther's theology of the passibility of God is anchored in the identity of God eternal with the incarnate Son of God, who is revealed to us by the power of the Holy Spirit.

It follows that there is in Luther no need to discuss the Spirit's role in relation to the cross in terms of the Spirit's "suffering." The divine works, with the cross as their centre, are completed and brought to their perfection in the Spirit. The *conformitas Christi* of the believer which Luther interpreted in terms of participating in the suffering of Christ is the work of the Spirit. Christian suffering, then, is a participation in Christ's incarnational soteriological reality on earth. Here Luther uses the German expression *Berufsanfechtungen*, the concept which appears in his *Sermon on Cross and Suffering*, preached at Coburg Castle in 1530.[138] What is unique about this sermon is the stress it lays on the *Anfechtungen* —trials and sufferings—which do not proceed from the conditions of the Christian as *totus peccator*; rather they are *Anfechtungen* that come from our condition as *totus iustus*.[139] Christians are called to be "Christ-bearers," living a life of discipleship in which Christ's work and burden, through the joyous exchange (*admirabile commercium*), become ours. Our trials and sufferings, for Luther, should not be self-chosen as the fanatics choose their own suffering. It should be the sort of suffering imposed upon us by the devil and the world. "The cause of our suffering is the same as that for which all the saints have suffered from the beginning. Of course, the whole world must bear witness that we are not suffering because of public scandal or vice such as adultery, fornication, murder, etc. Rather we suffer because we hold to the Word of God, preach it, hear it, learn and practice it."[140] What makes a true theologian of the cross is the willingness to live in God's passion, willingly suffering the opposition of the devil and world thereby giving a witness to the truth (Christ). "To believe in the cross always means to carry the cross. A 'yes' to the cross of Christ is also a 'yes' to my cross."[141] This kind of suffering flows not from our condition as *totus peccator* but from our communion and identification with the crucified Christ. There is no merit in our suffering. We suffer in order that we may be conformed to Christ. This conformity of ours to Christ's passion is the work of the Holy Spirit in us as the "active subject."[142] This explains why Luther says, in his *The Large Catechism*, that to affirm belief in the Holy Spirit is to "believe that the Holy Spirit makes me holy, as his name implies."[143] The Spirit makes us holy through: "The Christian church, the forgiveness of sins, the resurrection of the body, and the life everlasting."[144] Herms notes:

> Von früh an hat Luther den Umgestaltungsprozeß der menschlichen Existenz unter dem Wort und Sakrament bewärhrenden Wirken des Geistes als das real Umgestaltetwerden des Menschen zu Konformität mit Christus, als ein mit Christus Gekreuzigt—und Anferwecktwerden oder als "mortificatio carnis" bezeichnet Aus dem Vorstehenden ist nun klar, wie diese—verbal ganz traditionellen—Formeln der Sache nach verstanden werden müssen: Nicht als Beschreibung einer asketischen Nachfolgund Imitationspraxis, die der Mensch durch Anstrengung seiner eigenen Kräfte zu leisten hätte, und auch nicht als absage an den Leib.[145]

In his sermon *A Meditation on Christ's Passion*, Luther discussed the relationship between Christ's suffering and our suffering. To contemplate the suffering of Christ is to know that our sin has been nullified by Christ's passion.[146]   For Luther, as for Augustine, Christ as redeemer precedes Christ as a model.[147]   Tinder writes:

> But, on its own, such contemplation is bound to terrify us with the knowledge that it is on account of our sins that Christ has suffered. Thus, we must look beyond the cross to see that it was out of love that Christ died for us and this love is an expression of the Father's eternal love. When you know this, Luther tells his listeners, "Christ's passion must from that day on becomes a pattern for your entire life."[148]

The joyous exchange that makes of Christ the Righteous One, the sinner, and of us sinners, righteous ones, is an experiential and practical truth, not restricted to the sphere of subjectivity.   The believer through the happy exchange assumes the same form of life as his Saviour—namely, "the cross."   This is what Luther means: "Christ is our abstraction.   We are His concretion."[149] Luther's theology, thus, does not allow ethical passivity in the new life of those who have been redeemed by Christ.   "The provisional sign of the new life is not glory but the cross," thereby abandoning the medieval idea of the imitation of Christ.[150]   "Nothing makes a man good except faith."[151]   "Here faith is truly active through love, (finding expression) in works of the freest service, cheerfully and lovingly done, with which a man willingly serves another without hope of reward."[152]

To conclude this section, the Son suffers and dies.   The Son is God, assuming humanity and suffering in the act of His self-humiliation; the Holy Spirit is God, creating in us faith in and conformity to the incarnate and crucified Christ who achieved for us the divine "blessing" in His cross and Easter.   The love of God that suffers the sinful world and the divine wrath, and eventually suffers them into defeat is God's love in the incarnate Christ, in whom God's fatherly heart is mirrored and revealed through the Spirit. All three persons work together as the "one" God, the God of our salvation.   In Luther's own words in his *Confession*:

> These are the three persons and one God, who has given himself to us all wholly and completely, with all that he is and has.   The Father gives

himself to us, with heaven and earth and all the creatures, in order that they may serve us and benefit us. But this gift has become obscured and useless through Adam's fall. Therefore the Son himself subsequently gave himself and bestowed all his works, sufferings, wisdom, and righteousness, and reconciled us to the Father, in order that restored to life and righteousness, we might also know and have the Father and his gifts.

But because this grace would benefit no one if it remained so profoundly hidden and could not come to us, the Holy Spirit comes and gives himself also, wholly and completely. He teaches us to understand this deed of Christ which has been manifested to us, helps us receive and preserve it, use it to our advantage and impart it to others, increase and extend it. He does this both inwardly and outwardly — inwardly by means of faith and other spiritual gifts, outwardly through the gospel, baptism, and the sacrament of the altar, through which as through three means or methods he comes to us and inculcates the sufferings of Christ for the benefit of our salvation.[153]

The whole *Confession* is theocentric, speaking not of three different gifts from God, but rather of God's three-fold giving of Himself as one act in the economy of our salvation.[154] It is God as Father, Son and Holy Spirit who saves: the Father gives, the Son atones for us, and the Holy Spirit draws us to the Son through whom we are given access to the Father.[155]

Divine Suffering in the Economic Trinity vis-a-vis the Immanent Trinity

The question as to whether the polarity between the immanent Trinity and the economic Trinity may be that of impassibility and passibility is the focus of concentration in this section. We know that, for Luther, only in Christ is God revealed as a "suffering" God who bears the judgement of sin *pro nobis*. In the cross the Father surrenders the Son in love; the Son surrenders Himself as an act of His perfect obedience to the Father who sends. That God the Son became incarnate and suffered death and dereliction on the cross is the expression of God's self-giving love. The death of Jesus is, then, the definitive revelation of God, not only of the

Father but also of God the Son, which He is from eternity. If Jesus Christ is not eternally divine, as Arius claimed, there is no revelation of God. The death of Jesus is, for Luther, the definitive act of God going out of the Godself in self-giving love, going into the far country to perform the act of self-sacrifice on the cross. "God is most Himself" precisely in the act of the self-sacrificing death of His Son on the cross. In this act faith recognizes God's divine being, which is found and recognized in Christ's humble obedience, which achieves for us salvation. The Holy Spirit leads us into the accomplished act of redemption, into the "suffering" love of the cross, that is, of the Son through whom we are restored to the Father.

It is significant to recall that Luther's theology of the cross is primarily concerned with God as He wills to be found. God has designated a place and a person, showing us where and how He can be found. Luther instructs us to listen to God's Word alone if we wish to learn who God is and what His will is towards us. Hence we are to follow the way of the baby in the cradle, at His mother's breasts, through the desert, and finally to His death on the cross. Luther's doctrines of the incarnation and of the economic Trinity provides the conceptual framework in which Luther conceives of God's suffering, that is, God's suffering in the concrete unity of Christ's personal identity. As has been stated, God's eternal impassibility is presupposed in Luther's thought. Luther, in his *Disputation on The Divinity and Humanity of Christ*, states: "From eternity, He has not suffered, but since He became man, he is passible."[156] Just as one cannot assert "*in abstracto*" that humanity creates, for Luther, one also cannot assert that the divinity, that is, "*in abstracto*," suffers. "Inasmuch as he is God, he did not suffer, because God is incapable of suffering."[157] The assertion of God's suffering, for the reformer, can only be made "*in concreto*," that is to say, in the person of Jesus, the God-man *in toto*. Here we see that Luther addresses the passibility question from the perspective of the suffering of God in the incarnation of the Son. Though God *in abstracto*, that is, God "by Himself" does not suffer, God in His sovereign freedom has determined Himself in His "Word," and hence became "passible" in Jesus Christ out of His unfathomable love towards the sinner. That is why Luther insists that if we are to know God truly we "look at no other God than this incarnate and human God," the righteous One who has acted and suffered in His self-humiliation according to the *ratio vicaria* between the sinner and Christ. God as God does not suffer; but He suffers salvifically for us in the Son's concrete unity of the human and divine nature. Accordingly, Luther's understanding of God is against that which tends to anchor God's "suffering" love in the pre-Incarnation Trinity, and finally in an extra-Incarnation Trinity, where "suffering" loses all its meaning. Once we retreat to this sort of the divine aseity and sovereignty, we have little left for the Incarnation to do except to "reveal" a God who would have been what "He is" anyway, with or without the Incarnation. For Luther God as God, unlike human creatures, does not suffer because there is nothing in God's deity that gives rise to suffering. Divine suffering is affirmed when God constitutes humanity in Himself, bearing our sin and mortality ontically. The greatest marvel occurs when God in Christ "receives" that which is "alien" to Himself but "proper" to humanity—the "suffering" of the opposition or discontinuity between God and man. God in Christ "suffers" the opposition, and eventually suffers it into defeat, effecting for us reconciliation with God.

With respect to the issue of whether the suffering of Christ is attributable to God in His immanent life, it is helpful to recall that for Luther, the incarnate One is taken into the immanent life. "(T)he humanity in which God's Son is distinctively revealed is complete, it is united with God in one Person, which will sit eternally at the right hand of God."[158] For the reformer, God, who became incarnate, continues to be incarnately human. Christ's home-coming to the Father is his exaltation as the "whole person" of the God-man. If God continues to be incarnately human, the question must then be, concerning God's possibility, whether the still incarnately human Son of God continues to bear our sin and mortality. Luther answers with a "qualified" yes:[159] yes, but the sin and death which the once humiliated Lord now carries are the sin and death as "overcome" and "vanquished" in the cross and resurrection. As Luther argues in *A Sermon on Preparing to Die*

(1519):

> He (Christ) is the living and immortal image against death, which he
> suffered, yet by his resurrection from the death he vanquished death in
> his life. He is the image of the grace of God against sin, which he
> assumed, and yet overcame by his perfect obedience. He is the heaven-
> ly image, the one who was forsaken by God as damned, yet he con-
> quered hell through his omnipotent love, thereby proving that he is the
> dearest Son, who gives this to us all if we but believe.[160]

Since the incarnate One is eternally exalted, the Son of God therefore continues to bear our sin and mortality but in a "new" sense
that springs from their having been defeated and overcome in the
cross and Easter.[161] This incarnately human Son's return to the
Father is a return with our sin and mortality, which he has "suffered," "vanquished" and "overcome" in the cross and Easter. In
this way the cross as a "crisis" which the divine life wills to suffer
in the humiliated Lord is "eternally" in God, but not as a crisis
eternally; but as a crisis "overcome" in His "exaltation and glorifi-
cation after the resurrection."[162] Consequent upon Christ's victory, He, who "is" Lord over creatures from eternity, was "made"
Lord in time and as such was and is therefore crowned with glory
and honor.[163] God's eternal Son and the incarnate Son are one person, who continually bears our sin and mortality, although in the
form of sin and mortality overcome. Christ's suffering in human
history is thus introduced into the eternal nature of God. God not
only suffers in the economic Trinity, but this suffering reaches into
the immanent Trinity. This means God's capacity to suffer, in
Luther's view, has reached God's inner being, and he has avoided
driving a wedge between God *ad extra* and *ad intra*.[164] There is no
untouched hinterland in the inner-trinitarian life of God.
Suffering, an aspect of God's humble act in human history, is thus
carried into the divine life of God. God's love must be conceived
as "suffering" love inasmuch as the cross of the eternal and incarnately human Son exists in the divine life of God.

The burning question of Luther is not whether there is an intra-
trinitarian life in God's inner Being in the sense of how God might
be in-and-for-Himself, but rather what the Gospel of Christ

bestows upon us. Nevertheless, that there is an immanent Trinity as the God "beforehand in eternity" is affirmed by Luther. Luther has no wish to occupy himself with speculation upon the immanental relations within the Godhead for that smacks too much of a *theologia gloriae.* "These, then, are the differences between the Persons as given to us in the Gospel. Whoever wishes to do so can ponder it further, but he will find nothing of greater certainty. Therefore we ought to stay with this in all simplicity and be satisfied with it, until we arrive in heaven, where we shall no longer have to hear or believe it, but clearly see and apprehend it."[165] Thus Luther's emphasis is to know God in Jesus Christ, that is, in the triumphant act of loving and giving where He makes Himself our righteousness and salvation. The reality of Christ as God-with-us and God-for-us is that which concerns Luther, not how God may be in-and-for-Himself. Nevertheless, he does affirm that God's essence is located in the incarnate Son, and since this is what God really is in His revelation to man, Luther sees no need to inquire about some other essence, which by definition we cannot know.[166] Luther sees no need to dwell on the *ad intra* life of God. Thus he did not develop a theology of relationships in which the suffering and dying person of the Son affect God the Father and God the Spirit in the inner divine life. However this does not mean that he says nothing of the immanent Trinity at all.

Although Luther refrained from speculating upon the relational dynamism in the immanent life of God, he did assert that "the accomplishment of salvation, realized by the Father, the Son and the Spirit is determined in the very eternity of God."[167] Any division between the economic Trinity and the immanent Trinity would not only lead to modalism, but also calls salvation into question. In Lienhard's words:

> If there were two "Gods"—the God who saves and God in himself—the assurance of salvation would be put in question. And to that, modalism ultimately leads, wherein the Father, the Son, and the Holy Spirit are reduced to different modes by which the divinity is manifest in history. But in its essence it remains beyond revelation. A division arises between God as he is and God as he acts. That is why it is also necessary to speak of the "immanent" Trinity, even if, faced with mystery it

is only possible to speak with hesitation and inadequately. But it
appears that the saving act of God in history only translates what God is
from all eternity, that is, to say action between the Father, the Son, and
the Holy Spirit.[168]

On this basis it is necessary to say with hesitation and inade-
quacy that the humiliation in history mirrors in God's inner life an
eternal relation of obedience between the Father and the Son.
Luther said in his sermon *Meditation on Christ's Passion*, "Christ
would not have shown this love for you if God in his eternal love
had not wanted (willed) this, for Christ's love for you is due to his
obedience to God."[169] This text suggests that God has willed an
eternal obedience of the Son to the Father who sends. There
already in God's Being a relationship of obedience between the
Father and the Son, which, when the Son becomes incarnate,
entails the Son's suffering. The obedience of the Son to the Father
is an obedience rendered by God to Himself. God the Son is one
with the Father—one of essence and will: "I and the Father are
one" (cf. Jn.14). The obedience within the Godhead does not com-
promise the unity and equality of divine being, thereby avoiding
the heresy of subordinationism. Against modalism, the unity
within the Godhead is not a simple and an undifferentiated unity.
For Luther, as for Augustine before him, persons are differentiated
within the divine life by relations. The distinctions within the
Godhead ensure the particular characteristic of each person. A
modalistic form of patripassianism, that the Father comes and suffers as man, is denied. Because the Son comes, suffers and dies
there must be in God's relationships, in His eternal being and life,
the form of obedience, which makes incarnation and Calvary possible. For the reformer, there is an eternal relation of the Son's
obedience to the Father who sends, which constitutes the basis for
the suffering of the Son in human history. There is in God a send-
ing and an obeying, a giving and a receiving, an active as well as a
passive, obedient aspect. The Father gives the Son to death, as is
proper to a reflection of His eternal relationship to him, and the
Son willingly accepts and carries out the eternal plan of salvation.
This is evident in Luther's treatise on *The Last Words of David*:

This passage from Daniel (Chap. 7:13-14) also powerfully presents the doctrine of the Godhead in three Persons and of the humanity of the Son; for the Person who gives must be distinct from the Person who receives. Thus the Father bestows the eternal dominion on the Son, and the Son receives it from the Father, and this is from eternity; otherwise this could not be an eternal dominion. And the Holy spirit is present, inasmuch as He speaks these words through Daniel. For such sublime and mysterious things no one could know if the Holy Spirit would not reveal them through the prophets. It has been stated often enough above that Holy Scripture is given through the Holy Spirit. In addition, the Son is nevertheless also a Son of Man, that is, a true human being and David's Son, to whom such eternal dominion is given. Thus we note that the prophets did indeed respect and understand the word "eternal" which God used when He addressed David through Nathan and said (I Chron. 17:14): "I will install My Son and yours in My eternal kingdom."[170]

The same idea emerges when Christ speaks about this in John 16:15: "All that the Father has is Mine." "And of this 'all' of the Father which belongs to the Son the Holy Spirit also partakes as Christ says in the same passage: 'He will take what is Mine,' " which the Father has.[171] That is patently saying that the Holy Spirit takes from both, from the Father and the Son, the same single and complete Godhead from eternity. All three persons might be called "relational dynamism," in which there is a pole of bestowing, a pole of receptivity and a pole of reciprocity within the triune nature of God. Luther would be wary indeed of equating the pole of reciprocity within the Being of God, presumably the Holy Spirit, with passibility.[172] For the reformer the pole of receptivity, which is the Son, is identified as passibility. It is appropriate for God in the Son to be obedient unto death on the cross, to exhibit His deity in lowliness, for eternally there is a humility, a lowliness and a receptivity in the triune nature of God. God's relation to what is *ad extra* reflects the relation which He has within Himself from eternity. God's relation to man in the passion and death in His Son is, for Luther, a self-determined act of God. God says "yes" to Himself before He says "yes" to suffering. Luther has spoken of the foreordained will of God that the "lamb" should be slain *"in promissio"* before the foundation of the world. The

eternal will of God to suffer salvifically is seen in the Son's assuming the form of a servant, and becoming obedient unto death, even
death on the cross. The Son willingly receives and carries out the
role of an obedient servant to actualize reconciliation for humanity. The Son exhibits His "inexpressible humility" of the cross
(Matt. 11:29) until the Father "exalts" Him.[173] God has chosen to
be found in the suffering and the humiliation of the cross of Christ,
in which God is most divine. "God is to be found nowhere except
in suffering and in the cross."[174] This means the humiliation of
Jesus, in Luther's view, must not be distinct from His divine
nature. Jesus' suffering in his humiliation and weakness is actually God's suffering in his humiliation and weakness. On the cross
it is actually God who is there, God who suffers, and God who
dies. In the incarnate Son, the eternal God has entered the lowest
of the low, thereby exhibiting Himself as one who is not infinitely
removed from suffering and death. That the only suffering was
that of Jesus in His humanity is therefore, according to Luther, not
a satisfactory answer since it was the one Lord Jesus in the totality
of His being (God-man *in toto*) and work who suffered and died on
the cross. The older conception of *apatheia*, that God could not suffer since he exists in blessedness, joy and life, is discarded in the
light of the ontology constructed from within God's identification
with the crucified Jesus, this human and crucified God.[175]

What about the pole of bestowing, that is, the Father? If God
is one and yet three in one, how does the Father relate to the suffering of Jesus Christ? Was the Father absent from the Son's suffering and death? Is it the case that the Father has no part in the
suffering of Jesus Christ? As noted above, the nature of God is
inseparable from the act of Jesus Christ. The patristic idea of *perichoresis* accentuates Luther's view that God's essence and God's act
are inseparably one. Here, the trinitarian-theological axiom of
opera trinitatis ad extra sunt indivisa finds expression in the coinher-
ence of the three persons in the one divine essence. Luther understands the act of Jesus Christ in His suffering as integral to the one
essence of God. Because the Son is one undivided essence with the
Father (and the Spirit), where we grasp the Son of God we grasp
the Father too. For Luther, the Trinity is known in His Son. The

entire essence of God is found in the Person of Jesus Christ. "For in him the whole fullness of deity dwells bodily" (Col. 2:9). That the Father and the Son mutually coinhere in one another enables Luther to affirm a marvelous exchange between the Son's suffering and that of the Father. Furthermore, since the Father and the Son are one in essence, as Scripture says, the eternal Son's suffering is therefore also predicated of the Father, except that the Father suffers through the compassion that the Father has for the Son who assumes the destiny of man into the inner life of God. "The Father loves the Son," declares John the Baptist (cf. Jn. 3:35).[176] Christ's humiliation shows the eternal love of the Father; both the Father's love and the Son's love are identical.[177] It is here that God's trinitarian nature of love is demonstrated. From the perspective of the Father, He loves the only begotten Son, and therefore suffers the forsakenness of the Son, "the heavenly image," in order to communicate His eternal essence of love to the world.[178] The Son's true image is demonstrated in His willingness to accept this God-forsakenness, thereby also communicating the essence of God's love. Both the Father and the Son are united in their self-giving love, that gives up the Son on the cross. A modalistic doctrine of God endangers the trinitarian distinction of persons; a perichoretic doctrine of God allows Luther to see the differentiated ways in which God suffers uniquely as Father and Son. Whereas it is the Son who suffers dying on the cross to effect reconciliation for us, the Father participates as the "fellow-sufferer," indicating that the Father's heart is open to the suffering of His beloved Son. As Luther says, "rise beyond Christ's heart to God's heart," and "you will find the divine and kind paternal heart, and, as Christ says, you will be drawn to the Father through him."[179] For our Christ says, "Whoever beholds the Father's love also beholds Mine; for Our love is identical. I love you with a love that redeems you from sin and death. And the Father's love, which gave His only Son, is just as miraculous."[180] The Father of Jesus Christ suffers, not from any deficiency in being, but from the abundance of love. "For God so loved the world that he gave his only Son" (Jn. 3:16). This affirms that the God of Israel, the Father of Jesus Christ, was no apathetic being, whose essence is untouched by the pain and suffering of His beloved Son. Since the one undivided essence is located in the Son's act of self-humiliation, the redemptive act of Christ's suffering is integral to the one divine essence in the same Godhead. By *perichoresis*, the Father is said to suffer along with the Son through their divine unity.

Furthermore, Luther often declares that it is the love of the Father who sends the Son to suffer. The passion and death of Christ is then the revelation of God, i.e., the revelation of the immanent Trinity, and not only an external show of the eternal God. "God is love," says Luther; and the crucified God of history reveals the eternal being of God as "love". Luther, in the third part of the *Confession*, designates the person of the Holy Spirit as "a living, eternal, divine gift and grace."[181] With this Luther follows the old Western tradition that can be traced as far as Augustine, according to whom the Persons are distinguished from one another not in terms of substance but in terms of unchangeable relations to one another in their *intra* life: paternity, filiation and gift.[182] In *De trinitate* XV 19, Augustine provides an extensive account in which the Spirit is to be designated as *donum dei*. Thereby he seeks to establish speculatively the *processus a patre filioque*, by understanding the Holy Spirit as the Father's and the Son's mutual love. The Spirit, the "gift" of both the Father and Son, is "love," and thus, "He reveals to us the common love by which the Father and the Son mutually love each other."[183] Toward the end of the *De trinitate* Augustine argues from the mutual-love to the "communion" between the Father and the Son. This shows that the ideas of the mutual-love and communion become for him practically interchangeable:

> And if the love by which the Father loves the Son and the Son loves the Father ineffably demonstrates the communion of both, what is more suitable than that He should properly be called love who is Spirit common to both?[184]

Luther sought the scriptural foundation for Augustine's account of *filioque*. If, he concludes, the New Testament reveals to us that Jesus sends us as His own the Holy Spirit from the Father, as

Augustine had said, then in the immanent Trinity the Holy Spirit
must proceed from the Father and the Son as from a "single principle."[185] Since the Holy Spirit proceeds as a *hypostasis* from the
Father and the Son, he must be in His Person the "ontological communion" of love that exists between them.[186] Thus there already
is a mutuality of self-giving love in the immanent Trinity, awaiting
its actualization in human history: in love the Father surrenders
the Son and in love the Son surrenders Himself, and the Spirit of
love is between them. This is the conceptualization of the event of
the cross in trinitarian terms: the Son relates to the Father in obedient suffering and love, and the Father suffers the loss of the Son,
with the Spirit binding them, even in the loss. The identification of
God with the crucified Jesus is a rejection of untrinitarian speech
about God. Because it is the Father's love which gives up his
beloved Son, Luther can speak of the Father's "suffering" the Son's
suffering on the cross. In this patripassianism is affirmed as seriously as the Son's suffering except that the Son suffers dying on the
cross. Only one of the Trinity suffered and died on the cross. In
love the Father "suffers" over the Son's suffering. It must be
remembered that by "suffering" Luther means in the first place the
sort of suffering which God the Son undergoes by becoming a
"human sinner, and dying." Important in this context is the perception of God's suffering as the first-hand "cross-bearing" of our
sin and dying on the cross, according to which only the Son suffers
in obedience to the Father's foreordained will. That is why Luther
insists that the Father does not suffer as the Son does but suffers in
communion with the Son in the Spirit of love. The assertion that
the Father suffers is made possible because Luther assumed
Augustine's conception of the love of the Father for the Son,
according to which the Father is said to suffer in compassion with
the Son, sharing the fate of the Son. The passion and death of Jesus
Christ is thus the revelation of God, i.e., the revelation of the
immanent Trinity. The perception of the suffering Christ as the
lowly servant is thus carried into the inner life of God, allowing a
predication of Christ's suffering not only of the economic Trinity
but also of the immanent Trinity, the former being the self-manifestation of the latter.

The aforementioned tells us that Luther developed the Augustinian-Western tradition in a way which led him to affirm that the Father suffers in love over the death of his Son. However Luther did not exploit in detail the implications of the Father's love for the Son in the unity of the Spirit. That is to say, he did not fully develop a theology of an immanental relationship in which the suffering of Jesus Christ affects the Father and the Spirit. In keeping with his dominant emphasis on soteriology, the reformer concentrated his attention on the economic Trinity. This is evident in his explanation of the third part of the *Confession*, where we witness how quickly he shifts from a discussion of the immanent Trinity to that of the economic Trinity: "By this Holy Spirit, as a living, eternal, divine gift and grace, all believers are adorned with faith and other spiritual gifts. .. These are three Persons and one God, who has given himself to us all wholly and completely, with all that he is and has."[187] Following the confession of the Father's, the Son's and the Holy Spirit's divinity is a summary of the one indivisible work of the Trinity, whereby God's unity is again emphasized. In revelation God communicates "Himself" in the economy of salvation, in virtue of which "the one God in three Persons" has "given Himself" entirely to us. The three Persons and the gifts respective to each, in Luther's view, are perceived in a salvation-historical sequence. The meaning and purpose of their gifts are briefly described: the Father gives Himself to us with all creatures, so that we and they may serve Him; the Son gives Himself to us for reconciliation with the Father, for justification and for our knowledge of God; the Holy Spirit gives Himself to us so that we may appropriate the charity of Christ. Here the work of the Son and the work of the Holy Spirit are referred to one another. Luther deals with the doctrine of the Trinity, as he did with his Christology, by referring to justification; in declaring our justification to us God announces Himself three times, each one differently. This three-fold self-giving of God gives full expression to the three-fold revelation of God's love, which for Luther must not be understood "modalistically".[188]   More precisely, the economic Trinity stands in the foreground, by which we are told who God is and what He does *pro nobis*. However the stress that Luther's *the-*

ologia crucis lays on the economic Trinity must not be taken to imply that the immanent Trinity is left out of account. For the reformer the immanent Trinity is the presupposition for the economic *pro nobis* of his soteriology.[189] What we experience in this economy of salvation is indeed God in His essence and true relationship to us, and therefore is reliable. Our investigation has thereby shown how closely bound to each other are the doctrines of the Trinity, Christ and soteriology in Luther's theology of the cross in that none of them can be viewed independently of the others.

Conclusion

This present study seeks to demonstrate that the suffering of God has an "ontological status" in Luther's *theologia crucis*. The discussion circulated around three constituents of Luther's theology—Christology, soteriology and Trinity—to see how each of them establishes the assertion that God suffers. Christian theology, which for Luther is the theology of the cross, is concerned not with any *a priori* conceptions of God imported from elsewhere but with the identity of God as He has defined Himself in the cross of Christ. The identity of God is regulated by the content of the divine as revealed in Jesus. The Greek idea of divine impassibility has obscured the biblical revelation of God understood in Jesus Christ. Under the influence of hellenism the early church fathers tended to affirm the impassibility of the divine nature in Christ and the passibiltiy of the human nature of Jesus. This interpretation leads to a Nestorian Christology which the reformer repudiates. Luther's *theologia crucis* opens up an attack upon the understanding that only the humanity of Christ suffers on the cross, while Christ's divine nature is untouched. For Luther the nature of God is unveiled on the cross. God suffers on the cross in oneness with the person of Jesus Christ who is ontologically constitutive of God. The suffering of Christ as God's own suffering is established in the concretre unity of Christ's personal identity, which is to be explained according to the old doctrine of the *communicatio idiomatum*.

Soteriology is intergral to the reformer's Christology. Luther understood the person of Jesus Christ primarily in terms of what He does *pro nobis* as our redeemer. This means that his doctrine of the Incarnation is conceived in terms of the passion and death of Jesus. The divine suffering which God undergoes is consequent upon God's becoming a "human sinner and dying for us on the cross," according to which only the Son dies. This understanding of God's suffering may be called, as Jüngel termed it, "expiatory suffering."[1] The fundamental truth of the Christian faith consists in the fact that God in the passion history of Jesus Christ has suffered the curse of death and the misery of infinite suffering, and eventually suffered them into defeat. In the light of this "expiatory suffering" it becomes evident that God is nothing else but "love"—this "love" stands as the true condition for the possibility of God's suffering so long as the world is in sin and under God's wrath. Thus the "suffering" divine love cannot be perceived apart from the *communicatio idiomatum*. The divine imperative is to cling to the *deus revelatus*, the God with whom we have to do and the God who truly suffers for sin; on the contrary, the *deus absconditus* is non-salvific and thus does not suffer over the death of sinners. The antinomy between the impassible/naked God and the passible/clothed God is resolved in the cross of Christ but only for those who believe. Faith lays hold of the crucified Jesus as "the object of mercy"; unbelief encounters the wrathful deity (*ira dei*) and the impassible/naked God, from whom it must flee" and cleave to the passible/clothed God of mercy in Jesus Christ in order to be safe and saved.

Just as soteriology is intergral to Luther's Christology, the doctrine of the Trinity is also understood in soteriological terms. What God does in Jesus and through the Holy Spirit is, for Luther, the content of all theological thinking, and thus the weight of Luther's theology falls on the economic Trinity—the God who acts—which for Luther is the self-manifestation of the immanent Trinity—the God who is. For the reformer the triune God and the crucified Jesus belong together. That God is identified with the crucified Jesus compels theology to take seriously the trinitarian distinctions in God as Father, Son, and Holy Spirit. Emphasizing these distinctions, Luther rejects a modalistic version of "Patripassianism" which speaks of God in a simple untrinitarian fashion, but appropriates in some measure the theopaschite formula, that one of the Trinity suffered. It is the Son, Jesus of Nazareth, who suffers dying on the cross, not the Father. Though a modalistic version of patripassianism is rejected by Luther, there are ways in which Luther can speak of the Father's "fellow-suffering" with the Son: (i) First by way of *perichoresis*, the Father is said to suffer with the Son through their divine unity.   (ii) Second, Luther evidently assumes Augustine's understanding of the Spirit as the common bond of love (*vinculum caritatis*) between the Father and the Son within the inner being of God. So for Luther the Father suffers in compassion with the Son in the Spirit of love between them. However he did not develop the implications of this understanding of the Father who suffers with the Son in the unity of the Spirit (i.e., love). (iii) Finally God's being and God's act mutually and eternally coinhere in one another, and this understanding compels the affirmation that God suffers in eternity the cross of Christ. Since God is known through His acts, then God in His inner life is not different from God with us. The redemptive "act" of the suffering Christ is integral to the one undivided "essence" of God.   In the history of Christ's suffering passion we recognize who God is because God has identified Himself with this man Jesus. For Luther God continues to be incarnate for Christ's humanity has been taken up into the divine life "eternally". The incarnately human Son of God continues to bear our sin and mortality but as that which has been conquered and overcome in the cross and Easter. In this way Christ's suffering in human history is then carried into the eternal life of God, so that suffering is attributed at once to God with us and God in Himself.   God's capacity to suffer therefore has reached God's inner being, guaranteeing that the "economic" God of the Gospel corresponds to the "immanent" God.

Our study has shown that the passibility of God in the Incarnation goes deeper than the traditional *communicatio idiomatum* between Christ's human nature and his person. Luther's vehement repudiation of Zwingli's linguistic understanding of the *communicatio idiomatum* demonstrates that Luther would not have a Christ in which the divinity does not suffer. Otherwise Christ would be too weak a "Saviour" for us. Thus, the suffering of God in Jesus Christ has a "soteriological" point and is for Luther directly connected with his doctrine of justification. Luther's *theologia crucis* begins from "below"—the humanity of Jesus whose suffering is then predicated of His divine nature, affirming that Christ suffers in the concrete unity of His two natures. Then he moves from the "who" that suffers—the incarnate Son—to the "why" of Christ's suffering—for atonement. Finally, though Luther did not preoccupy himself with a discussion of the immanent Trinity, it can be discerned, as this study seeks to show, that Luther moves from the redemptive "act" of Christ's suffering to the acknowledgement, recognition and confession that Christ's suffering belongs to the *intra* trinitarian life of God. Accordingly, God, for Luther, ceases to be God in a Platonic sense that denies suffering and death to God's heavenly divinity.

Notes

Introduction

1   This book will use Althaus' term "dei-passionism" (God suffers) as descriptive of the Reformer's passibility position.   See Paul Althaus, *Theology of Martin Luther*, trans. Robert Schultz (Philadelphia: Fortress Press, 1966), p.197.   See also Marc Lienhard, *Luther: Witness to Jesus Christ* trans. J.A. Bouman (Minneapolis: Augsburg Publishing House, 1982), p.171.

Chapter One: Divine Suffering in Early Church History

1   For further discussions on the passibility - impassibility debate, see John Mozley, *The Impassibility of God: A Survey of Christian Thought* (Cambridge: Cambridge University Press, 1926); Jospeh Hallman, *The Descent of God: Divine Suffering in History and Theology* (Minneapolis: Fortress Press, 1991); Lester, J. Kuyper, "The Suffering and Repentance of God," *Scottish Journal of Theology* 22 (Sept., 1969): 3-16; T.E. Pollard, "The Impassibility of God," *Scottish Journal of Theology* 8 (Dec., 1955): 353-364; Wolfhart Pannenberg, "The Appropriation of the Philosophical Concept of God as a Dogmatic Problem of Early Christian Theology," in *Basic Questions in Theology*, vol. 2., trans. George H. Kehm (Philadelphia: The Westminster Press, 1971), pp. 119-183; Gerald Wondra, "The Pathos of God," *The Reformed Review* 18 (Dec., 1964): 28-35; Richard Bauckham, " 'Only the Suffering God can Help' : Divine Passibility in Modern Theology," *Themelios* 9 (1984):6-12; Ronald Goetz, "The Suffering God: The Rise of a New Orthodoxy," *The Christian Century* 103 (April 16, 1986): 385-289, and his "Karl Barth, Jürgen Moltmann and the Theopaschite Revolution," in *Festschrift: A Tribute to Dr. William Hordern*, ed. Walter Freitag (Saskatoon: University of Saskatchewan Press, 1985); B.H. Streeter, "The Suffering of God," *The Hibbert Journal* (April 1914): 603-611; H. Wheeler Robinson, *Suffering, Human and Divine* (New York: Macmillan, 1939); Warren McWilliams, *The Passion of God: Divine Suffering in Contemporary Theology* (Macon: Mercer University Press, 1985); Kenneth J. Woollcombe, "The Pain of God," *Scottish Journal of*

Theology 20 (June, 1967): 129-148; Marcel Sarot, "Patripassianism, Theopaschitism and the Suffering of God. Some Historical and Systematic Considerations," *Religious Studies* 26 (1990): 363-385; Francis House, "The Barrier of Impassibilit Theology 83 (1980): 409 - 415; R.S. Franks, "Passibility and Impassibility," in *Encyclopaedia of Religion and Ethics*, Vol. 9, ed. James Hastings, (New York: Charles Scribner's Son, 1917), 658-659; Paul Fiddes, *The Creative Suffering of God* (Oxford: Clarendon Press, 1988); Werner Elert, "Die Theopaschite Formel," Theologische Literaturzeitung 75 (1950): 195-206; Edward Burnley, "The impassibility of God," *The Expository Times* 67 (1955/56): 90-91; Peter Forster, "Divine Passibility and the Early Christian Doctrine of God," in *The Power and Weakness of God: Impassibility and Orthodoxy*, ed. Nigel M. de S. Cameron (Edinburgh: Rutherford House Books, 1989); Lucien Richard, *What are they saying about the theology of Suffering?* (New York: Paulist Press, 1992).

2   See Jung Young Lee, *God Suffers for Us; A Systematic Inquiry into a concept of Divine Passibility* (The Hague: Martinus Nihhoff, 1974), p.28.

3   John Russell, "Impassibility and Pathos in Barth's Idea of God," *Anglican Theological Review* LXX:3 (1988), p.222.

4   *Ibid.*, p.233. See also Francis House, "The Barrier of Impassibility," Theology 83(1880), pp. 410-411; Colin Grant, "Possibilities for Divine Passibility," *Toronto Journal of Theology* 4 (1988), pp.6-8; Charles Taliaferro, "The Passibility of God," *Religious Studies* 25 (1989), p.218. The attributes of immutability and impassibility are closed related, but not equivalent. Immutability means that God does not change in any way, even from within, while impassibility suggests the impossibility of being affected by any other realities, even in the emotional sense.

5   Jürgen Moltmann, *The Crucified God: The Cross of Christ as the Foundation and Cricitism of Christian Theology*, trans. R.A. Wilson & John Bowden (New York: Harper & Row, Publishers, 1973), p.228.

6   For further studies on the influence of Greek ideas upon classical Christianity, see Charles Hartshorne and William L. Reese, *Philosophers Speak of God* (Chicago: University of Chicago Press, 1953), pp. 38-106; Edwin Hatch, *The Influence of Greek Ideas and Usages upon the Christian Church*, ed. A. M. Fairbairn (London: William and Norgate, 1892), pp. 3-5, 114-115; Pannenberg, "The Appropriation of the Philosophical Concept of God," pp. 134-137; Fiddes, *The Creative Suffering of God*, p.47. See also Pollard, "The Impassibility of God," p.354 who comments properly the consequences for the early church's embrace of the Platonic idea of the absolute: "much that was distinctive in Christianity was either lost

or falsely expressed, and alien elements which (were) imported into Christian thought have cursed theological thought ever since their time."

7   See McWilliams, *The Passion of God*, pp.10-11.

8.   Bauckham, " 'Only the Suffering God can help'," p.7. See also Hatch, *The Influence of Greek Ideas and Usages upon the Christian Church*, p.182. It is Hatch's observation that the writings of Philo have largely contributed to the sublimation of the Christian doctrine of God into the hellenistic worldview. For further study on Philo, see Joseph C. McLelland, *God the Anonymous. A Study in Alexandrian Philosophical Theology* (The Philadelphia Patristic Foundation, Ltd., 1976), pp.23-44; Hallman, *The Descent of God*, pp.23-29.

9   Pollard, "The Impassibility of God," p.357. See also Cyril C. Richardson, ed. *Early Christian Fathers*, in *The Library of Christian Classics*, vol. 1 (Philadelphia: Westminster Press, 1853), pp.105, 118-119; Elert, "Die Theopaschite Formel," p.195.; Robert Jenson, *The Triune Identity* (Philadelphia: Fortress Press, 1982), p.63.

10   *Ibid.*

11   Pollard, "The Impassibility of God," p.357.

12   *Ibid.*, cf. Hallman, *The Descent of God*, p.33: "Irenaeus' view of God (late second century) is virtually the same. God is uncreated, unbegotten, incomprehensible, without figure, has no beginning or end, is impassible and immutable. The *Adversus Haereses* raises the question of divine impassibility because of the Gnostic creation myth. In his critique of the myth, the impropriety of divine feelings becomes Irenaeus' major theme."

13   McWilliams, *The Passion of God*, pp.11-12: "As the *via negativa* and Neoplatonic thought exercised more influence in doctrinal development, God's transcendence was further accentuated and anthropopathic language was summarily dismissed. Very early theologians began to distinguish between Christ's divine and human nature: his divine nature was impassible and his human nature was passible." See also Franks, "Passibility and Impassibility," p.658.

14   See Mozley, *The Impassibility of God*, pp.30-332; Jaroslav Pelikan, *The Emergence of the Catholic Tradition* (100-600), vol. 1 (Chicago: University of Chicago Press, 1971), pp. 176-180; John N. D. Kelly, *Early Christian Doctrines* (London: Harper & Row, 1968), pp.100-123; Aloys Grillmeier,

Christ in Christian Tradition: From the Apostolic Age to Chalcedon (451), vol. 1., trans. J. S. Bowden (New York: Sheed & Ward, 1964), pp.133-54.

15   See Hippolytus of Rome, *Contra Noetum*, ed. & trans. Robert Butterworth (London: Heythrop Monographs, 1977), p.42.

16   Tertullian, *Against Praxeas*, trans. A. Souter (London: The MacMillan Co., 1920), 1, p.25.

17   See *Against Praxeas* 27. Tertullian means by '*Pater*' the first person of the Trinity, whereas the modalists use '*Pater*' in the sense of 'God *simpliciter*.' Cf. Kelly, *Early Christian Doctrines*, pp.100, 112-113, 119-123. Franks, in his "Passibility and Impassibility," reports concerning the modalists that "there was only one God, impassible and invisible when He does not suffer and die, passible and visible when He suffers and dies" (p.658). This Patripassian Monarchianism only draws a distinction between the visible and the invisible "modes" of the one God, refusing to maintain a distinction between the Son and the Father.

18   See *Against Praxeas*, ch.1 as quoted in Pollard, "The Impassibility of God," p.358. Franks, in his "Passibility and Impassibility," p. 658, quotes Tertullian's *Adversus Marcionem* ii. 27: "Whatever attributes therefore you require as worthy of God, must be found in the Father, who is invisible and unapproachable, and placid, and(so to speak)the God of the philosophers; whereas those qualities which censure as unworthy must be supposed to be in the Son, who has been seen, and heard, and encountered, the Witness and Servant of the Father, uniting in Himself man and God."

19   See *Against Praxaes*, ch. 29 as quoted in Pollard, *ibid.*

20   Mozley, *The Impassibility of God*, p.38.

21   Clement, *Stromateis*, VI.9 as cited in Pollard, "*The Impassibility of God*," p.358. See also Hallman, *The Descent of God*, pp. 36-37.

22   Origen, *Contra Celsus* 8:384-85 as quoted in Hallman, *The Descent of God*, Cf. Jürgen Moltmann, *The Trinity and the Kingdom: The Doctrine of God*, trans. Margaret Kohl (San Francisco: Harper & Row Publishers) pp. 23-25. Moltmann argues on the basis of this text that in the patristic period, Origen is the "only one" who speaks theologically about God's suffering. But Moltmann ignores the developed theology of Origen.

23   See Hallman, *The Descent of God*, p.42 where *Contra Celsus* 7. 211-214 is quoted. Cf. Mozley, *The Impassibility of God*, p.60, where *Contra Celsus* 4.

71-72 is quoted: "We do not therefore ascribe human passions to God, nor do we hold impious opinions about Him."

24 See Mozley, *The Impassibility of God*, pp.63-72 where Gregory Thaumaturgus' monograph on divine impassibility was quoted and summarized. See also Hallman, *The Descent of God*, pp.46-48 and Forster, "Divine Passibility and the Early Christian Doctrine of God," pp.36-37.

25 McWilliams, *The Passion of God*, pp.12-13.

26 Hallman, *The Descent of God*, p.47.

27 *Against the Arians*, III. xxvi. 34 as cited in Pollard, "*The Impassibility of God*," pp. 258-259. Cf. Hallman, *The Descent of God*, p.83. Hallman recognized that the issue of divine impassibility became important in the fourth century because of Arianism. He writes: "If the Logos was changeable and capable of suffering, it could not have divine status."

28 Pollard, "*The Impassibility of God*," p.359. See also Justo Gonzálec, *A History of Christian Thought* (Nashville: Abingdon Press, 1970-75), vol. 1, p.309; Kelly, *Early Christian Doctrine*, pp.381ff.

29 Hallman, *The Descent of God*, p.83.

30 Athanasius, *Four Discourses Against the Arians* 3.26. 32-33, in *The Nicene and Post-Nicene Fathers of the Christian Church*, 14 vols., ed. Philip Schaff (Grand Rapids: William B. Eerdmans, 1980), vol. 4, pp.410-412. See also Gonzaléc, *A History of Christian Thought*, pp.298 & 300.

31 *Theological Oration*, IV.5 as cited in Pollard, "*The Impassibility of God*," p.359 and Bauckham, " 'Only the Suffering God can help'," p.8. See also John Egan, "God-forsaken: The Crucified Christ or Suffering Humanity? Current Evaluation of Jürgen Moltmann's and Gregory Nazianzen's comments on the Crucified Christ's Cry of Abandonment," in *Tradition and Innovation*, ed. Jos. B. Gavin, S.J. (Regina: Campion College Press, 1983), p.63.

32 Gregory of Nazianzus, *Panergyric on his Borther S. Caesarius*, 7.23, in *The Nicene and Post-Nicene Fathers of the Christian Church* , vol. 7, 237.

33 Mozley, *The Impassibility of God*, pp. 87ff. See also Grillmeier, *Christ in Christian Tradition*, pp.278-290.

34 Millard J. Erickson, *Christian Theology* (Grand Rapids: Baker Book House, 1984), vol.2, p.727.

35 *Ibid..*, p. 728. See also Kelly, *Early Christian Doctrines*, pp. 311-312.

36 See Grillmeier, *Christ in Christian Tradition*, pp. 363-388.

37 See Henry Bettenson, ed., *Documents of the Christian Church* (London: Oxford Uni. Press, 1981), p.46.

38 Grillmeier, *Christ in Christian Tradition*, p. 405.

39 *Ibid.*

40 See Cyril of Alexandria, *The Epistle of Cyril to Nestorius with the XII Anathematisms* in *Patrologia Graeca* (Paris: 1857-1866), vol. 77, col. 105. See also Grillmeier, *Christ in Christian Tradition*, pp.406-412.

41 Grillmeier, *Christ in Christian Tradition*, p. 365. Cf. Bettenson, ed., *Documents of the Christian Church*, pp. 47-48. See also Grant, "Possibilities for Divine Passibility," p.4

42 Cyril of Alexandra, *The Epistle of Cyril to Nestorius with the XII Anathematisms*, vol. 77, col. 105.

43 See Bettenson, ed., *Documents of the Christian Church*, pp. 50-52.

44 See George Miucumakes, "Monophysitism," in *The New International Dictionary of the Christian Church*, ed., J.D. Douglas (Grand Rapids: Zondervan Publishing House, 1978), pp. 672-673.

45 A.A. Luce, *Monophysitism Past and Present: A Study in Christology* (New York: The MacMillan Co., 1920), p.69.

46 Pelikan, *Emergence of the Catholic Tradition*, pp. 270-272; see also Mozley, *The Impassibility of God*, pp. 95-96.

47 See J.A. McGuckin, "The 'Theopaschite Confession: (Text and Historical Context)': A Study in the Cyrilline Reinterpretation of Chalcedon," *Journal of Ecclesiastical History* 35:2 (1984), p.240.

48 *Ibid.*, p.250. See also Sarot, "Patripassianism, Theopaschitism and the Suffering of God," p.373.

49 *Second Council of Constantinople* (553), *anathema* 12 as cited in Norman Nagel, " 'Heresy, Doctor Luther, Heresy!' The Person and Work of Christ, "in *Seven-headed Luther. Essays in Commemoration of a*

Quincentenary 1483-1983, ed. Peter Newman Brooks (Oxford: Clarendon Press, 1983), p.31

50   See Pelikan, *Emergence of the Catholic Tradition*, pp. 270-271; McGuckin, "The 'Theopaschite Confession', " pp. 239ff.

51   See Hallman, *The Descent of God*, pp. 101-102, where he quoted Hilary's *De Synodis* 49, in Migne, *Patrologia Latina*, 10. 516B-517A.

52   Saint Augustine, *The City of God*, trans. Marcus Dods (New York: Random House, 1950), p.263.

53   See Hallman, *The Descent of God*, p. 122, where he quoted *Contra Advers. Legis et Prophet* 1.20.40 in Migne, *Patrologia Latina*, Paris. 42, 627. Hallman comments that "although God is immutable and impassible for (Augustine), the Incarnate Word is *Deus humilis*. This points the way to another view, one that could have taken divine mutability and passibility seriously on the philosophical level. Obviously Augustine did not develop this view" (p.123).

54   See Rem. B. Edwards, "The Pagan Dogma of the Absolute Unchangeableness of God," *Religious Studies* 14 (1978), pp.307-308.

55   See Anselm, *Proslogion*, ch. 8. in *Saint Anselm: Basic Writings*, p.13 as cited by Elizabeth Johnson, *She Who is. The Mystery of God in Feminist Theological Disourse* (New York: Crossroad, 1992), p. 248. Also quoted in MacWilliams, *The Passion of God*, p.13 and Edwards, "The Pagan Dogma of the Absolute Unchangeableness of God," pp.13-14.

56   *Ibid.*

57   Mozley, *The Impassibility of God*, pp. 113-114. See also Fiddes, *The Creative Suffering of God*, pp. 49-50.

58   *Ibid.* See also Michael Dodds, "Aquinas, Human Suffering and the Unchanging God of Love," *Theological Studies* 52 (1991): 330-344. Cf. Grillmeier, *Christ in Christian Tradition*, pp. 361-391.

59   See Russell, "Impassibility and Pathos in Barth's Idea of God," p.223.

60   *Ibid.* p.223. Russell further explains: "God's love involves only intellectual desire (for Thomas). Hence an immaterial God's intellectual desires concern neither sense-grounded nor bodily actions. Thomas thus reasons that God's love—an intellectually rooted desire—represents an *actio* rather than a *passio*. Thus God experiences love and nonetheless

186 Notes

remains impassible" (Cf. *Summa Theologica* 1.20.1).

61   Mozley, *The Impassibility of God*, p.119.

62.   See John Calvin, *Institutes of the Christian Religion*, trans. Ford Lewis Battles & ed. John T. McNeill in *The Library of Christian Classics*, vol. 20 (Philadelphia: Westminster Press, 1960), vol. 1, bk. II. xiii. 2, p.484. Also quoted in Wondra, "The Pathos of God," p.28.

63.   Mozley, *The Impassibility of God*, p.121.

64.   *Ibid.* See also McWilliams, *The Passion of God*, p.14, who sees in Luther the communication between the two natures. Cf. Wondra, "The Pathos of God," p.34. Wondra says that biblical revelation portrays God as one who has suffered in the cross of His Son, concerning whom "there is no talk ... of suffering only in the human nature. Moreover, there is no formulation of two natures in Christ. It belongs to His person as the mediator, the eternal High priest, that He is the God-man."

65   *Ibid.* See also Lienhard, *Witness to Jesus*, p.341.

66   See Woollcombe, "The Pain of God," pp. 137-138: "All the experiences of the Incarnate One, however endured, were experiences of the One Divine Person; and it was just because the cross was not the cross of a man but of the Lord Jesus Christ that the Cross saved." Cf. Franks, "Passibility and Impassibility," p. 658, who sees the cross as "a fresh point of contact between God and passibility in so far as the man Jesus Christ is regarded as the Incarnation of God." See also Galen Tinder, "Luther's Theology of Christian Suffering and Its Implications for Pastoral Care," *Dialog* 25:2 (1986), p.111. Tinder correctly perceives that Luther's notion of the *communicatio idiomatum* allows him to assert that in Christ, God himself suffered on the cross. "This proved an intolerable thought to those of Luther's age who were imbued with the Greek assumption that God is impassible and free of limitation and imperfection."

67   Mozley, *The Impassibility of God*, p.121. Mozley indicates that Luther's "retention of the doctrine of impassibility is crossed by his Christology."

68   See Wondra, "The Pathos of God," p.34. Wondra quotes Emil Brunner favorably: "It is hardly an exaggeration to say that the theological doctrine of the Divine attributes, handed on from the Early Church, has been shaped by the Platonic and neo-Platonic idea of God, and not by the Biblical Idea" (p.31). Cf. Emil Brunner, *The Christian Doctrine of God*, trans. Olive Wyon (London: Lutterworth Press, 1949), p. 153. See also

H.M. Relton, *Studies in Christian Doctrine* (London: MacMillan, 1960), p. 79, where he makes a remarkably far-sighted statement: "There are many indications that the doctrine of the suffering of God is going to play a very prominent part in the theology of the age in which we live."

Chapter Two: Luther's *Theologia Crucis*

1   Joseph Lortz, *The Reformation in Germany*, trans. Ronald Walls (London: Darton, Longman & Todd, 1968), vol. 1, p. 167.

2   See W. Pauck's introduction in *Luther: Lectures on Romans, in The Library of Christian Classics*, XV (Philadelphia: Westminster Press, 1961), pp. xxxviii-xxxix.

3   Dietmar Lage, *Martin Luther's Christology and Ethics* (Queenston: Edwin Mellen Press, 1990), p.9.

4   See Aquinas, *Summa Theologica*, I-II, quest. 109-112 as cited in Lage, *Martin Luther's Christology and Ethics*, p.10.

5   Lage, *Martin Luther's Christology and Ethics*, p.11.

6   *Ibid.*, p.11.

7   *Ibid.*, p.12.

8   *Ibid.*, p. 13.

9   See Heiko A. Oberman, *The Harvest of Medieval Theology: Gabriel Biel and Late Medieval Nominalism* (Mass.: Harvard University Press, 1963), p.65.

10   See Aquinas, *Summa Theologica*, I-II, quest. 94, art. 2 (Pegis edition), p.636 as cited in Lage, *Martin Luther's Christology and Ethics*, p.13.

11   *Ibid.*, pp. 634-645.

12   Lage, *Martin Luther's Christology and Ethics*, pp.13 & 19.

13   Ockham, *Summa Totius Logicae*, in *Ockham: Philosophical Writings*, ed. & trans P. Boehner (London: Thomas Nelson & Sons, 1957), pp. 92 - 95.

14   See Steven Ozment, "Mysticism, Nominalism and Dissent," in *The Pursuit of Holiness in Late Medieval and Renaissance Religion* . Papers from the University of Michigan Conference, Vol. X of the series *Studies in Medieval and Reformation Thought*, ed. Charles Trinkhaus & Heiko A.

Oberman (Leiden: E. J. Brill, 1974), p. 78.

15   Lage, *Martin Luther's Christology and Ethics*, p.12.

16   For a thorough discussion of *de potentia absoluta* and *de potentia ordinata*, see Oberman, *Harvest of Medieval Theology*, pp. 30-38; and his, "Notes on the Theology of Nominalism with attention to its relation to the Renaissance," *Harvard Theological Review* 53 (1976): 47-76.

17   McGrath, *Luther's Theology of the Cross*, p. 56. McGrath is mistaken here in equating the necessity that involves force (*coactionis*) with the necessity of consequence (*consequentiae*). The necessity of consequence means that if God wills something, that event or thing will necessarily happen, not as a voilation of the divine freedom but rather as a consequence of the divine will. This is not the same as the necessity that involves compulsion, which is inapplicable to God for it violates the divine freedom.

18   Heiko Oberman, "Facientibus Quod in se est Deus not denegat Gratiae: Robert Holcot, and the Beginning of Luther's Theology," in *The Reformation in Medieval Perspective*, ed. Steven Ozment (Chicago: Quandros Books, 1971), pp.119-141.

19   See McGrath, *Luther's Theology of the Cross*, pp. 28-34. See also Lage, *Martin Luther's Christology and Ethics*, p.17: "The primary Ockhamist influence on the faculty at Erfurt, and thus indirectly upon the young Martin Luther, came from Gabriel Biel (c. 1420-1495)."

20   See Gabriel Biel, *Collectorium circa quattuor libros sententiarum*, Lib. II. dist. 27, art. 2, as cited in Bengt Hägglung, "The Background of Luther's Doctrine of Justification in Late Medieval Theology," *Lutheran World* 8 (1961), p.30.

21   Biel, *Collectorium*, Lib. II, dis. 22, art. 3, as quoted by Hägglund, *ibid.*, pp. 31-32. See also *Collectorium*, Lib. II, dist. 28, art 2, as quoted by Lage, *Martin Luther's Christology and Ethics*, p.23.

22   Timothy George, *Theology of the Reformers* (Nashville: Broadman Press, 1988), p.66.

23   See Biel, *Collectorium*, Lib. II, dist. 29, quest. 7, art. 2, Concl. 1, as quoted by Loewenich, *Luther's Theology of the Cross*, p. 53.

24   Oberman, *Harvest of Medieval Theology*, pp. 65-68.

25   As quoted by Lage, *Martin Luther's Christology and Ethics*, p.21;

Oberman, *Harvest of Medieval Theology*, p.268.

26   See Oberman, *"Facientibus Quod in se est Deus not denegat Gratiam,"* pp. 130-134; Oberman, *Harvest of Medieval Theology*, pp. 176-177: "It is clear that Biel has aremarkable doctrine of justification: seen from different vantage-points, justification is at once *sola gratia* and *solis operibus*. ... It is therefore evident that Biel's doctrine of justification is essentially Pelagian." McGrath argues against Oberman's position that Biel's doctrine of justification is "not only not Pelagian, but is actually strongly anti-Pelagian." See his *Luther's Theology of the Cross* p.62 and his article, "The Anti-Pelagian Structure of 'Nominalist' Doctrine of Justification, "*Ephemerides Theologicae Lovanienses* 57 (1981): 107-119.

27   See *WA* 4, 262 as cited in George, *Theology of the Reformers*, p.66.

28   See *WA* 3, 603 as cited in Lage, *Martin Luther's Christology and Ethics*, p.26.

29   *LW* 25, 157; *WA* 56, 177.

30   *LW* 11, 453; *WA* 3, 453.

31   *WA* 1, 32 as cited in Lage, *Martin Luther's Christology and Ethics*, p. 26.

32   *LW* 31, 1; *WA* 1, 225.

33   *Ibid.*

34   Lage, *Martin Luther's Christology and Ethics*, pp. 30-33.

35   See *WA* 2, 394; *WA* 2, 303 as quoted in Lage, *ibid.*, p.33.

36   See *WA* BR 1, 66 as translated and quoted in E. Gordon Rupp, Luther's *Progress to the Diet of Worms* (New York: Harper & Row, 1964), p.46.

37   *LW* 25, 262; *WA* 56, 275.

38   *LW* 25, 222; *WA* 56, 237.

39   *LW* 25, 262; *WA* 56, 273.

40   *LW* 25, 262; *WA* 56, 275.

41   *LW* 31, 13.

42   *LW* 31, 10.

43   See "Luther to John Lang," 1517, *LW* 48, 36-38; *WA BR* 1 no. 12, pp. 88-89, where Luther argues against adherence to Aristotelian principles (such as *habitus infusus*), particularly those of the scholastic theology.

44   See *LW* 31, 9-16; *WA* 1, 221-228, where Luther repudiated the semi-Pelagian doctrine of the will of some scholastics. Cf. Loewenich, *Luther's Theology of the Cross*, pp. 52-58; Rupp, *The Righteousness of God: Luther Studies* (New York: Philosophical Library, 1953), pp. 150-152.

45   See Pauck, *Luther: Lectures on Romans* (1515-16), p. xxxix where *WA* 12, 414, 22 was quoted.

46   See *WA BR* I, 99 as quoted in Rupp, *Luther's Progress to the Diet of Worms*, p.46.

47   Oberman, *Harvest of Medieval Theology*, p.16. See also his "Gabriel Biel and Late Medieval Mysticism," *Church History* 20 (1961), p.261.

48   Hägglund "The Background of Luther's Doctrine of Justification in Late Medieval Theology," pp.25-46 for a summary of scholarship on Luther's relation to mysticism. See also Oberman, "*Simul Germitus et Raptus*: Luther and Mysticism," in *The Reformation in Medieval Perspective*, pp. 219-251.

49   Uuras Saarnivaara, *Luther Discovers the Gospel* (St. Louis: Concordia Publishing House, 1951), pp. 76-77; Loewenich, *Luther's Theology of the Cross*, pp. 152ff for a historical discussion of Tauler in relation to Luther.

50   George, *Theology of the Reformers*, pp. 66-67.

51   Steven Ozment, *Homo Spiritualis: A Comparative Study of the Anthropology of Johannes Tauler, Jean Gerson and Martin Luther in the Context of their Theological Thought*. Studies in *Medieval and Reformation Thought*, vol. 6 (Leiden: E. J. Brill, 1969), pp. 234-237.

52   Ozment, ed., "*Homo Viator*: Luther and Late Medieval Theology," in *The Reformation in Medieval Perspective*, pp. 145 & 149.

53   *LW* 25, 287-288; *WA* 56, 300; cf. "Explanation of the Ninety-five Theses", 1518, *LW* 31, 128ff; *WA* 1, 37, 14ff.

54   *Ibid.*

55   *LW* 27, 308-309; *WA* 40^2, 548 (Galatians, 1519).

56   *LW* 10, 405; *WA* 3, 463 (Psalms, 1532)

57   See Bernard, *Sermons* LXXXIII.3 as cited in Lage, *Martin   Luther's Christology and Ethics*, p.51.

58   *Ibid.*

59   See Bernard, *Sermons* XXIV.I as cited in Lage, *ibid.*.

60   See Rupp, *Luther's Progress to the Diet of Worms*, p.15. See also David Steinmetz, "Hermeneutic and Old Testament Interpretation in Staupitz and the Young Martin Luther," *Archiv für Reformationsgeschichte* 70 (1979): 24-58. Both Rupp and Steinmetz argue that Augustine and Staupitz provided Luther with the hermeneutical distinction between "letter" (*littera*) and "spirit" (*spiritus*) for the reading of the Scripture.

61   *Ibid.*

62   See Stapulensis, "Introduction to the Commentary on the Psalms," in Oberman, ed., *Forerunners of the Reformation: The Shape of Late Medieval Thought* , ed. Heiko Oberman (U.S.A.: Holt, Rinehart & Winston, 1966), p.298.

63   *Ibid.*

64   For a brief study of Stapulensis' influence upon Luther, see Lage, Martin *Luther's Christology and Ethics*, pp. 57-62.

65   See *WA* 1, 32 as cited in Lage, *ibid.*, p.61.

66   *Ibid.*

67   See *WA* 4, 110 as cited in lage, *ibid.*, p.62.

68   *Ibid.*

69   *LW* 25, 370; *WA* 56, 380.

70   See "The Disputation Concerning Justification", 1536, *LW* 34, 178; *WA* 39^1, 109, 1-3.

71   See Carter Lindberg, "The Mask of God and Prince of Lies: Luther's Theology of the Demonic," in *Disguises of the Demonic*, ed. Alan M. Olson

(New York: Association Press, 1975), p. 89; Heinrich Bornkamm, *Luther's World of Thought*, trans. Martin H. Bertram (St. Louis: Concordia Publishing House, 1958), p.73; David R. Scaer, "The Concept of *Anfechtung* in Luther's Thought," *Concordia Theological Quarterly* 47 (Jan., 1983): 15-30.

72   See *WA* 40^2, 582, (Psalm. 45, 1932) as quoted in Bornkamm, *Luther's World of Thought*, p.73.

73   See *WA* 9, 95ff as cited in Lage, *Martin Luther's Christology and Ethics*, p.76.

74   See McGrath, *Luther's Theology of the Cross*, pp. 169-175; Paul Büehler, *Die Anfechtung bei Martin Luther* (Zurich: Zwingli Verlag, 1942), pp. 7-8.

75   Loewenich, *Luther's Theology of the Cross*, pp. 129 & 134. See also Ozment, ed. *"Homo Viator,"* p.148, where he notes a "permanently irreconcilable difference" between Luther and mysticism.

76   *LW* 51, 15; *WA* 1, 111 (Sermon on Luke 18:9-14, 1516).

77   See Erwin Iserloh, "Luther's Christ-Mysticism," in *Catholic Scholars Dialogue with Luther*, ed. Jared Wicks (Chicago: Loyola University Press, 1970), pp.43ff.

78   See *WA* 3, 504 as cited in Lage, *Martin Luther's Christology and Ethics*, p.85.

79   See *WA* 7, 25 as cited in Lage, *ibid.* See also *LW* 26, 168; *WA* 40^1,285.

80   *LW* 26, 4-5; *WA* 40^1, 41. See also *WA* 33, 566.

81   *LW* 26, 264; *WA* 40^1, 414.

82   *LW* 34, 111; *WA* 39^1, 45.

83   *WA* 44, 135.

84   *LW* 35, 370.

85   *LW* 27, 30; *WA* 40^2, 37.

86   See *WA* 39^2, 248 as quoted in *Martin Luther's Christology and Ethics, ibid.*, p.153.

87   *LW* 34, 111.

88.   *LW* 26, 274; *WA* 40^1, 428.

89   *LW* 26, 270; *WA* 40^1, 424.

90   *LW* 26, 155; *WA* 40^1, 266.

91   *LW* 27, 35; *WA* 40^2, 43.

92   *LW* 27, 34; *WA* 40^2, 42..

93   *LW* 27, 35; *WA* 40^2, 43.

94   Rupp, *The Righteousness of God*, p.92.

95   *Ibid*. See note 4.

96   Lienhard, *Witness to Jesus*, pp. 25 & 79, note 22.

97   *LW* 28, 42; *WA* BR 1, no. 41, 99.

98   *LW* 31, 75; *WA* 1, 378, 21ff.

99   While Luther in his early career esteemed Augustine as the truest inter-
        preter of Paul, his later assessments are marked by reserve, particularly
        pertaining to the doctrine of justification. See Anders Nygren, *Agage and
        Eros*, trans. Philip S. Watson (New York: Harper & Row, Publishers,
        Harper Torchbooks, 1969), pp. 513-518, where Augustine's emphasis on
        human love (*caritas*) through its seven stages of virtue necessary for fel-
        lowship with God is discussed. Augustine is credited with the doctrine
        of *synteresis*, the anti-thesis of Luther's doctrine of justification.

100   See Lienhard, *Witness to Jesus* , p. 36 where he cites Iserloh, "Luther und
        die Mystik," in *Kirche, Mystic, Heiligung und das Natürliche bei Luther*
        (Göttingen: Asheim, 1967), p.61.

101   *LW* 25, 310; *WA* 56, 321.

102   *LW* 29, 124; *WA* 57^3, 114, 13-19.

103   See Regin Prenter, *Spiritus Creator*, trans. John Jensen (Philadelphia:
        Mühlenberg Press, 1953), p.210.

104   See *LW* 31, 342-378 (The Freedom of a Christian, 1520); Jaroslav Pelikan, *Reformation of Church and Dogma*, in *The Christian Tradition: A History of the Development of Doctrine*, vol. 4 (Chicago: University of Chicago Press, 1984), p.163.

105   See *LW* 27, 128 (Galatians, 1519)

106   See Lage, *Martin Luther's Christology and Ethics*, p.100: "For a faith rooted in an historical incarnation, to preach the cross event as *sacramentum* alone is to slip into spiritualism or intellectual abstraction. The danger is that ultimately Christ's sacrifice may be reduced to simply a formula or a slogan of merely symbolic validity and a rationale for a hidden self-justification."

107   *LW* 27, 238; *WA* 2, 501. For further discussion, see Norman Nagel, "*Sacramentum et Exemplum* in Luther's Understanding of Christ," in *Luther for an Ecumenical Age*, ed. Carl S. Meyer (St. Louis: Concordia Publishing House, 1967), pp. 172-199, where he notes Augustine's Christology has been finally appropriated by Luther in his lectures on Romans and Hebrews.

108   Lienhard, *Witness to Jesus*, p.137.

109.   For a detailed study of Gregory of Rimini and Johannes von Staupitz, see Gordon Leff, *Gregory of Rimini: Tradition and Innovation in Fourteenth Century Thought* (Manchester: Manchester University Press, 1961); David C. Steinmetz, *Luther and Staupitz, An Essay in the Intellectual Originals of the Protestant Reformation*, Duke Monographs in *Medieval and Renaissance Studies* 4 (Durham: Duke University Press, 1980).

110   See Rupp, *The Righteousness of God*, p.140; McGrath, *Luther's Theology of the Cross*, p.67. See also Oberman, "Headwaters of the Reformation," in *Luther and the Dawn of the Modern Era* (Leiden: E. J. Brill, 1974), pp. 80-82.

111   *LW* 31, 322.

112   See David Steinmetz, *Misericordia Dei: The Theology of Johannes von Staupitz in its Late Medieval Setting*, studies in *Medieval and Reformation Thought*, ed. Heiko Oberman, vol. 4 (Leiden: E. J. Brill, 1968), p.93.

113   McGrath, *Luther's Theology of the Cross*, pp. 66-67. St. Thomas Aquinas and Giles of Rome taught that justification is based on "a created habit of grace within the soul."

114   *LW* 48, 66; *WA* 1 525 (Letter to John von Staupitz: Wittenberg, May 30, 1518).

115   See *Johannis Staupitii Opera*, I, p.62, as quoted in Lage, *Martin Luther's Christology and Ethics*, p.49.

116   The concept of "Joyous exchange", says Steinmetz, is particularly associated with Staupitz. See his *Luther and Staupitz*, p.106. See also McGrath, *Luther's Theology of the Cross*, p.173.

117   See *WA* 58^1, 27 as cited in George, *Theology of the Reformers*, p.63.

118   *LW* 23, 271; *WA* 33, 431.27-432.5 (Eighth Sermon on John 7, 1530-1532).

119   *LW* 16, 55; *WA* 31^2, 29, 5-8 (Isaiah, 1532).

120   *LW* 26, 114; *WA* 40^1, 204-205 (Galatians, 1535).

121   *LW* 5, 47; *WA* 43, 461, 11-16 (Genesis, 1535-45). See also *Luther: Letters of Spiritual Counsel*, ed. T. G. Tappert, in *The Library of Christian Classics*, vol. 18 (Philadelphia: Westminster Press, 1955), p.116, where Luther, in April 30, 1531, exhorted Barbara Lisskirchen, who was troubled by the doctrine of predestination, to contemplate the "wounds of Jesus".

122   *LW* 54, 9; *WA* TR I, 245, no. 526 (1531-32).

123   See *WA* TR 2, 242, 4, no. 1868, referring to Rom. 1:2.

124   See *WA* 4, 365, 5-14 as quoted in John R. Loeschen, *The Divine Community: Trinity, Church, and Ethics in Reformation Theologies* (Missouri: Northeast Missouri State University, 1981), p.19. Loeschen notes that Luther's distinction between "letter" and "spirit" finds its origin in the fathers, chiefly St. Augustine. See also Roland Bainton, *Here I stand: A Life of Martin Luther* (Nashville: Abingdon-Cokesburg Press, 1950), p.39, where he remarks that Staupitz exerts "a determinative influence" on Luther's theological development.

125   Pelikan, *Luther the Expositor*, Companion Volume to Luther's Works (St. Louis: Concordia Publishing House, 1959), p. 42. Cf. Pauck, *Lectures on the Romans*, p.xx.

126   Ebeling, "The New Hermeneutics and the Early Luther," *Theology Today* 21:1 (1964), p.36.

127   See *WA* 9, 65 as analyzed by Oberman, "*Facientibus Quod in se est Deus*

non denegat Gratiam," pp.119ff.

128   James Atkinson, ed., *Luther: Early Theological Works* in *The Library of Christian Classics,* XVI (Philadelphia: Westminster Press, 1962), pp. 269-270. See also Heinrich Boehmer, *Luther in the Light of Recent Research* (New York: The Christian Herald, 1916), p.87. By 1515, Luther referred to the nominalists as "hog-theologians"*(ibid).*

129   See *LW* 14, 284; *WA* 5, 21-23 (Preface to Psalm 1.2, 1519-1521)

130   See *Commentary on Genesis,* 2 vols., trans. & ed. J. Thedore Mueller (Grand Rapids: Zondervan, 1968), Vol. I, p.358.

131   See Pelikan, *Luther the Expositor,* pp. 149-189, where he observes four components of Luther's exegesis: the Scripture as the Word, the church tradition, the history of God's people and the defense of the doctrine.

132   See Pauck, *Lectures on Romans,* p.xxxii; Ebeling, "The New Hermeneutics and the Early Luther," p.41. For a thorough study of Luther's hermeneutics, see James Preus, *From Shadow to Promise : Old Testament Interpreter from Augustine to the Young Luther* (Cambridge: Harvard University Press, 1969), pp.142ff; A. Skevington Wood, *Captive to the Word* (Grand Rapids: Eerdmans, 1969). See also Jerry K. Robbins, ed. *The Essential Luther. A reader on Scripture, Redemption, and Society* (Grand Rapids: Baker Book House, 1991), p.26: "All the books of the Bible are to be evaluated in terms of Christ ... The Old Testament not only has great value in and of itself, but is 'the ground and proof of the New Testament'. Further, the New Testament unlocks the Old Testament ..." See *LW* 35, 236-237 (Prefaces to the Old Testament, 1545).

133   Thomas, "Luther's Canon: Christ Against Scripture," *Word and World* 8:2 (1988):142-143; cf. Jack Rogers and Donald McKim, *The Authority and Interpretation of the Bible* (New York: Harper & Row, 1979, pp.73-78. See *LW* 26,295: "Christ is Lord over Scripture and all works."

134   *LW* 35, 236; (Prefaces to the Old Testament, 1545).

135   *Ibid.*

136   Pelikan, *Luther the Expositor,* pp. 112-113. Cf. *LW* 26, 435; *WA* 40^1, 657, 13-14 (Galatians).

137   *Ibid.*

138   *Ibid.,* p.68; cf. *LW* 1, 331; *WA* 42, 243 (Lectures on Genesis, 1535)

139   See David W. Lotz, "The Proclamation of the Word in Luther's Thought,"
       Word and World 3:4 (1983):347: "In 18th century Lutheran theology, ...
       everything came to focus on the 'inscripturation' of the Word, its past
       encoding in a supernaturally perfect Book—thus leading to an almost
       complete identification of Word of God with the Bible and so to a static
       concept of the Word." Cf. Pelikan, *Luther the Expositor*, p.68:" ... While he
       (Luther) simply identified the Bible as 'the Word of God,' the Word as
       deed and the Word as proclamation were still included in the definition
       of what he meant by 'word.' For the Word as deed al*w*ays circumscribed
       the Word as proclamation. The proclamation was entitled to be called
       the 'Word of God,' only if it recited those deeds which were the 'Word of
       God.' And to do this task of reciting those deeds which were the 'Word
       of God' the oral proclamation had to rely on the 'Word of God' as
       Scripture."

140   Pelikan, *Luther the Expositor*, p.54.

141   *LW* 26, 29; *WA* 40^1, 77, 28 (Lectures on Galatians, 1535).

142   *LW* 14, 105; *WA* 31, 181 (Psalm 118, 1530). Moltmann, in his book, *The
       Crucified God*, borrowed Luther's phrase, *"gekreuzigte Gott,"* to develop
       his theology of the cross. This phrase appears more in Luther's homilet-
       ical and devotional writings. In his theological writings he distinguish-
       es its proper use from its improper use (see footnote 70 in *LW* 14, 105).

143   *LW* 41, 19; *WA* 50, 519, 18-27 (On the Councils and the Church, 1539).
       Also quoted in Lienhard, *Witness to Jesus*, p.78.

144   See Pelikan, *Luther the Expositor*, pp. 46-65; James Atkinson, *Martin
       Luther and the Birth of Protestantism* (Pelican Books, 1968), pp. 11-12;
       Heinrich Bornkamm, *Luther and the Old Testament*, trans. Eric W. & Ruth
       Gristsch (Philadelphia: Fortress Press, 19679), pp. 225-260. All three
       scholars concur upon Luther as a biblical theologian.

145   See Joseph Sittler, *The Doctrine of the Word in the Structure of Lutheranism*
       (Philadelphia: Fortress Press, 1948), pp. 3-4. Also quoted in Pelikan,
       Luther the Expositor, pp. 42-43.

146   See Walter von Loewenich, *Luther's Theology of the Cross*, trans. Herbert
       J. A. Boumann (Minneapolis: Augsburg Publishing House, 1976), pp. 13,
       17-18; Regin Prenter, *Luther's Theology of the Cross* (Philadelphia: Fortress
       Press, 1966), p.2; McGrath, *Luther's Theology of the Cross*, pp. 1-2;
       Lienhard, *Witness to Jesus* , pp. 65-66; Lortz, *The Reformation in Germany*,
       vol. 1, pp. 208 - 210; Althaus, *Theology of Luther*, p. 34; Gerhard Forde,

"Luther's Theology of the Cross," in *Christian Dogmatics,*. 2 vols, eds. Carl Braaten & Robert Jenson (Philadelphia: Fortress Press, 1984), vol. 2, pp. 47ff.

147   Loewenich, *Luther's Theology of the Cross*, p.13.

148   *Ibid.*, pp. 17-18. See also Charles Cousar, *A Theology of the Cross. The Death of Jesus in the Pauline Letters* (Minneapolis: Fortress Press, 1990), pp. 7-8.

149   See McGrath, *Luther's Theology of the Cross*, p.174; Althaus, *Theology of Luther*, p.34.

150   Quoted by Gerhard Ebeling, *Luther: An Introduction to His Thought*, trans. R.A. Wilson (Philadelphia: Fortress Press, 1970), p.248.

151   *LW* 31, 52-53; *WA* 1, 353-365. See Bainton, *Here I Stand*, p.51, where he says that Luther was lecturing on the Psalms at the time when he coined the term *"theologia crucis."* See also Atkinson, *Martin Luther and the Birth of Protestantism*, p.159. See also Hermann Sasse, "Theologia Crucis," *Lutheran Theological Journal* 11 (1968), p. 121-122.

152   Atkinson, *Martin Luther and the Birth of Protestantism*, p. 158, finds it unacceptable for the historians to put more emphasis on the 95 theses than on the Heidelberg Theses.

153   Vercruysse, "Luther's Theology of the Cross at the time of the Heidelberg Theses," *Gregorianum* 57 (1976):524.

154   *Ibid.*, pp. 524-525. The *Resolutions* or *Explanations of the 95 theses* were probably written in the early part of 1518, and finished around March of the same. The *Asterisci* was written between March 5th and 24th, according to the introductions of the critical edition of the Weimar. The *Lectures on Hebrews* was probably written towards the end of the course, so also around March 1518.

155   *Ibid.*, pp.526ff. See also Gordon Rupp, "Luther's Ninety-five These and the Theology of the Cross," in *Luther for an Ecumenical Age*, pp. 67 - 81.

156   The *Asterisci* in found in *WA* 1, 281-314 as quoted in Vercruysse, "Luther's Theology of the Cross", pp. 526 -528.

157   *WA* 1, 290, 39-291.2: "He (Eck) is so ignorant of the theology of the cross, that he believes it is certain for them that they will be saved, because they are God's friends and separated from the body" (Translation is

Vercryusse's).

158   *WA* 1, 291, 1ff; cf. *WA* 1, 294, 10: "I (Luther) don't deny some are saved."

159   Vercryusse, "Luther's Theology of the Cross," p. 527.

160   See "Ninety-Five Theses", 1517, *LW* 31, 27.

161   Vercryusse, "Luther's Theology of the Cross," p.528; cf. *WA* 1, 281, 28-31: "One does not find any scripture, nor any church father, nor any canon, but is scholastic (*scholasticissima*) and conjectural (*opioniossima*) and all bare fancies and exactly what I (Luther) am arguing against" as quoted in *ibid.*, p. 526.

162   *WA* 573, 79; cf. Atkinson, *ibid.*, pp. 233-234.

163   Vercryusse, "Luther's Theology of the Cross," p.530.

164   *LW* 31, 83-252; *WA* 1, 525-628.

165   See Lienhard, *Witness to Jesus*, p.63, where he observes that the *Lectures on Hebrews*, particularly in his emphasis on the cross, is close to the "*Resolutions*."

166   *WA* 1, 613, 7 as cited in Vercryusse, "Luther's Theology of the Cross", p.531.

167   *LW* 31.225; cf. Rupp, "Luther's Ninety-Five Theses," p.76; Vercryusse, *Ibid.*

168   See Thesis 7 of Ninety-five Theses in *LW* 31, 99: "... God works a strange work in order that he may work his own work" (I Kings 2 and Deut. 32-39 are quoted). Cf. Heidelberg Thesis 4, in *LW* 31, 44: "And that it is which Isaiah 28.21 calls the alien work of God that he may do his work..."

169   As quoted in Loewenich, *Luther's Theology of the Cross*, p.23. Also quoted in Carl Braaten, *Shadows of the Cross* (Toronto: Regis College, 1983), pp. 7-8; See Atkinson's Introduction to "Disputation against Scholastic Theology," in *Early Theological Works*, p. 265: "His (Luther) attack on Aristotelian scholasticism was in the interest of a true Christology, so that Christ be allowed to do his proper work."

170   Vercryusse, "Luther's Theology of the Cross," p.533. Cf. *LW* 31, 223; *WA* 1, 612, 22-4; *LW* 31, 224; *WA* 1, 614, 18.

171   *Ibid.*, p.533; Rupp, "Luther's Ninety-five Theses," p.76.

172   *WA* 1, 355, 30-32; Atkinson, *ibid*, p.281.

173   *Ibid.*

174   Prenter, *Luther's Theology the Cross* , p.4, identifies the doctrine of justifi-
        cation by faith with the theology of the cross: "The theology of the cross
        according to which the cross in my life destroys all my self-righteous-
        ness so that I am judged solely in the light of Christ's action on my
        behalf, through him alone I am made righteous before God, is identical
        with the main Lutheran doctrine of the justification of sinners through
        faith alone."

175   See McGrath, *Luther's Theology of the Cross*, pp. 146-147.   See also
        Loewenich, *Luther's Theology of the Cross*, p.116: "In this point Luther's
        doctrine of justification is a concrete application of his theology of the
        cross."

176   *WA* 1, 357-358; Atkinson, *ibid*, pp. 284-286.

177   *WA* 1, 360-361; Atkinson, *ibid.*, pp. 287-89; 295-304.

178   *Ibid.*

179   Rupp, *The Righteousness of God*, pp. 150-153. See also Harry J. McSorley,
        *Luther: Right or Wrong: An Ecumenical—Theological Study of Luther's Major
        Work, "The Bondage of the Will"* (New York: Newman Press, 1969), pp.
        224-273.

180   *LW* 10, 197; *WA* 3, 238.

181   *LW* 11, 453; *WA* 3, 453, 1-5

182   See *LW* 25, 157; *WA* 56, 177, where Luther says that "this theological
        'insight of the conscience' is in all men and cannot be obscured."

183   *LW* 25, 222; *WA* 56, 237.

184   *LW* 25, 245; *WA* 56, 345.

185   *LW* 25, 262; *WA* 56, 275.

186   *WA* 1, 359, 32-33; Atkinson, *ibid.*, p.287. See *WA* 1, 360; Atkinson, *ibid.*,

p.288.

187   *LW* 25, 274; *WA* 56, 287. See also Carter Lindberg, *The Third Reformation?*
      Charismatic Movements and the Lutheran Tradition (Macon, Georgia:
      Mercer University Press, 1983), pp. 47-48, who says that justification is,
      for Luther, to be understood in terms of God's "descent" to the level of
      the human under the rubric "theology of the cross," thereby conversely
      rejecting all theologies of human "ascent" to God which Luther labeled
      "theologies of glory."

188   *WA* 1, 364, 23-224; Atkinson, *ibid*, p.294.

189   *LW* 31, 52ff; *WA* 1, 362.

190   *WA* 1, 362, 21-22; Atkinson, *ibid*., p.290. See Philip Watson, *Let God Be*
      God. An interpretation of the Theology of Martin Luther. (London: Epworth
      Press, 1948), p.85. For a discussion of Luther's thought against scholas-
      ticism, see Brian Gerrish, *Grace and Reason* (Oxford: Clarendon Press,
      1962), pp.43ff.

191   *LW* 31, 52; *WA* 1, 361, 36.

192   *WA* 1, 362, 21-22; Atkinson, *ibid*, p.290.

193   *Ibid.*

194   Pannenberg, "A Theology of the Cross, "*Word and World* 8:2 (1988),
      p.162. Pannenberg notes that what Luther rejected as *theologia gloriae*
      was the self-glorification of works righteousness. This theology was
      broadened to include "the method of philosophical theology, because in
      Luther's opinion it was this method that led to the definition of justice as
      virtue and finally to works righteousness" (p.163). See *LW* 31, 227; *WA*
      1, 614, 17-22 (Explanation of the 95 Theses, 1518): "The theologian of
      glory, however, learns from Aristotle that the object of the will is good
      and the good is worthy to be loved, while the evil, on the other hand, is
      worthy of hate. He learns that God is the highest good and exceeding
      loveable." See also his "Disputation Against Scholastic Theology", 1517,
      LW 31, 9-10; *WA* 1, 224, where Luther rejects the efficacy of the will: "One
      must concede that the will is not free to strive toward whatever is
      declared good. This is in opposition to Scotus and Gabriel" (thesis 10).

195   See *LW* 51, 26; *WA* 1, 138, 13-14.

196   *LW* 31, 53; *WA* 1, 362, 14.

197   *WA* 1, 354. See McGrath, *Luther's Theology of the Cross*. p. 146-148.

198   *WA* 1, 362, 21-22; Atkinson, *ibid*, p.290.

199   *LW* 31, 52-53; *WA* 1, 362, 18-19.

200   *Ibid.*

201   *Ibid.* In speaking of God's self-revelation in Christ, however, Luther does
        not reject the revelation of God that comes through natural reason and
        knowledge. Both his 1515-1516 Romans commentary and his 1535
        Galatians commentary speak positively about natural knowledge of
        God (See *LW* 25, 157; *WA* 56, 177, 11-14; *LW* 27, 53; *WA* 40^2, 66, 34-37).
        Such knowledge of God, though useful in the worldly realm, is corrupt-
        ed by sin, and therefore must not be construed as God's self-revelation
        of God, leading humanity to justification *coram Deo*. See also *LW* 44, 336;
        WA 8, 629, 24-27 (On Monastic Vows, 1521): "Reason can do this much:
        it can recognize God as a terrible, wrathful judge, who leaves us no place
        to hide, neither in this world or in hell." When reason seeks to take the
        place of faith, Luther says, *"ratio adversatur fidem"* (See *LW* 34, 160; *WA*
        39^1, 90, 23—"Disputation on Justification", 1536). Luther accepts the
        understanding of "reason, illumined by faith" which grasps the victory
        of Christ (See *LW* 26, 284; *WA* 40^1, 443-444).

202   *LW* 31, 53; *WA* 1, 362, 21-22.

203   *WA* 1, 362, 4-14; Atkinson, *ibid*, pp. 290-291.

204   See *WA* 5, 176, 32-33 as quoted in McGrath, *Luther's Theology of the Cross*,
        p.1. See also McGrath, *The Making of Modern German Christology* (Oxford:
        Basil Blackwell, 1986), pp. 187-188.

205   Pelikan, *Reformation of Church and Dogma*, p.155.

206   McGrath, *Luther's Theology of the Cross*, p.150.

207   Loewenich, *Luther's Theology of the Cross*, p.113.

208   McGrath, *Luther's Theology of the Cross*, p.150. See also Douglas John
        Hall, *Lighten Our Darkness : Toward An Indigenous Theology of the Cross*.
        (Philadelphia: Westminster, 1976), p.117, where he speaks of the unity of
        the cross of Christ and that of the Christian: "the theology of the cross
        can never be a brilliant statement about life's brokenness, because it par-
        ticipates in what it seeks to describe. Apart from that participation, it

would be empty chatter."

209   *Ibid.,* p.151.

210   *LW* 31, 53; *WA* 1, 362, 30ff.

211   McGrath, *Luther's Theology of the Cross,* p.151. See also John Strelan, *"Theologia Crucis, Theologia Gloriae:* A Study in Opposing Theologies," *Lutheran Theological Journal* 23 (Dec., 1989): 89-100.

212   *WA* 1, 365, 9-24; Atkinson, *ibid,* p.295.

213   *Ibid.*

Chapter Three: Christology and Divine Suffering

1   See *LW* 26, 28-29; *WA* 40^1, 77-78 (Galatians, 1535).

2   *LW* 24, 23; *WA* 45, 481-482 (John, 1537-38).

3   *LW* 34, 208; *WA* 50, 267, 18 (The Three Symbols or Creeds of Christian Faith, 1538). See also Nagel, "Heresy, Doctor Luther, Heresy!" pp.26ff.

4   For a detailed study on Luther's Christology, see Lienhard, *Witness to Jesus* and Siggins, *Luther's Doctrine of Christ.*

5   *LW* 24, 23; *WA* 45, 481-482.

6   See *WA TR* 2, 16:1265 (Table Talk Recorded by John Schlaginhaufen, 1531-1532) as quoted in Siggins, *Luther's Doctrine of Christ,* p.209.

7   See *LW* 41, 121 (On the Councils and the Church, 1539). Also quoted by Carl Braaten, "The Fundamentals of Dogmatics," in *Christian Dogmatics,* p.47.

8   See Leslie Prestige, *God in Patristic Thought,* (London: S. P. C. K., 1952) p.76. Lienhard, *Witness to Jesus,* pp. 28-29; Siggins, *Luther's Doctrine of Christ,* p.223, notes that Luther doubted the adequacy of the Chalcedonian orthodoxy; for instance, the traditional meaning of "person" presents a difficulty for Luther since "person" may carry more than one sense, even in Christological statements.

9   Lienhard, *Witness to Jesus,* p.28.

10   See *LW* 22, 110, footnote 83; *LW* 24, 90-91, footnote 52.

11 *LW* 29, 111; *WA* 57, 111 (Hebrews, 1516). See also "On the Councils and the Church," 1539, *LW* 41, 100-110.

12 *Ibid.*

13 See *WA* 10^{1,1}, 208, 24 as cited in Lienhard, *ibid*, p.155.

14 See *WA* 12, 585-591 (Church Postils, 1523) as cited in Lienhard, *ibid.*, p.189 (his translation). See also Victor C. Pfitzer, "Luther as Interpreter of John's Gospel with special reference to his Sermons on the Gospel of John," *Lutheran Theological Journal* 18(1984):65-73; John T. Pless, "Martin Luther: Preacher of the Cross," *Concordia Theological Quarterly* 51(1987), pp.97-98. Althaus, in his *Theology of Luther*, pp.181-188, identifies a movement in Luther's Christology, that is "from below to above": "from Christ as man to Christ as God and thereby to God."

15 See *LW* 37, 72 (Confession on Christ's Supper, 1528): "But the glory of our God is precisely that for our sakes he comes down to the very depths, into human flesh, into the bread, into our mouth, our heart, our bosom;..." See also William Hordern, *Experience and Faith. The Significance of Luther for Understanding Today's Experiential Religion* (Minneapolis: Augsburg Publishing House, 1983), pp. 89-90.

16 See *LW* 24, 23; *WA* 45, 481-482 (John, 1538).

17 See *LW* 22, 492-493 (John, 1537).

18 Watson, *Let God Be God*, p.152.

19 See *WA* 10^{1,1}, 158, 16 (Church Postil, on Heb. 1:2-3, 1522); Cf. *LW* 29, 155; *WA* 57^3, 151, 14-15 (Hebrews, 1517-1518): "For through faith a man becomes like the Word of God, but the Word is the Son of God." See also M. J. Harran, *Luther on Conversion: The Early Years* (London: Cornell University Press, 1983), p.116.

20 See Prenter, *Spiritus Creator*, pp. 107ff, where he noted Augustine's influence upon Luther's Christological hermeneutics.

21 *LW* 22, 9; *WA* 46, 544, 3-10 (John 1:1, 1537).

22 Watson, *Let God Be God*, p.152.

23 See *LW* 52, 20, 23 (The Gospel for Christmas Eve, LK.2:1-14, 1522).

24   Lotz, "The Proclamation of the Word in Luther's Thought," p.346.

25   *LW* 35, 237 (Prefaces to the Old Testament).

26   *Ibid.*

27   *Ibid.*

28   See *LW* 35, 123 (A Brief Instruction on what to Look for and Expect in the Gospels, 1521) as cited in Lotz, "The Proclamation of the Word in Luther's Thought," pp. 346-347.

29   *LW* 35, 236 (Prefaces to the Old Testament).

30   *LW* 52, 205 (The Gospel for the Festival of the Epiphany, Matt. 2:1-12).

31   *LW* 52, 206.

32   *Ibid.*

33   See *LW* 35, 22; *WA* $10^{1,1}$, 181 as cited in John Wilch, "Luther as Interpreter: Christ and the Old Testament," *Consensus* 9:4 (1983), p.11.

34   See *WA BR* 5:2-3 as cited in Wilch, *ibid.*, p.12.

35   See *WA* 24, 16 as cited in Wilch, *ibid.* See also Bornkamm, *Luther and the Old Testament*, pp. 84-85.

36   See *WA* 17^2, 132; *WA* 19, 595-7; *LW* 14, 257-259 as cited in Wilch, *ibid.*, p.13.

37   Bornkamm, *Luther and the Old Testament*, pp. 202-203.

38   See *LW* 1, 18; *WA* 42, 14-15; *WA* 14, 100; *WA TR* 5, 361 (#5800) as cited in Wilch, "Luther as Interpreter," p.12.

39   *LW* 12, 33.

40   *LW* 15, 328; *WA* 54, 79.

41   See Bornkamm, *Luther and the Old Testament*, pp. 202-203, 206; cf. *LW* 15, 313; *WA* 54, 66-67.

42   For a study of Luther's view of *promissio*, see Preus, *From Shadow to Promise*. See also Pelikan, *Luther the Expositor*, p.59.

43   *LW* 12, 54; *WA* 402, 300, 27-36 (Psalm 2, 1532).

44   See Thomas F. Torrance, *The Trinitarian Faith* (Edinburgh: T. & T. Clark Ltd., 1988), p.170.

45   *LW* 12, 49.

46   See *LW* 12, 54.

47   See McGuckin, "The 'Theopaschite Confession'," p.250.

48   *LW* 12, 55.

49   *LW* 12, 52.

50   *Ibid.*

51   *Ibid.*

52   *LW* 26, 273; *WA* 40^1, 427, 21-22.

53   *Ibid.*

54   See Sayers, "The Shattering Dogmas of the Christian Tradition," in *Christian Letters to a Post-Christian World* (Grand Rapids: Wm. B. Eerdmans, 1969), p.14.

55   See *LW* 15, 293; *WA* 54, 49-50 (Last Words of David, 1543) as cited in "The Formula of Concord" 8:85, in *The Book of Concord: The Confessions of the Evangelical Lutheran Church*, trans. & ed. Theodore G. Tappert (Philadelphia: Fortress Press, 1959), p.608.

56   *LW* 26, 273; *WA* 40^1, 427.

57   *Ibid.*

58   See *WA* 39^2, 99, 10-15 (Die Disputation de divinitate et humanitate Christi, 1540): "Schwencfeld does not see this; so when he hears the Fathers say that Christ is a creature according to His humanity, he immediately attacks, distorts, and misuses the phrase for his own ends. Even if the Fathers should say: Christ is a creature according to His humanity, this can be tolerated in some way; but Schwencfeld wickedly remarks: Therefore Christ is simply a creature. Why do you not add: Christ is a creator according to His divinity?"

59   *Ibid.*

60   *LW* 13, 228; *WA* 41, 80, 13-16 (Psalm 110, 1532).

61   *Ibid.*

62   *LW* 12, 282 (Psalm 45, 1532).

63   *LW* 12, 98 (Psalm 8, 1537).

64   *LW* 12, 50 (Psalm 2, 1532).

65   *LW* 24, 97; *WA* 45, 549, 5-8 (John, 1537). See also Siggins, *Luther's Doctrine of Christ*, p.223.

66   *LW* 13, 313 (Psalm 110:4).

67   *LW* 12, 45.

68   *LW* 13, 240.

69   See Lienhard, *Witness to Jesus*, p.378.

70   *WA* 39^2, 98, 6ff (on the disputation on the Divinity and Humanity of Christ, 1540).

71   *WA* 39^2, 95, 32; 34. Also quoted in Lienhard, *Witness to Jesus*, p. 329.

72   See *WA* 39^2, 98, 6ff; 101, 19; 102, 3; 106, 26ff; 114, 15ff as cited in Lienhard, *ibid.*, p.329.

73   *WA* 39^2, 100, 6-12: "M. Lutheri contra Schwenkfeldi Argumenta contraria. Alia est persona Deus, alia homo. Christus et homo et Deus. Ergo sunt in eo duae personae. R. In Philosophia est verum."

74   *WA* 39^2, 100, 9-23: "One is the person of humanity, the other is the person of divinity. However, both humanity and divinity are in Christ. Therefore, there are two persons in Christ. Response (Luther's). This is the fallacy of composition and division. In the former you divide human and divine nature; in the latter you join them. This is a philosophical solution, but we express it theologically. I refute the consequence because the humanity and divinity constitute one person in Christ. But these two natures are distinct in theology according to their

natures and not according to the person. They are indistinct, but two distinct natures, although indistinct persons. They are not two distinct persons, but are distinct and indistinct; that is they are distinct natures but indistinct persons."

75   See *LW* 38, 253 (The Word Became Flesh, 1539).

76   *LW* 38, 272.

77   *LW* 38, 247.

78   *LW* 38, 274.

79   *LW* 38, 239.

80   *LW* 38, 273.

81   See *WA* 39², 117,35.

82   See *WA* 39², 117,33.

83   See *WA* 39², 116,3.

84   See *WA* 39², 118,3-4.

85   See Lienhard, *Witness to Jesus*, p.342. It must be borne in mind that Luther did not use the term "hypostatic union," rather he used the term "personal union." However both carry the same meaning. For a study of *extra-calvinisticum*,see E. David Willis, *Calvin's Catholic Christology. The Function of the So-called Extra Calvinisticum in Calvin's Theology* (Leiden: E.J. Brill, 1966). See also Braaten, "Classical Christology and its Criticism," p. 509, where he quotes the Heidelberg Catechism: "Because the divinity is everywhere present, it must follow that it is indeed outside its adopted humanity and yet none the less also in the same and remains in personal union with it." The Logos, for the Calvinists, is infinite, and thus must exist *extra carnem*, unlimited by its union with the flesh. The Lutherans countered the *extra-Calvinisticum* by coining the phrase "*totus intra carnem and numquam extra carnem.*"

86   See Nagel, "Heresy, Doctor Luther, Heresy!" p.46

87   *LW* 26, 265; *WA* 40¹, 415, 30.

88   See *WA* 25, 106, 33-107 (1532-34) as quoted in Lienhard, *Witness to Jesus*,

p.342. See also *LW* 24, 5; *WA* 45, 520.

89   See *WA* 39^2, 25, 17.

90   *LW* 26, 266; *WA* 40^1, 416,10-12; cf. *LW* 24, 65; *WA* 45, 520.

91   See Gerhard O. Forde, *Where God Meets Man: Luther's Down-to-Earth Approach to the Gospel* (Minneapolis: Augsburg Publishing House, 1972).

92   *LW* 24, 65; *WA* 45, 520.

93   See *LW* 22, 361-362 as cited in Hordern, *Experience and Faith*, p.90.

94   See Isao Kuramatsu, *"Die gegenwärtige Kreuzestheologie und Luther, besonders in Rüecksicht auf die Theologie des Schmerzes Gottes von Kazo Kitamori," Kerygma and Dogma* 36 (1990), p.281, where he, in agreement with Lienhard, affirms *"Luther als Deipassionist in dem Sinne, daß Gott der persönliche, in Christus gegenwärtige und am Leiden des Menschen mitbeteiligte Gott ist."* According to Kuramatsu, Kitamori was the first advocate of God's suffering in the later 20th century. Kuramatsu seems to forget the reformed theologian, Karl Barth, whose theopaschite position preceded Kitamori's. See Russell, "Impassibility and Pathos in Barth's Idea of God," pp. 221-222.

95   Loewenich, *Luther's Theology of the Cross*, p.36. See also *LW* 17, 131-133; *WA* 25^2, 363-365 (Isaiah, 1529).

96   *LW* 21, 340; *WA* 7, 585, 86 (The Magnificat, 1521).

97   Kasper, Jesus the Christ, trans. V. Green (New York: Paulist Press, 1976), p.180.

98   See *LW* 22, 362 where it said: "crucify the Son of God," "the Lord of glory."

99   Siggins, *Luther's Doctrine of Christ*, pp.234ff.

100 Lienhard, *Witness to Jesus*, p.336. See also Grillmeier, *Christ in Christian Tradition*, pp.122 & 131. It was above all John of Damascus who developed the *communicatio idiomatum*.

101 See Robert Jenson, *The Unbaptized God. The Basic Flaw in Ecumenical Theology* (Philadelphia: Fortress Press, 1992), p.122.

102 Lienhard, *Witness to Jesus*, p.336. Both Thomas and Calvin affirm that

the communication is indeed real with respect to the person, designated by the deity or humanity. On Calvin's view on the doctrine of *communicatio idiomatum*, see his *Institutes of the Christian Religion*, II, xiv. 2ff. On Thomas' view, see Michael Dodds, "Aquinas, Human Suffering, and the Unchanging God of Love," *Theological Studies* 52 (1991): 330-344.

103   Jenson, *The Unbaptized God*, p.122.

104   See WA 10^{1,1}, 150, 21 as cited in Lienhard, *Witness to Jesus*, p.171.

105   *LW* 30, 222-223; *WA* 20, 603, 19.

106   *LW* 37, 210-211; *WA* 26, 321-322 as quoted in Martin Chemnitz, *The Two Natures in Christ*, trans. J.A.O. Preus (St. Louis: Concordia Publishing House, 1971), p.193. The above translation is Preus'.

107   *Ibid.* This thesis does not concern Luther's eucharistic theology as a whole except to deal briefly with the suffering of God in relation to the *communicatio idiomatum*.

108   Lienhard, *Witness to Jesus*, pp. 337ff. See Wolfhart Pannenberg, *Jesus-God and Man*, trans. Lewis L. Wilkins & Duane A. Priebe (Philadelphia: Westminster Press, 1977), p. 299: "Zwingli said nothing of a real community between Christ's divine and human natures lying at the basis of that figurative speech (*a praedicatio verbalis*)." That "God suffers", for Zwingli, has no "ontological status." See also Althaus, *Theology of Luther*, pp.196ff.

109   *LW* 37, 212; *WA* 26, 319 as quoted by *The Formula of Concord,*, p. 599.

110   *Ibid.*

111   See *LW* 23, 101-103; *WA* 33, 153-155 (John, 1537).

112   *LW* 37, 214. Cf. Moltmann, *The Crucified God*, pp. 232-233.

113   See *LW* 37, 209-210 as quoted in, Article VII, in *The Formula of Concord*, p. 598. *Alloeosis* is defined by Zwingli in 1527: "an exchange or substitution of two natures that are one person, by which one is named and the other is meant, or that is named which they both are and yet one of them is meant." See also *LW* 23, 101; *WA* 33, 153-154.

114   See *WA* 26, 319 as cited in Jenson, *The Unbaptized God*, p.129.

115   See *LW* 37, 209-210.

116   See *LW* 27, 212.

117   See *WA* 26, 321 as quoted in Jenson, *The Unbaptized God*, p.129.

118   See *WA* 26, 322 as quoted in Jenson, *ibid*, p.129. See also Lienhard, *Witness to Jesus*, pp. 214-215.

119   See *WA* 40³, 87, 16 (Schwabach Articles, 1529) as cited in Werner Elert, *The Structure of Lutheranism*, vol. 1., trans. Walter Hansen (St. Louis: Concordia Publishing House, 1962), p.227.

120   See *LW* 22, 321.

121   See *WA* 45, 300, 37ff as quoted in Lienhard, *Witness to Jesus*, p.338.

122   See *WA* 45, 301, 21-25 as cited in Lienhard, *Ibid.* .

123   See *LW* 24, 105; *WA* 45, 556 (John, 1538).

124   *LW* 24, 106; *WA* 45, 557.

125   *Ibid.*

126   See *LW* 38, 254. See also Elert, *The Structure of Lutheranism*, p.228.

127   See *WA* 10, 579-581 (Briefwechsel No: 3994, 1544).

128   See *LW* 22, 491-492. See also John Loeschen, *Wrestling with Luther* (St. Louis: Concordia Publishing House, 1976), pp. 133ff; Yves M.J. Congar, "Considerations and Reflections on the Christology of Luther," in his *Dialogue Between Christians*, trans. Philip Loretz (Westminster: The Newman Press, 1966), pp. 393-395; J.A. Dorner, *History of the Development of the Doctrine of the Person of Christ* (Edinburgh: T & T Clark, 1839), vol. 1., p.104.

129   *Ibid.*

130   See *WA* 50, 590 (On the Councils and the Church, 1539) as cited in *The Formula of Concord*, p. 599. Also cited in Ted Peters, *God—the World's Future* (Minneapolis: Fortress Press, 1992), p.198, where he argues, on the basis of this text, that "for Luther the divine nature was present throughout the earthly life of Jesus, suffering the slings and arrows of human fortune."

131   See *WA* 10^{1,1}, 11ff as cited in Reiner Jansen, *Stuiden zu Luthers Trinitätslehre* (Frankfurt: Peter Lang, 1976), p.115.

132   Jansen, *Studien zu Luthers Trinitätslehre*, p. 120.

133   Peters, *God —the World's Future*, p. 198.

134   *LW* 41, 100.

135   Jansen, *Studien zu Luthers Trinitätslehre*, p.116.

136   *LW* 41, 101.

137   *Ibid.*

138   *LW* 41, 105 & 102.

139   *LW* 41, 101-102.

140   *LW* 41, 103. For Luther the Council at Ephesus "condemned far too little of Nestorius, for it dealt with only one *idioma*, that God was born of Mary. Thus the histories relate that it was resolved in this council, in opposition to Nestorius, that Mary should be called *Theotokos*, 'bearer of God,' even though Nestorius denied to God in Christ all *idiomata* of human nature such as dying, cross, suffering and everything that is compatible with the Godhead. This is why they should not have just resolved that Mary was *Theotokos*, but also Pilate and the Jews were crucifiers and murderers of God..." (p.104).

141   *LW* 15, 341-342; *WA* 54, 91-92; *LW* 41, 117-118. See also *WA* 594,7; 602,12 as cited in Lienhard, *Witness to Jesus*, p.317. According to the Patristic evidence, Eutyches does not refuse to ascribe the attributes of the divine nature to the human nature; he does not accept that there is a human nature, but affirms the one nature of the *Logos*. Here Luther seeks to reconstruct the heresy of Eutyches in his own direction, especially when he applies the doctrine of the *communicatio idiomatum* to his Christology. He reapproaches Eutyches, notes Lienhard, "for failing to bind sufficiently strongly the humanity and the divinity, since, according to Luther, he refused to apply the attributes of the divinity to the humanity." Lienhard further remarks: "In reality, Eutyches had so strongly bound them together that humanity disappeared! This is a point that Luther did not see...because he was above all attached to the idea of the unity of Christ" (*Ibid*).

142   See *WA* 50, 596, 16; 598, 15 as cited in Siggins, *Luther's Doctrine of Christ,*

p.236.

143   *LW* 15, 341-342; *WA* 54, 91-92.

144   See *WA* 40^3, 707, 22-27 (Isaiah 53, 1544) as cited in Lienhard, *Witness to Jesus*, p.456 and Chemnitz, *The Two Natures in Christ*, pp. 191-192.

145   See Mozley, *The Impassibility of God*, p.133.

146   See Lienhard, *Witness to Jesus*, p.341. See also *LW* 26, 267; *WA* 40^1, 416, 10-12, where the Cappadocian image of iron/fire is employed by Luther to express the mutual penetration of the divine and human properties in Christ: "Whoever touches the heat in the heated iron touches the iron; and whoever has touched the skin of Christ has actually touched God."

147   See Lienhard, *Witness to Jesus*, p.341; Mozley, *The Impassibility of God*, p.121: Cyril's "distinction between the proper nature of the Word and the body which the Word has made His own vanishes in Luther's exposition."

148   See Graham White, "Luther's view on Language," *Literature and Theology* 3 (1989): 188-218, for a study of Luther's use of the new language.

149   *Ibid.*, p.189.

150   See *WA* 39^2, 93ff (On the divinity and humanity of Christ, 1540). I shall use translations of White and Nagel.

151   See *WA* 39^2, 93, 3-9; 94, 7-8, 11-12, 17-18.

152   See *WA* 39^2, 343 as cited in Nagel, "Heresy, Doctor Luther, Heresy!" p. 46.

153   See *WA* 39^2, 94, 17-18.

154   Nagel, "Heresy, Doctor Luther, Heresy!" p.47.

155   See *WA* 39^2, 120, 8 as cited in Nagel, "Heresy, Doctor Luther, Heresy!" p.46 (Nagel's translation).

156   See *WA* 39^2, 107, 27-29; 101.4—102.8 as cited in Nagel, *Ibid.*

157   Braaten, "Classical Christology and its Criticism," pp. 508-510. See also

Althaus, *Theology of Luther*, pp. 197-198. Martin Chemnitz developed three-fold ideas of *communicatio idiomatum* —a form of speaking about Christ (*genus idiomatum*), a form of Christ's working (*genus apoteles-maticum*), a description of Christ's person (*genus maiestaticum*)—to understand the mystery of our Lord's divine-human person. See his The *Two Natures in Christ*; Pannenberg, *Jesus—God and Man*, p.300.

158   See *WA TR* 6, 67ff (Aurifaber, 1541). See also *WA* 47, 199, 20-28 (Sermon on John 3, 1538-1540): "You know that there is a *communicatio idiomatum*, that in the Lord Christ there are two natures, and yet one person, and that these two natures have and hold each other's properties and even share them with each other." Cited in Lienhard, *Witness to Jesus*, p. 356, and Mozley, *The Impassibility of God*, p.122.

159   *LW* 22, 346; *WA* 47, 42 (John, 1537). See Thomas G. Weinandy, *Does God Change? The Word's Becoming in the Incarnation* (Still River, Massachusetts: St. Bede's Publications, 1985), p. 105, says of Luther: The *communicatio* motif is "not divine and human attributes predicated of the one person of the Logos, but rather the mutual interchange and com-munication of the divine and human properties from the one nature to the other." On Calvin's rejection of a real communication of properties between the natures, see his *Institutes of the Christian Religion*, II. xiv. 2ff as cited in Pannenberg, *Jesus-God and Man*, pp. 299-300.

160   *LW* 26, 265; *WA* 40^1, 416, 10-12 (Galatians, 1535).

161   *Ibid.*

162   Pannenberg, *Jesus-God and Man*, p.299.

163   *LW* 26, 267; *WA* 40^1, 418, 14.

164   *LW* 26, 265; *WA* 40^1, 416, 10-12.

165   *LW* 26, 267; *WA* 40^1, 416, 10-12: "Therefore faith is the 'do-all' in works...."

166   *Ibid.*

167   *WA* 39^2, 117, 35.

168   See *WA* 39^2, 13, 13; cf. *WA* 392, 26, 4 and 29, 33 (The Word was Made Flesh, 1539) as cited in Nagel, "Heresy, Doctor Luther, Heresy!" p.47.

169   See *WA* 39², 9, 9 as cited in Nagel, *ibid.*

170   Nagel, *ibid.*, p. 43.

171   See *WA* 39², 94, 17-22. Cf. *LW* 38, 253 (The Word was made Flesh, 1539): "... man according to philosophy is an existing person, but in theology he is certain divinity in Christ."

172   See *WA* 39², 105, 4-7: "In the old language a creature is that which the creator creates and separates from himself, but this signification has no place in the creature Christ (in theology). There the creator and creature are one and the same."

173   See *WA TR* 6, 68, 18ff as cited in Lienhard, *Witness to Jesus*, p.357; also cited in Mozley, *The Impassibility of God*, p.122.

174   See *Tischreden* 7:551 (von dem Herrn Christo, 1541) in vol. 58, 35-40 (Erlangen Edition) as cited by Mozley, *The Impassibility of God*, p. 122 (Translation is Mozley's). See also *WA TR* VI. 6600, 67-70.

175   *Ibid.*, cf. *LW* 22, 492-492. See also Hordern, *Experience and Faith*, p.90.

176   Althaus, *Theology of Luther*, p.197. See also Andrew Sung Park, *The Wounded Heart of God. The Asian Concept of Han and the Christian Doctrine of Sin*(Nashville: Abingdon Press, 1993),pp.115-116.

177   See *WA* 39², 120, 21-2; 121, 1-2: "The divinity in Christ did not feel pain. God is divinity. Therefore, he did not feel pain on the cross, and accordingly he did not suffer. Response: This is the communication of attributes. Those things which Christ suffered are attributed to God since they are one."

178   See *WA* 39², 121, 6-12: "Whatever is subject to death is not God. Christ was subject to death. Therefore, Christ is not God. Response: There is the communion of properties, and there is also a philosophical argument. The Scripture does not say: This man created the world. God suffered. Therefore, these attributes must not be used. Response: The error lies not in the words but in the meaning; although the Scripture does not use these words, nevertheless it has the same force."

179   See *WA* 39², 101, 24-28 as quoted in Siggins, *Luther's Doctrine of Christ*, p.236 (Siggins' translation).

180   See *WA* 39², 112. 13-21 as cited in Nagel, "Heresy, Doctor Luther,

Heresy!" pp. 44-45 (Nagel's translation).

181   See *WA* 39^2, 102, 24-27.

182   See *WA*39^2, 103, 24-31.

183   *LW* 22, 492.

184   *WA* 39^2, 112, 13-16.

185   Jansen, *Studien zu Luthers Trinitätslehre*, p. 116: "However, Scripture wit-
       nesses now that God's Son suffers. Though this refers first of all to
       Christ's human nature, His divine nature is meant at the same time. For
       Scripture does not neatly distribute its remarks on Christ between both
       natures, but rather refers them to the Person of Christ. The person of
       Christ however is—by the power of *enhypostasis* of Christ's human
       nature in God—God's Son, 'truly God.' Luther therefore is thinking of
       the unity of the two natures in such a way that every interpretation of
       the one nature immediately touches upon the other. All that happens to
       Christ's human nature also happens to the divinity and vice-versa.
       When Christ's human nature suffers, then His divine nature suffers also
       with it."

186   See *WA* 39^2, 279, 26 (*Promotionsthesen für Georg Major*, 1544). Also cited
       in Althaus, *Theology of Luther*, p.197 and Lienhard, *Witness to Jesus*, p. 341.

187   See Lienhard, *ibid., p.344.*

188   See *LW* 22, 352; cf. *LW* 22, 291-298.

189   *LW* 22, 491-492: "... these two natures are so united that there is only one
       God and Lord, that Mary suckles God... that Pilate and Herod crucified
       and killed God. ..."

190   See *WA* 50, 590 as quoted in *The Formula of Concord*, p. 599; also quoted
       in Braaten, *Shadows of the Cross*, p.10.

191   Cf. Lienhard, *Witness to Jesus*, pp. 317, 344-346, where he argues that the
       doctrine of the *communicatio idiomatum* is so emphasized that Luther's
       thought departs from the Chalcedonian tradition, bringing him danger-
       ously near to monophysitism and docetism. Luther is certainly aware of
       the danger. How Luther faces the charges of monophysitism and
       docetism remains an open question.

192   See Jansen, *Studien zu Luthers Trinitätslehre*, pp. 118-119: "In emphasizing also that God in his nature cannot suffer Luther stands of course in the theopaschite tradition. As is shown by his criticism of Nestorius, he knows the apathy axiom 'that God and suffering do not rhyme with one another.' Nevertheless he admits that one should answer to the charge of reason 'certainly the divinity cannot suffer and die': 'That is true.' This does not hinder the reformer from making the theopaschite statement that God and dying come together and belong in the one person of Jesus Christ." Cf. Jenson, *The Unbaptized God*, pp. 128-129, who notes that Luther was "driven by the doctrine of justification to amend the standard Christology drastically,... (but) in a hyper-Alexandrian direction," and sees "no fortitude to attack the axiom of impassibility directly." However Jenson's observation falls within the period where Luther countered Zwingli on the issue of omnipresence of the humanity of Christ, i.e. in 1528. A direct attack on the axiom of impassibility is evident in his interpretation of the Council of Ephesus (AD 431) where he countered Nestorius' Christology. (See his "On the Councils and the Church," 1539).

193   See *LW* 28, 264-267; *WA* 26, 37-40 (I Timothy, 1528).

194   *Ibid.*

195   Cf. Jüngel, *God as the Mystery of the World*, pp. 35ff. Jüngel holds that Christian theology is fundamentally the theology of the crucified Jesus. He asserts: "God is not necessary in a worldly sense; God is groundless in the worldly sense." Jüngel opts for a theology of revelation in which God is radically free to determine Himself in the cross of Jesus Christ. See also his, "The Christian Understanding of Suffering," *Journal of Theology for Southern Africa* 65 (1988), pp. 8-9: "... the bright light of the Gospel is cast upon the question about God and about suffering from that work of God in which he has made himself known—yes, from that work in which he has wholly and definitely made himself known: from out of God's revelation in that human being called Jesus we recognize God has to do with the suffering humanity. For this man Jesus is the essence of suffering humanity. His history is the history of suffering, passion history. In his history we recognize who God is because God has identified himself with this man. Whoever sees him sees God (Jn. 12:45; 14:7,9)."

196   See *The Formula of Concord*, 8:85, p.608. Siggins, in his *Luther's Doctrine of Christ*, p.236, holds that for Luther, God suffers only after the Incarnation.

197   See *LW* 24, 97; *WA* 45, 548 (John, 1538). See also *LW* 15, 341; *WA* 54, 90-

91 (Last Words of David, 1543).

198   Nagel, "Heresy, Doctor Luther, Heresy!" pp. 38-39. See also Hermann
       Sasse, *We Confess Jesus Christ*, trans. Norman Nagel (St. Louis: Concordia
       Publishing House, 1984), pp. 39-41.

Chapter Four: Soteriology and Divine Suffering

1   This study follows the thesis of Ian Siggins, who holds that while motifs
       from all the historic astonement theories are present in Luther's thought,
       there is no single "nucleus" in his atonement thought. See Siggins,
       Luther's Doctrine of Christ, pp. 113-143. It has been argued that either the
       penal-substitution or the *Christus Victor* motif is dominant. See H.D.
       MacDonald, *The Atonement of the Death of Christ* (Michigan: Baker Book
       House, 1985), p.182, where the penal motif is seen as primary. Aulen, in
       his *Christus Victor*, sees the *Christus Victor* as dominant (pp. 101-104).
       Althaus, however, sees a combination of the classical and Latin concepts,
       but leans more toward the latter. See his *Theology of Luther*, p.222.

2   See Luther's "The Small Catechism,"1529, in *The Book of Concord*, p.345.

3   See LW 37, 362; WA 26, 501, 29-35; also cited in Nagel, "Heresy, Doctor
       Luther, Heresy!" pp. 48-49. That "this man became true God" must be
       taken in concreto, and can be said not in philosophy but only in theolo-
       gy. Cf. Chapter Three of this book.

4   See LW 23, 129; WA 33, 200 (John, 1537-1538): "This article of justification
       is the chief doctrine. St. John expounded it especially. In this he proved
       himself a master. St. John cannot be sufficiently praised for treating this
       doctrine of justification. I cannot discourse on it more clearly and more
       forcefully than John here through the Holy Spirit." Pfitzner argues, in his
       article, "Luther as Interpreter of John's Gospel," that Luther's under-
       standing of the gospel has a Johannine character. Congar, in his article,
       "Christology of Luther," argues that for Luther the real mystery of the
       Incarnation lies not so much in St. John's statement: "The Word was
       made flesh" (Jn. 1:1) as in St. Paul's phrases: "Christ *was* made sin for us"
       (2 Cor. 5:21), "Chist redeemed us from the curse of the law, having
       become a curse for us" (Gal. 3:13). Elert, in his noteable book, *The
       Structrure of Lutheranism*, argues for the primacy of the Pauline concept
       of justification in Luther's thought (see pp.72ff). See also Luther's own
       account of his indebtedness to Paul in his "Table Talk Recorded by John
       Mathesius", 1540, in LW 54, nos. 335 and 347.

5   LW 12, 310; WA 40^2, 328, 1ff (Psalm 51). See also Bernhard Lohse, *Martin
       Luther: An Introduction to His Life and Work*, trans. Robert C. Schultz

(Philadelpha: Fortress Press, 1986), p.144. Lohse notes Luther's practical *way* of doing theology, within which individual theological problems must be viewed. Consequently the question of the *way* in which one systematizes Luther's theology, says Lohse, is of far less important. "Only on this basis can we succeed in avoiding both the danger of an orthodox systematiztion of Luther on the one hand and the danger of an attempt to reinterpret Luther in order to make him existentially relevant to a particular contemporary situation on the other." *Watson* points out that Luther had a dominant concern with what he termed "the theological knowledge of man and the theological knowledge of God". See his *Let God Be God* , p.23 where he quoted *LW* 12, 310.

6   Congar, "Christology of Luther," p.377.

7   See marginal gloss on *Sentences.*, lib. III, d. 23: *WA* 9, 91, 22-24 as cited in Congar, "Christology of Luther," p.376. See also Pfitzner, "Luther as Interpreter of John's Gospel," pp.70-71.

8   See Robert Bertram, "Luther on the Unique Mediatorship of Christ," in *The One Mediator, The Saints, and Many,* eds. H. George Anderson, J. Francis Stafford & Joseph A. Burgess (Minneapolis: Augsburg Publishing House, 1992), pp. 249-262.

9   *LW* 22, 324. See also *LW* 24, 104 (Gospel of John).

10   See *WA* 16, 217, 33ff as quoted in Congar, "Christology of Luther," p.374. See also Elert, *The Structure of Lutheranism*, p.68.

11   *LW* 26, 176; *WA* 401, 299 (Galatians, 1535). See also *WA* 31^2, 431 as cited in Siggins, *Luther's Doctrine of Christ*, p.110. Cf. Philip Melanchthon asserted: "To know Christ is to know his benefits" (Melancthon and Bucer, *Library of Christian Classics*, vol. 19, ed. Wilhelm Pauck (Philadelphia: Westminster Press, 1969), pp. 21-22.

12   Nagel, "Heresy, Doctor Luther, Heresy!" p.43.

13   *LW* 26, 32; *WA* 40^1, 83.

14   *LW* 26, 288; *WA* 40^1, 448.

15   *Ibid.*

16   *LW* 26, 288; *WA* 40^1, 443 (Galatians, 1535).

17   *Ibid.*

18   *LW* 26, 267; *WA* 40^1, 417-418.

19   *LW* 26, 267; *WA* 40^1, 417.

20   *LW* 26, 265; *WA* 40^1, 415.

21   *Ibid.*

22   *LW* 41, 100-111. Cf. *LW* 24, 106; *WA* 45, 557 (John, 1548). See Gerhard
      Forde, "Caught in the Act: Reflections on the Work of Christ," *Word and
      World* 3:1 (1983), p.31.

23   *LW* 26, 369-370; *WA* 40^1, 564.

24   See Bertram, "Luther on the Unique Mediatorship of Christ," p. 256,
      where he cites *LW* 26, 288; *WA* 40^1, 448.

25   *LW* 26, 277; *WA* 40^1, 432-434.

26   *Ibid.*

27   *LW* 26, 280; *WA* 40^1, 437-438. See also Siggins, *Luther's Doctrine of Christ*,
      p.241.

28   *LW* 26, 369-370; *WA* 40^1, 564.

29   *LW* 26, 272; *WA* 40^1, 567-578.

30   *LW* 26, 369-370; *WA* 40^1, 564.

31   *LW* 26, 373; *WA* 40^1, 568-570. See also Burnell F. Eckardt, "Luther and
      Moltmann: The Theology of the Cross," *Concordia Theological Quarterly*
      49:1 (1985), p.19: "So also man is justified not by works, but through
      faith in the suffering of Christ."

32   *LW* 26, 373; *WA* 40^1, 568-570.

33   *Ibid.* See also Pelikan, *Reformation of Church and Dogma* (1300-1700), pp.
      162-163.

34 *LW* 26, 265; *WA* 40^1, 415-416.

35 *LW* 26, 29; *WA* 40^1, 77-78.

36 *LW* 26, 278; *WA* 40^1, 434-435.

37 *LW* 26, 277; *WA* 40^1, 432-434.

38 *LW* 26, 284; *WA* 40^1, 443-444.

39 *Ibid.*

40 *LW*26, 287-288; *WA* 40^1, 446-448.

41 *LW* 26, 284; *WA* 40^1, 443-444.

42 *LW* 26, 278, *WA* 40^1, 434-435. See Forde, "Luther's Theology of the Cross," pp. 52-53.

43 See Pelikan, *Reformation of Church and Dogma*, p.163, where he notes that Luther echoed Augustine's phrase "fortunate exchange."

44 *LW* 26, 278; *WA* 40^1, 434-435.

45 *LW* 48, 12; *WA* BR 1, 35, 24-27.

46 *LW* 26, 278; *WA* 40^1, 434-435.

47 *Ibid.* See also "The Large Catechism," p.442.

48 *LW* 26, 284; *WA* 40^1, 443-444.

49 *LW* 26, 284; *WA* 40^1, 443-444.

50 *Ibid.*

51 See Loewenich, *Luther's Theology of the Cross*, p. 106.

52 See *LW* 25, 287. See also *LW* 26, 129.

53 *LW* 26, 284; *WA* 40^1, 443-444.

54   See *WA* 10^3, 432 (Church Postill, 1522) as cited in Lienhard, *Witness to Jesus*, p,175. Lienhard notes that Luther finds above all in Philippians 2 the affirmation of the love of Christ, which "drives Christ to the incarnation and animates him during the whole of his earthly life. It is from the point of view of this redemptive love that one must consider Christ and not be preoccupied with the mystery of the person as such."

55   *LW* 26, 177; *WA* 40^1, 296-298.

56   *LW* 26, 178-179; *WA* 40^1, 298-299.

57   *LW* 26, 281-282; *WA* 40^1, 440-441.

58   See Bertram, "Luther on the Unique Mediatorship of Christ," pp. 259-260. Cf. *LW* 26, 281-282; *WA* 40^1, 440-441.

59   *Ibid.*

60   *LW* 26, 282; *WA* 40^1, 440-441. See Lienhard, *Witness to Jesus*, pp. 109-110, where he notes that Luther did not establish a theory of atonement in the line of Anselm. "With Anselm, the suffering of the man Jesus Christ, united with the Son, had acquired a meritorious character for all persons, being the work of a just person, because of his union with the Son of God, of a person representing other persons." With Luther, it is not so much a question of the person Jesus acquiring merit, thereby satisfying God's wounded honor; rather it is a question of "Jesus Christ, God and man, interposing himself between sinful human beings and the wrath of God, bearing the punishment and thus dissipating the wrath of God. Such a work is not the achievement of the man Jesus considered in isolation, but of the Son became human, so that he is 'the happening of divine love among human beings living under the wrath of God'." Cf. *LW* 42, 107; *WA* 2, 691, 18-19 (Preparing to die, 1519).

61   *LW* 26, 283; *WA* 40^1, 441-442.

62   *LW* 26, 278; *WA* 40^1, 434-435.

63   *Ibid.*

64   *LW* 26, 42; *WA* 40^1, 97-98.

65   *Ibid.*

66 *LW* 26, 182; *WA* 40^1, 303-304.

67 *LW* 26, 292; *WA* 40^1, 454-455.

68 See *WA* 23, 157, 30 (That these Words of Christ, 1527) as cited in Nagel, "Heresy, Doctor Luther, Heresy!" p.41. Cf. *LW* 27, 72 (This is My Body, 1527).

69 See *WA* 10^1, 277, 18-292, 3 as cited in Nagel, *ibid*.

70 Nagel, "Heresy, Doctor Luther, Heresy!" p.37.

71 See *WA* 12, 285, 9 (Chruch Postil, 1523).

72 See Lienhard, *Witness to Jesus*, pp. 172-175. Luther differs from the kenotic theologians such as Thomasius and Frank, who conceive that Jesus Christ, by becoming incarnate, renounces certain of his divine properties." See also *WA* 17^2, 242, 7: "... it (deity) is within him, this is his form... he has it by birth." See also Siggins, *Luther's Doctrine of Christ*, pp. 217ff.

73 See *WA* 17^2, 243, 19 (Sermon on Philippians, 1525), as cited in Lienhard, *Witness to Jesus*, p. 174.

74 See *WA* 17^2, 243, 4, as cited in Lienhard, *ibid*.

75 See *WA* 17^2, 243, 5, as cited in Lienhard, *ibid*, p.,192, footnote no. 46. Cf. *WA* 11, 76: "Christ's emptying of himself thus consists in serving us with his 'divine form' and using it for us and not for himself." See also Althaus, *Theology of Luther*, p. 196.

76 See *WA* 17^2, 243, 30, as cited in Siggins, *Luther's Doctrine of Christ*, p.217, where the implications of Christ's voluntary self-abasement are discussed.

77 Peters, *God-the World's Future*, p.198.

78 *WA* 40^3, 707.

79 *Ibid*. See also Elert, *The Structure of Lutheranism*, p.228: "It is true ... that in his nature God can neither suffer nor die. But because of the personal union with Christ He was present when Christ suffered and died as if

He Himself were suffering and dying. And He is not affected by it in any other *way*."

80   See Siggins, *Luther's Doctrine of Christ*, p.241.

81   See Forde, *"Luther's Theology of The Cross,"* p.55. Cf. p. 59: "(Christ) is not paying God according to some celestial bookkeeping scheme. He is dying—suffering the punishment of being found 'among the thieves,' because He willed it so. Nor is he a religious hero, demonstrating the potency of his God-consciousness or his faithfulness to his calling to the end, thus becoming the example for our religious aspirations. He was dying: feeling in himself and in his conscience the agony of the ultimate separation. God is hidden in his death; indeed, God dies. What that means is that all the systems by which theology has sought to rescue Jesus from death, making a meaning of it which obscures the fact of it, are suddenly cut away."

82   See *LW* 26, 287; *WA* 40^1, 446-447: "The speculation by which Christ is grasped is not the foolish imagination of the sophists and monks about marvelous things beyond them; it is a theological, faithful, and divine consideration of the serpent hanging from the pole, that is, of Christ hanging on the cross for my sins, for your sins, and for the sins of the entire world.... Hence it is evident that faith alone justifies."

83   See *WA* 10^3, 162, 10 as quoted in Forde, *"Luther's Theology of The Cross,"* p.59.

84   *LW* 12, 126ff; *WA* 45, 239ff (Psalm 8, 1537). See Althaus, *Theology of Luther*, p.198. Cf. Eberhard Jüngel, *The Doctrine of the Trinity. God's Being is in Becoming* (Grand Rapids: (William B. Eerdmans Publishing Co., 1976), p.87, where he quotes favorably Barth's *Church Dogmatics*, ed. G.W. Bromiley & trans. T. F. Torrance (Edinburgh: T. & T. Clark, 1975), vol. IV/1, pp. 246-247. "In his (Christ's) passion and death," says Jüngel, "he did not therefore somehow 'waive his divinity (somewhat like the emperor of Japan in 1945)', but was rather 'in such a humiliation supremely God, in this death supremely alive', so that 'he has actually maintained and revealed his deity precisely in the passion of this man as his eternal Son'." Moltmann, in his of *The Crucified God*, pp. 214ff, says ... the cross must be 'evacuated' of deity, (if) by definition God cannot suffer and die...".

85   *LW* 12, 126ff; *WA* 45, 239ff (Psalm 8, 1537). See also Siggins, *Luther's Doctrine of Christ*, p. 218.

86   *Ibid.*

87   Althaus, *Theology of Luther*, p.198.

88   See *LW* 38, 254 (The Disputation "The Word was made Flesh", 1539).

89   *LW* 51, 14 (Sermon on the Tenth Sunday after Trinity, 1516).

90   See Douglas John Hall, *Lighten Our Darkness. Toward an Indigenous Theology of the Cross* (Philadelphia: Fortress Press, 1976), p.149. See also Sasse, *We Confess Jesus Christ*, p.39: "Obviously the 'theology of the cross' does not mean that for a theologian the church year shrinks together into nothing but Good Friday, Rather it means that Christmas, Easter, and Pentecost cannot be understood without Good Firday...."

91   *LW* 12, 310ff; *WA* 40^2, 327 (Psalms, 1537).

92   Mühlen, "Luther II: Theologie," in *Theologische Realenzyklopädie.* 21 volumes. Ed. Leonardo da vinci-Malachias von Armagh (Berlin: Walter de Gruyter, 1991), vol. 21, p.537: "God's essence is accessible only insofar as God has defined Himself in His revelation in Jesus Christ."

93   See *LW* 37, 56 & 61 (This is my Body, 1527).

94   See William Ockham, *Summa Logicae* I.C. XIV. XV (St. Bonaventure N.Y.: The Franciscan Institute, 1957), vol. 1, pp. 43-49 and pp.98-100.

95   *LW* 21, 331; *WA* 7, 577, 26.

96   See Peters, *God—the World's Future*, pp. 200-201. Cf. Moltmann, *The Crucified God*, p. 205: "When the crucified Jesus is called the 'image of the invisible God,' the meaning is that this is God, and God is like this. God is not greater than he is in this humiliation. God is not more glorious than he is in this self-surrender. God is not more powerful than he is in this helplessness. God is not more divine than he is in this humanity. However, Moltmann refuses to identify his position as theopaschite, notes Peters, he prefers to speak of "death in God" rather than the "death of God" (See his *God—the World's Future*, p.201).

97   See Carl Braaten, "The Problem of God-Language Today," in *Our Naming of God. Problems and Prospects of God-Talk Today*, ed. Carl Braaten (Minneapolis: Fortress Press, 1989), p.31. See also his "Let's Talk About the 'Death of God'," *Dialog* 26 (1987): 209-214.

98   See *LW* 26, 314; *WA* 40^1, 488, 15 (Galatians, 1535); *LW* 30, 300-301; *WA* 20, 756 (I John, 1527); *LW* 12, 406; *WA* 40^2, 462, 27 (Psalm 51, 1532); *LW* 3,

137-138; *WA* 42, 646, 9 (Genesis, 1539); *WA* 10 ^{1,1}, 100-101, 98 (1522).

99   See *WA* 36, 425 as quoted in Althaus, *Theology of Luther*, p.116.

100   *WA* 36, 424 as quoted in Althaus, *ibid.* See also *LW* 14, 47; *WA* 31^1, 68(Psalm 118:1, 1532). Cf. Nygren, *Agape and Eros*, trans. Philip Watson (Chicago: University of Chicago Press, 1953), p. 681 where he calls the rediscovery of the agape-love in his discussion of God, which has been evaded in scholasticism, the "copernican revolution."

101   See Althaus, *Theology of Luther*, p.116. See also *LW* 26, 127; *WA* 40^1, 244.

102   *Ibid.*, p.191

103   *Ibid*, p.116.

104   *LW* 30, 300-301; *WA* 20, 756 (I John, 1527).

105   See *LW* 13, 319 (Psalm 110, 1532). Cf. Lienhard, *Witness to Jesus*, p.110.

106   *LW* 42, 13; *WA* 2, 140, 30. See Siggins, *Luther's Doctrine of Christ*, p.221.

107   *LW* 23, 61-63; *WA* 33, 91 (John, 1537).

108   *LW* 26, 178; *WA* 40^1, 298 (Galatians, 1535).

109   *LW* 24, 115; *WA* 45, 556 (John, 1538).

110   *LW* 52, 42; *WA* 10^1, 188 (The Gospel for the Main Christmas Service, John 1:1-14, 1522).

111   See *WA* 21, 477, 24 as cited in Siggins, *Luther's Doctrine of Christ*, p. 221.

112   *LW* 22, 157; *WA* 47, 673.

113   See *LW* 40,215 (Against the Heavenly Prophets, 1525): "The lamb of God was slain before the foundation of the world." *LW* 34, 115; *WA* 39^1, 49 (Thesis Concerning Faith and Law, 1535); *LW* 40, 214; *WA* 18, 203 (Licentiate Examination, 1545): "Christ was not in reality slain from the foundation of the world, except in promise only."

114   See *WA* 57^3, 193, 18; *Library of Christian Classics*, Vol. 16, p. 144 (Hebrews, 1517-1518).

115   See *The Bondage of the Will*, trans. J. I. Packer & O.R. Johnson (London: Clarke, 1957), p. 176 (Hereafter cited as *BOW*).

116   *LW* 35, 89; *WA* 6, 358, 14-20 (A Treatise on the New Testament, 1520). See also *LW* 26, 386; *WA* 40^1, 587-588 (Galatians, 1535).

117   See *LW* 22, 354 (John, 1537). For a study of Luther's understanding of Testament, see Kenneth Hagen, *A Theology of Testament in the Young Luther. The Lectures on Hebrews* (Leiden: E. J. Brill, 1974).

118   *WA* 1, 365, 9-25; Atkinson, *ibid*, p.295.

119   See Watson, *Let God Be God:*, p.159; Julius Köstlin, *The Theology of Luther in its Historical Development and Inner Harmony*, 2 vols, trans. Charles E. Hay (Philadelphia: Lutheran Publication Society, 1897), vol. 2, pp. 290ff.

120   Watson, *Let God Be God*, p. 159.

121   *LW* 20, 175; *WA* 23, 517, 2ff (Zechariah, 1527). Also quoted in Watson , *Let God Be God*, p. 182. See also Elert, *The Structure of Lutheranism*, p. 276 quoting *WA* 36, 428, 3: *"Deus an yhm selber est mera charitas..."*

122   *LW* 2, 134; *WA* 42, 356 (Genesis).

123   See *LW* 12, 134; *WA* 42, 356; *LW* 25, 44-45; *WA* 56, 19-20 (On Rom. 2:8); *LW* 16, 233-234; *WA* 31^2, 167-1687 (On Isa. 28:21); *LW* 17, 88; *WA* 31^2, 331 (On Isa. 43:4).

124   See *WA TR* 1, 117 as cited in Lage, *Martin Luther's Christology and Ethics*, p.66.

125   See Watson, *Let God Be God*, p.159; Althaus, *Theology of Luther*, p. 116.

126   Althaus, *Theology of Luther*, p.116. See *LW* 12, 34: "Our sins stirred up God's wrath against us." For an extended study on God's wrath, see Egil Grislis, "Luther's Understanding of the Wrath of God," *Journal of Religion* 42 (1961): 277-292.

127   *LW* 42, 13 (Meditation on Christ's Passion, 1519). See also his "Introductrory Meditations" in *Sermons on the Passion of Christ*, trans. Prof. E. Smid (Rock Island: Lutheran Augustana Book Concern, 1873), pp. 12-13, where Luther wrote on how to preach rightly on the passion of Christ: "... Above all we must know and believe, as John preaches, that Christ suffered on account of our sins, which God cast upon him, and which He bore in obedience to His Father's will and from love

toward us."

128   *LW* 2, 44ff; *WA* 42, 294ff (Genesis, 1539).

129   See Robert D. Shofner, "Luther on '*The Bondage of the Will*': An Analytical-Critical Essay," *Scottish Journal of Theology* 26(1973), pp. 34-35.

130   See *LW* 33, 194-195 (The Bondage of the Will, 1525) where Luther discussed two sorts of necessity: an absolute necessity and a conditional necessity.

131   *Ibid.*, p.68.

132   See *LW* 21, 328; *WA* 7, 574 (Comments on Luke 1:49) for Luther's understanding of the word "mighty": "For the word ... does not denote a quiescent power, as one says of the temporal king that he is mighty, even though he may be sitting still and doing nothing. But it denotes an energetic power, continuous activity, that works and operates without ceasing." Cf. *LW* 1,25; *WA* 42, 20 (Genesis 1:6); *WA* 18, 718; *BOW*, 217: "By the omnipotence, 1 mean, not the power by which he omits to do many things that he could do, but the active power by which he mightily works all in all. It is in this sense that Scripture calls him omnipotent." Also quoted in Althaus, *Theology of Luther*, p.108.

133   *LW* 14, 52; *WA* 31, 77-80 (Psalm 118:2, 1530).

134   *LW* 31, 350ff (The Freedom of A Christian, 1520).

135   *Ibid.* See "The Large Catechism", p.366 as cited in Timothy Lull, "God and Suffering: A Fragment," Dialog 25:2 (1986), p.94. See also Bornkamm, *Luther's World of Thought*, p.65.

136   *LW* 18, 413; *WA* 13, 696-697 (Malachi, 1526). See Rem B. Edwards, "The Pagan Dogma of the Absolute Unchangeableness of God," p. 306. Edwards notes, "Taken in context, Malachi and James affirm only that God does not change with respect to His goodness and righteousness."

137   *LW* 18, 12-13; *WA* 13, 11-12 (Hosea 2:19-20, 1545). See also Pelikan, *The Emergence of the Catholic Tradition*, p.22; Wondra, "The Pathos of God," p. 32: "The God of the Bible ... is unchangeable ... in terms of 'faithfulness'... He steps into the historical process as the unchaning faithful God. This is closer to the meaning of the name Jahweh. ... It also fits the prophets' picture of God's faithfulness to His covenant people despite their disobedience. His faithfulness solves the otherwise insoluble dialectic of holiness and love."

138   Cf. Torrance, *The Trinitarian Faith*, p.185.

139   *LW* 14, 106 (Psalm 118:29: "... God is good; for His steadfast love endures forever.").

140   *Ibid.*

141   See Richard Creel, *Divine Impassibility: An Essay in Philosophical Theology* (Cambridge Uni. Press, 1986), p.11: "It seems, then, that the most consistent element of meaning across these definitions of impassibility is that which cannot be affected by an outside force. Hence, impassibility is imperviousness to causal influence from external factors." Cf. Sarot, "Patripassianism, Theopaschitism and the Suffering of God," p.366, who observes in Creel's definition a distinction between "to be affected by" and "to be causally influenced by". "To be affected by," in Sarot's view, means that God may be influenced in a "personal" way; on the contrary, "to be causally influenced" means God cannot be influenced in a "causal" way.

142   Cf. Abraham Heschel, *The Prophets* (New York: Harper & Row, Publishers, 1962), p.225: "The divine reaction to human conduct does not operate automatically. Man's deeds do not necessitate but merely occasion divine *pathos*. Man is not the immediate but merely the incidental cause of pathos in God, the *'occasio'* or *'causa occaionalis'*, which freely calls forth a pathetic state in God. There is no nexus of causality, but only one of contingence between human and divine attributes, between human character and divine *pathos*. The decisive fact is that of divine freedom."

143   *LW* 14, 106.

144   See Forde, *"Luther's Theology of The Cross,"* p.37.

145   *LW* 35, 89ff.

146   See *LW* 22, 9: "Whatever we are, we received from Him and not from ourselves. He alone has everything from Himself." This understanding appears first in Anselm of Canterbury, *Monologium* ch. 6, which is the medieval scholastic doctrine of the "aseity" of God. See footnote 5, *LW* 22, 9.

147   See *LW* 17, 221; *WA* 31^2, 431-432 (Isaiah 53:4, 1529).

148   See his *Letters of Spiritual Counsel*, p.69 as cited in Tinder, "Luther's

Theology of Christian Suffering and Its Implications for Pastoral Care,"
pp. 111-112. Karl Rahner makes much the same point as does Luther.
See his, "Why Does God Allow Us To Suffer?" in *Theological
Investigations* XIX (New York: Crossroads, 1983), p. 207: "... in our present concrete state, the acceptance of suffering without an answer other
than the incomprehensibility of God and his freedom is the concrete
form in which we accept God himself and allow him to be God. If there
is not directly or indirectly this absolute acceptance of the incomprehensibility of suffering, all that can really happen is the affirmation of our
own idea of God and not the affirmation of God himself."

149   *LW* 31, 40.

150   See Lull, "God and Suffering," p.96.

151   *LW* 26, 178-179; *WA* 40^1, 288-289 (Galatians).

152   *LW* 14, 300 (Psalm 1:3, 1532).

153   *LW* 26, 178-179; *WA* 40^1, 288-289. See also *LW* 18, 13; *WA* 13, 11 (Hosea
2:19, 1545): "There is on earth no love more ardent than that between a
groom and his betrothed. The groom gives his bride not gift but himself.
the deepest love of his heart and all his property. He goes ahead of his
bride; he seeks her out, etc."

154   *LW* 26, 178-179; *WA* 40^1, 288-289. Cf. Braaten, "The True Divinity of
Jesus Christ,"in *Christian Dogmatics*, p.532: "God was not bound to suffer as an essential predicate of his being. Rather, God was free to suffer
as a function of divine love. Suffering cannot be predicated of God as a
metaphycsical attribute implied by God's immanence in the world
process, nor as an ontological limitation of God's being and nature, out
of the need to be fulfilled. The Greeks were right; there is no deficit in
God. But they wrongly concluded that for this reason there can be no
pain in God." See also Lee E. Snook, "A Primer on the Trinity: Keeping
our Theology Christian," *Word & World* 2:1 (1982), pp. 14-15.

155   *LW* 26, 277-278; *WA* 40^1, 432-433. The theme of a "joyous exchange" also
appears in "The Freedom of a Christian," 1520, in *LW* 31, 342-378.

156   See *LW* 22, 355, where Luther says that God in Jesus Christ has "entered
the belly of death and the devil..." so as to conquer them. See Dietrich
Bonhoeffer, *Letters and Papers from Prison*, ed. Eberhard Bethge & trans.
Reginald H. Fuller (New York: MacMillan, 1953), p. 220: "Only a suffering God can help."

157   See *LW* 1, 13; *WA* 42, 11 (Genesis, 1539); *LW* 42, 13; *WA* 2, 140 (Meditation on Christ's Passion, 1519); *LW* 26, 29; *WA* 40[1], 77.

158   See *LW* 5, 45 (Genesis 26:9, 1545). The distinction between the hidden God and revealed God does not mean two deities. Luther has God say: "For an unrevealed God I will become a revealed God. Nevertheless I will remain the same God". See also Otto Weber, *Foundations of Dogmatics*, trans. Darrell Gruder (Grand Rapids: William B. Eredmans, 1981), vol. one, p.405.

159   See *LW* 33, 139-140; *WA* 18, 684-685 (The Bondage of the Will, 1525); *LW* 1, 10-11; *WA* 42, 8-10 (Lectures on Genesis, 1535-1545); *LW* 2, 46-47; *WA* 42, 294-295 (Lectures on Genesis, 1535-1545). Luther mentions two "wills" of God (as he) deals with man: The Will of the Sign as the way of revealed God and the Will of His Good Pleasure as the way of the unrevealed God.

160   Brian Gerrish, " 'To the unknown God': Luther and Calvin on the Hiddenness of God," *Journal of Religion* 53 (1973), p.267. See also Egil Grislis, "Martin Luther's View of the Hidden God: The Problem of the *Deus Absconditus* in Luther's Treatise *De Servo Arbitrio*," *McCormick Quarterly* 21.1 (1967): 81-94. For a major study of this concept, see John Dillenberger, *God Hidden and Revealed: The Interpretation and its Significance for Religious Thought* (Philadelphia: Muhlenberg Press, 1953).

161   Gerhard Forde, *Theology is for Proclamation* (Minneapolis: Fortress Press, 1990), p.25.

162   See Eberhard Jüngel, "Quae supra nos, nihil ad nos," in his *Entsprechung. God-Wahrheit Mensch* (München: Kaiser, 1980), pp. 238ff. See also his *The Freedom of a Christian. Luther's Significance for Contemporary Theology*. Trans. Roy A. Harrisville (Minneapolis: Augsburg Publishing House, 1988), pp. 33-35, where he speaks the "human" hiddenness as the "specific hiddenness of God under His opposite."

163   Gerrish, " 'To the Unknown God'," p.268.

164   See *BOW*, p.101 as quoted in Grislis, "Luther's View of the Hidden God," p.85.

165   Althaus, *Theology of Luther*, p.277. See also, A. Skevington Wood, *Captive to the Word. Martin Luther: Doctor of Sacred Scripture* (Grand Rapids: Wm. B. Eerdmans Publishing Co., 1969), pp. 130-131. Gerrish, in his" 'To the Unknown God'," identifies three groups of interpreters of the *Deus*

absconditus: (i) those who see the hidden and revealed God as antitheti-
cal: Theodosius Harnack, the two Ritschls, Reinhold Seeberg, Hirsch,
Elert, Holl; (ii) those who see them as identical: Kattenbusch and Erich
Seeberg; (iii) those who simply find both: Althaus, Heim, and
Loewenich (pp. 266-267). The problematic nature of hiddenness and the
question of election cannot be fully considered in this study. For an
extensive study of the doctrine of predestination, see Fredrik Brosché,
Luther on Predestination (Sweden: Uppsala University, 1978).

166   *LW* 33, 139.

167   *LW* 33, 136.

168   Forde, *Theology is for Proclamation*, p.24.

169   *Ibid.*

170   *LW* 33, 138-139.

171   *Ibid.* For a discussion of Luther's dictum—"*Quae supra nos, nihil ad nos*"
which has its roots in Socrates, see Jüngel, "Quae supra nos, nihil ad
nos," pp. 268ff.

172   *LW* 5, 44; *WA* 43, 458-459.

173   See Forde, *Theology is for Proclamation*, p.26. See also Ebeling, *Luther*, pp.
230ff, where he writes of the "speculative mystical theology of
Neoplatonism which seeks to penetrate to the innermost darkness, to
hear the uncreated Word, and to be submerged in it. Here the desire is
to seek God in his divinity, God in his majesty, in total immediacy, naked
man meeting naked God."

174   *LW* 33, 139-140.

175   See *WA* 17[1], 404, 1 as cited in Lowell C. Green, "Luther on Revelation:
Foundation for Proclamation and Worship," *Consensus* 9:3(1983), p.9.

176   *LW* 6, 148; *WA* 44, 110, 23ff (Genesis).

177   Robert Jenson, *The Triune Identity*, p. 27.

178   *LW* 2, 46; *WA* 42, 294 (Genesis): "For what God is in His nature, we cannot define. We can well determine what He is not."

179   *Ibid.*

180   *Ibid.* See also *LW* 3, 122; *WA* 42, 635.

181   *Ibid.*

182   Jenson, *The Triune Identity*, p.28.

183   *LW* 5, 45; *WA* 43, 459. See also Gerrish, " 'To the Unknown God'," p.273, and Eberhard Jüngel, *God as the Mystery of the World. On the Foundation of the Theology of the Crucified God in between Thesim and Atheism*, trans. Darrell L. Gruder (Grand Rapids: William B. Eerdmans, 1983), p.346; "Briefly, the differentiation between God and God can never be understood as a contradiction in God."

184   *LW* 33, 145-146; *WA* 18, 638, 24-25. Also cited in Brosché, *Luther on Predestination*, p.164.

185   *LW* 5, 45; *WA* 43, 459-450. The above quotation suggests that the revealed God is Trinitarian, while the hidden God in His absolute hiddenness is not known by us as such.

186   *LW* 2, 45; *WA* 42, 294-295.

187   *Ibid.*

188   *LW* 12, 312.

189   *Ibid.*

190   Jüngel, "Quae supra nos, nihil ad nos," p.241: "The revealed God is hostile to that person who has become his own enemy. For whoever elevates himself above the preached God so as to rise to the God beyond us thereby rises above the (revealed) one, and elevates himself. In this self-elevation, he fails. He makes himself God's enemy, even that of the revealed God. So in this lies the identity of the hidden God and the revealed God. The hidden God directs us away from himself, so that the person elevating himself to Him must necessarily become God's enemy and insofar likewise directs us away from the hidden God. The revealed God points us to himself and insofar likewise directs us away from the hidden God. The revealed God directs us to his revelation in the man Jesus, where he awaits people as a friendly God. The hidden God and the revealed God correspond to each other, precisely in the centre of this apparent contradiction. Both teach us to understand: 'What is beyond us is no business of ours'."

191   Jenson, *The Triune Identity*, p.28.

192   *LW* 3, 139; *WA* 42, 645-646.

193   Jenson, *The Triune Identity*, p.28.

194   *BOW*, p.170.

195   *LW* 1, 13; *WA* 42, 10-11. Cf *LW* 33, 140; *LW* 26, 42-43.

196   See *WA* 40³, 337, 11 as cited in Mühlen, "Theologie: Luther II," p.537.

197   Klaus Schwarzwäller, *Theologia Crucis: Luthers von Prädestination nach De servo arbitrio*, 1525 (München: Chr. Kaiser Verlag, 1970), p. 127: "Precisely for this reason, (Luther) holds onto the Gospel: here and here alone God is evidently known as the savior who is wonderful to us because of his boundless mercy and unwavering love, towards whom there can only be faithful trust and humble obedience."

198   See *WA TR* 5, no. 5658a: 294.24.34; 295.5; 294.4 as cited in Gerrish, " ' To the Unknown God'," p.279.

199   See Gerrish, " 'To the Unknown God'," p.222.

200   See *WA* 45, 370 (Vyl fast nutzlicher punkt Ausbezogen auss etzlichen Predigen des Gottes gelahrtn Doctoris Martin Lutheri, 1547).

201   Gerrish ," 'To the unknown God'," p.278.

202   *LW* 42, 107; *WA* 2, 691, 18-19.

203   Forde, "*Luther's Theology of The Cross*," p.51.

204   *LW* 42, 107; *WA* 2, 691, 17.

205   *LW* 26, 235; *WA* 40¹, 371-372.

206   Forde, *Theology is for Proclamation*, p.27.

207   *Ibid.*, p.22. See also his "Reconciliation with God," in *Christian Dogmatics* p.71: "The *deus nudus*, the *deus absconditus*, the God of wrath, has virtually to be overcome by the 'clothed,' the revealed God of mercy in Jesus Christ. ... Theological theory cannot tear the mask from the face of the hidden God. One cannot see through God's wrath."

208   See *LW* 33, 293-295; *WA* 18, 786-787.

209   See *WA* 5, 204, 26 (Operationes in Psalmos): "*Proinde alia omnes tenta-tiones sunt huius perfectissimae delut rudimenta et praeludia, in quibus assuescamus and deum contra deum confugere*," as cited in Gerrish, " 'To the Unknown God'," p.291; Grislis, "Luther's view of the Hidden God," p.87; McGrath, *Luther's Theology of The Cross*, pp. 171-172.

210   Gerrish, " ' To the Unknown God'," p.291.

211   *Ibid.*

212   *Ibid.*

213   Forde, *Theology is for Proclamation*, pp.29-30. See also Loewenich, *Luther's Theology of The Cross*, pp. 50-51.

214   Cf. Gerrish, " 'To the Unknown God'," p.273, where he states, "Admittedly, Luther does not consider the antithesis within his conception of God to be indicative of a contradiction in God himself, although he grants the appearance. The problem is noetic, not ontic -- in our understanding, not in God's being." Gerrish's reading of Luther is inaccurate. For Luther the problem is indeed ontic because he locates the contradiction in God's being itself: a contradiction which God assumes but simultaneously conquers that contradiction "in himself". Bertram says rightly of Luther's position: "There the 'awesome conflict' (*mirabile duellum*) between the 'curse' and the 'blessing,' in both instances God's own, becomes the 'joyfullest of conflicts' (*iucundissimum duellum*). There the (contradiction) becomes ... 'the sheer immensity of what all the God of the gospel rescues us from, namely, God's own self, even though it took being triune to do that, because it took Christ'." See Bertram, "Again on the Trinity: Bertram Responds," *Dialog* 29(1990), p.61. See also Jüngel, "Quae supra nos, nihil ad nos," pp.240ff.

215   Cf. Lohse, *Martin Luther*, p.171, where he argues that Luther's distinction between God hidden and God revealed "corresponds" to his distinction between law and gospel.

216   *LW* 26, 335; *WA* 40^1, 516-518.

217   *LW* 25, 9; *WA* 46, 10-11(Romans, 1516). For more on Luther on the wrath of God, see Grislis, "Luther's Understanding of the wrath of God," pp. 277ff.

218   *LW* 25, 12-13; *WA* 46, 14-16.

219   See Grislis, "Luther's view of the Hidden God," p.287. See also *LW* 26, 337; *WA* 40[1], 520-521 (Galatians).

220   See Grislis, "Luther's view of the Hidden God," p.287.

221   *LW* 25, 260; *WA* 46, 273.

222   *LW* 26, 133; *WA* 40[1], 233-234.

223   *BOW*, p.278.

224   *LW* 26, 337; *WA* 40[1], 520.

225   *LW* 26, 338; *WA* 40[1], 520-521.

226   *Ibid.*

227   *LW* 26, 337; *WA* 40[1], 519-520.

228   *LW* 26, 339; *WA* 40[1], 521-523. Cf. *LW* 16, 260; *WA* 32, 190 (Isaiah, 1529): "God strikes in order to show mercy."

229   See Althaus, *Theology of Luther*, p.32.

230   See *LW* 33, 175ff: *WA* 18, 709ff; where Luther discusses how God's omnipotence can be said to work evil, without attributing evil acts to God.

231   See Goetz, "The Suffering of God," p.285.

232   Luther's corrective to Goetz's thesis would be: the polarity between the passible/clothed God and impassible/naked God corresponds to faith and unbelief. Cf. Schwarzwäller, *Theologia Crucis*, p.176, who says Luther did not attempt to systematize the two assertions: The revealed God is the hidden God, and the revealed God is distinguished from the hidden God. Ebeling, *Luther*, p.240, says that the contradiction between the two assertions is "resolved by the fact that in order that God may truly be God Luther maintains to the utmost the contradiction between God in Jesus Christ and the God of omnipotence and omniscience, between faith and experience." It is therefore necessary, says Ebeling, to speak of the *deus absconditus* in order that the revealed God may be taken seriously as God in his revelation. Althaus, *Theology of Luther*, p.197, says of Luther's paradox: God is "nothing else than that God is at once

completely above and completely below."

233 See *LW* 12, 322.

234 See *LW* 12, 323.

235 See *WA* 30^1, 133, 1 (Large Catechism) as cited in Gerrish, " 'To the Unknown God'," p.278.

236 Siggins, *Luther's Doctine of Christ*, p.84.

237 See *LW* 19, 60 & 44 (Treatise on Jonah, 1525).

238 *Ibid.*, 46.

239 *Ibid.*, 48.

240 Forde, *Theology is for Proclamation*, p.29.

241 *BOW*, p.217.

242 See *WA* 18, 684, 32 as cited in Gerrish, " 'To the Unknown God'," p.272.

243 See *LW* 54, 377 (Table Talk, 1540) where Augustine's *Confession* XI, 10 was quoted.

244 Forde, *Theology is for Proclamation*, p.20.

245 *LW* 33, 292-293. See also Lohse, *Martin Luther*, p.170, who rightly identifies that Luther's formulation of the distinction between God hidden and God revealed presupposes faith in Christ as the basis for its understanding.

246 *Ibid.*

247 *Ibid.*

248 See "Preface to the Epistle of St. Paul to the Romans, 1522" in *Martin Luther. Selections from His Writings*, ed. & with an introduction by John Dillenberger (New York: Doubleday & Co., Inc. 1961), p.32.

249 See *BOW*, pp. 234ff and p.315 where Luther discusses "faith" and "vision".

250 See Wolfhart Pannenberg, *Systematic Theology*, vol. 1., trans. Geoffrey W.

Bromiley (Grand Rapids: William B. Eerdmans Co., 1991), pp. 339-340.

251   See Lohse, *Martin Luther*, p.170.

252   See *WA* 39[1], 370, 12-371, 1 (Disputation gegen die Antinomer, 1537-1540) as quoted in Lohse, *Martin Luther*, p.170. For a discussion of the tension between the hidden God and the doctrine of the Trinity, see Albrechts Peters, *"Verborgener Gott-Dreieiniger.Beobachtungen und Überlegungen zum Gottesverständnis Martin Luthers,"* in *Martin Luther Reformator 'Und Vater im Glauben',* ed. Peter Manns (Stuggart: Franz Verlag Wiesbaden GMBH, 1985), pp. 87-98.

253   See Lohse, *Martin Luther*, p.170. He notes that Luther did not discuss how the doctrine of the Trinity is related to his discussion between God hidden and God revealed.

Chapter Five: Trinity and Divine Suffering

1   For a detailed study of Luther's trinitarian theology, see Jansen, *Studien zu Luthers Trinitätslehre.*

2   See Lohse, *Martin Luther*, pp. 166-167; Rowan Williams, *Christian Spirituality: A Theological History from the New Testament to Luther and St. John of the Cross* (Atlanta: John Knox, 1980), p.48, where he noted that Athanasius uses the trinitarian language to assure us of the longstanding conviction that "God and Christ were to be held together, and the work of Christ was in some sense the work of God."

3   See *LW* 32, 244 (Against Latomus, 1521); cf. *LW* 41, 82-83 (On the Councils and the Church, 1539). *"Homoousios"* means "of one substance or essence or nature."

4   *LW* 22, 16 (John, 1537). See also Lienhard, *Witness to Jesus*, p.321. For a historical study of these trinitarian terms, see Jenson, *The Triune Identity,* pp.57ff, and his "The Triune God," in *Christian Dogmatics,,* pp. 83ff. For a detained study of the Trinity in church history, see Betrand de Margerie, *The Christian Trinity in History,* trans. Edmund Fortman (Still River, Massachusett: St. Bede's Publications, 1981); Edmund Fortman, *The Triune God: A Historical Study of the Doctrine of the Trinity* (Philadelphia: Westminster, 1972); Harry Austryn Wolfson, *The Philosophy of the Church Fathers,* vol. 1. *Faith, Trinity, Incarnation* (Massachusetts: Harvard University Press, 1970); Torrance, *The Trinitarian Faith.*

5   *LW* 22, 16. Cf. Augustine, *On the Trinity,* V. ch. 8, par. 9-10.

6   See Lohse, *Martin Luther*, p.166 quoting *WA* 46, 436, 7ff.

7   *Ibid.*

8   *Ibid.*

9   Jansen, *Studien zu Luthers Trinitätslehre*, p.195: "Luther, therefore, 'only when driven by necessity' makes use of the 'old dogmatic terms' of the Trinity. According to Luther, they are not able to express adequately the matter (i.e., God is three and yet One)."

10   See *LW* 34, 199ff; *WA* 50, 262-283 (The Three Symbols); *LW* 41, 3ff; *WA* 50, 547, 12ff (On the Councils and the Churches); *LW* 15, 265ff; *WA* 54, 28-100 (On the Last Words of David). These texts are dealt with by Klaus Schwarzwäller, *Theologia Crucis*, pp. 201-212.

11   Althaus, *Theology of Luther*, p.200.

12   *LW* 22, 5; *WA* 46, 538 (Preface to John, 1537); *LW* 24, 8; *WA* 45, 468 (John, 1538). See also *LW* 1, 9; *WA* 42, 8 (Genesis, 1535-45).

13   See *WA* 39^2, 303, 12ff (Promtionsdisputation von G. Major und J. Faber, 1544): "Here the whole grammar must adopt new words, if it speaks of God." Also cited by Mühlen, "Luther II. Theologie," p.538.

14   See *WA* 39^2, 340, 12ff as cited by Mühlen, *ibid*: "Through philosophy and reason one can say and believe nothing correctly concerning these things of the Divine Majesty; however, through faith one can say and believe everything correctly."

15   *LW* 15, 302; *WA* 54, 57.

16   *Ibid.*

17   *LW* 34, 205 (Three Symbols). See also Siggins, *Luther's Doctrine of Christ*, p. 226; Kelly, *Early Christian Doctrines*, pp. 263ff; Torrance, *The Trinitarian Faith*, pp. 67-68. Torrance's thesis is that "the basic revolution in the knowledge of God that has taken place in Jesus Christ" requires that the true God is triune. In the Incarnation of the Son God "has opened up himself to our knowledge in his own being as Father, Son and Holy Spirit for what he has revealed himself to us through Christ and in the Spirit he is in himself."

18   *LW* 15, 302; *WA* 54, 58 (Last Words of David). See also "The Smalcald

Articles, 1537" in *The Book of Concord*, p.291, where Luther made similar statements.

19   *LW* 15, 303; *WA* 54, 58. Cf. *LW* 37, 361(Confession Concerning Christ's Supper, 1528), where Luther made his confession of faith in the "sublime article of the majesty of God" (i.e., the Trinity).

20   See Lienhard, *Witness to Jesus*, p.322; Lohse, *Martin Luther*, p.166, also asserts that Luther, following Augustine, expressed strong reservations about the concept of "person", preferring the concept of "relationship."

21   *LW* 15, 303; *WA* 54, 58.

22   Jansen, *Studien zu Luthers Trinitätslehre*, p. 197: *"Damit hat Luther also dargelegt, daß der reale Unterschied zwischen den drei göttlichen Personen nicht in ihren opera ad extra, sondern nur in ihren opera ad intra, den intertrinitarischen Relationen, zu finden ist."*

23   *LW* 15, 306; *WA* 54, 60.

24   *WA* 39^2, 95, 19-21. See Colin Brown, "Trinity and Incarnation: In Search of Contemporary Theology," *Ex Auditu* 7(1991): 83-100.

25   *LW* 15, 306; *WA* 54, 60.

26   *LW* 15, 397; *WA* 54, 61.

27   *LW* 15, 308; *WA* 54, 62. Luther quotes favourably Augustine's distinction between *res* and *signum*, especially in his work, *Christian Doctrine*, I.2. He illustrates this as follows: "Smoke is a reality, a thing per se and at the same time a sign of something else, something which it is not but which it indicates and reveals, namely, fire."

28   *LW* 15, 307; *WA* 54, 61.

29   *Ibid.*

30   *LW* 15, 308; *WA* 54, 62.

31   *Ibid.*

32   *LW* 1, 58; *WA* 42, 44 (Genesis).

33   See "The Apostle's Creed," in *LW* 24, 202ff and The Creed in *"The Small Catechism"* and "The Large Catechism," in *The Book of Concord*, pp. 344-

345 & pp. 411-420 respectively. See also Fortman, *The Triune God*, p.143, where Augustine's concept of "appropriations" is discussed.

34   *LW* 15, 309; *WA* 54, 63.

35   *LW* 1, 49-50; *WA* 42, 36-37; cf. *LW* 1, 60-61; *WA* 42, 45-46 (Genesis): *LW* 22, 19ff (John 1). See also Loeschen, *The Divine Community*, p.25.

36   *LW* 1, 58; *WA* 42, 44.

37   Though Luther did not coin the term "*Dreieinigkeit*", he facilitated its origin.

38   See *WA* 41, 276, 39-277, 16 as quoted in Jansen, *Studien zu Luther Trinitätslehre*, p.199: "These are like different clothes, that one does not mix together among the Persons. For however creating and sustaining all things, atoning for sins, forgiving sins, awakening from death and giving the gift of eternal life are works that no one other than God can do, nevertheless there are special works here that are ascribed to each Person distinctly, so that Christians have one simple, certain understanding, that there is only one God, and nevertheless three Persons in the one unified Divine Essence, just as the holy fathers read diligently in Moses, the Prophets and the writings of the Apostles and have held intact against all heretics."

39   See Bornkamm, *Luther and the Old Testament*, pp. 114-120.

40   See Jansen, *Studien zu Luthers Trinitätslehre*, p.200. Jansen is dependent on Bornkamm. Cf. Bornkamm, *ibid.*

41   *LW* 15, 316; *WA* 54, 69.

42   Lienhard, *Witness to Jesus*, p.165.

43   See Fortman, *The Triune God*, pp. 75-76.

44   *LW* 34, 216ff; *WA* 50, 274 (The Three Symbols).

45   *Ibid.* See also *LW* 12, 49; *WA* 40^2, 249-250 (Psalm, 1532).

46   *LW* 34, 217. See also de Margerie, *The Christian Trinity in History*, pp. 165ff, for a discussion of the "*filioque*" concept.

47   *Ibid.*

48   *LW* 34, 217.

49   See Augustine's *de Trinitate*, IV. 20, 29, as cited in Margerie, *The Christian Trinity in History*, p.48.

50   See Margerie, *The Christian Trinity in History*, p.48. Augustine affirmed the eternal procession and the termporal missions in his view of the Trinity.

51   *LW* 34, 216-217. See also *LW* 12, 49; *WA* 40^2, 249-250.

52   *LW* 34, 218.

53   *LW* 34, 219.

54   Schwarzwäller, *Theologia Crucis*, p.207.

55   *LW* 34, 219. See also Köstlin, The *Theology of Luther*, pp. 310ff.

56   *LW* 34, 218. Cf. Karl Barth, *Church Dogmatics*, vol. 1.1, p.383. Barth insists that "as Father, Son and Holy Spirit God is, so to speak, ours in advance," thereby bringing together the inner and outer being of God.

57   Torrance, *The Trinitarian Faith*, p.67.

58   See Karl Rahner, *The Trinity*, trans. J. Donceel (London: Burns & Oats, 1970), pp. 21-22, where he asserted: "The 'economic' Trinity is the 'immanent' Trinity, and the 'immanent' Trinity is the 'economic' Trinity." See also Moltmann, *The Trinity and the Kingdom of God*, p. 154, where Moltmann accepts Rahner's thesis. For contemporary discussions on the Trinity, See Ted Peters, "Trinity Talk: Part 1," and "Trinity Talk: Part II," *Dialog* Vol. 26 (1987):44-48, 133-138, and his monograph, *God as Trinity Relationality and Temporarily in Divine Life* (Louisville: Westminster/John Knox Press, 1993); Catherine Mowry LaCugna, *God For Us. The Trinity and Christian Life* (San Francisco: Harper & Row, 1991).

59   Eilert Herms, *Luthers Auslegung des Dritten Artikels* (Tübingen: J. C. B. Mohr, 1987), p.118: "*Older: die ökonomische Trinität ist die Selbsmanifestation der immanenten.*"

60   See Mühlen, "Luther II. Theologie," p.538: "*Doch ist die immanente Trinität die Voraussetzung für die ökonomische.*" For further dialogue on the doctrine of the Trinity, see Robert W. Bertram, "When is God triune?" *Dialog* 27 (1988):133; Paul R. Hinlicky, "Some Questions to Bertram on the Trinity," *Dialog* 28 (1989): 307-308; Ann Pederson, "A Question to

Bertram and Luther on the Trinity," *Dialog* 28 (1989): 308-309; Bertram, "Again on the Trinity : Bertram Responds," *Dialog* 29 (1990): 60-61. For Bertram, Luther's theological thinking is strictly concrete: in Jesus Christ we know *Deus revelatus qua Trinitas*, revealed as Jesus Christ, his Father and their common Spirit. Outside of this particular context, we just do not know an immanent Trinity. Bertram's point is that it is counter-productive to speak of the immanent Trinity. Bertram's view seems to be at odds with Luther's, for Luther did assert an immanent Trinity, though his emphasis is on the economic Trinity, which he proclaimed as the distinctive glory of the Gospel.

61   *LW* 34, 218; cf. *LW* 24, 292-293; *WA* 45, 727-728 (John, 1538).

62   This interpretation has been offered by Jansen, *Studien Zu Luthers Trinitätslehre*, pp. 204-205: "*In den Johannespredigten von 1538 interpretiert er den gleichen Vers sowohl als inner-trinitärisches Geschehen als auch als Sendung des Geistes an die Glaubigen. Wenn Luther die gleiche Bibelstelle sowohl immanent-trinitarisch als auch ökonomisch-trinitarisch interpretieren kann, so ist das ebenfalls ein Indiz däfür, daß für ihn die immanent-trinitarische Aussagen nur die notwendigen theologischen Vordersatz für die ökonomisch-trinitarischen Satze theologischen Vordersatz für die ökonomish-trinitarischen Sätze sind. Die opera trinitatis ad extra und die opera trinitatis ad intra lassen sich zwar unterscheiden, nicht aber scheiden.*" Cf. Torrance, *The Trinitarian Faith*, pp. 67-68. See also Eberhard Jüngel, "The Relationship between 'economic' and 'immanent' Trinity," *Theology Digest* 24 (1976): 179-184. Jüngel's reflection is based on Rahner's thesis that the economic Trinity is the immanent Trinity, and vice versa.

63   Loeschen, *The Divine Community*, p.18.   Loeschen accepts Regin Prenter's understanding of the Trinity in terms of the "motion" analogy. Both develop, on the basis of Luther's Christmas sermon on Trinity of 1514, an image of the Trinity in terms of the "moving, the moved and rest" (p.20). See Prenter, *Spiritus Creator*, pp.173ff, where he discusses on *WA* 1, 20ff.

64   See *WA* 7, 214, 27ff as quoted in Mühlen, "Luther II: Theologie," p.437; Elert, *The Structure of Lutheranism*, p.217.

65   See *WA* 50, 266, 37 as quoted in Elert, *The Structure of Lutheranism*, p.217.

66   Mühlen, "Luther II: Theologie," p.537; cf. *LW* 22, 246; *WA* 46, 555 (John):" Whoever comes in touch with the man Christ also comes in touch with the Son of God. In fact, the whole Trinity is found in this man."

67   Elert, *The Structure of Lutheranism*, p.217.

68   See The Creed in "The Large Catechism," p.419. See also The Creed, in *"The Small Catechism,"* pp. 344-345. Cf. Friedrich Mildenberger, *Theology of the Lutheran Confessions,* trans. Edwin L. Lueker (Philadelphia: Fortress Press, 1983), p.147.

69   See Lohse, *Martin Luther,* p.167, who observes that Luther understood the dogma of the Trinity in the light of the doctrine of salvation. "To this extent, (Luther) was part of the line of theological development begun by Athanasius. Athanasius felt that the Arians' rejection of the doctrine that the Son was of one substance with the Father (*homoousios*) called the meaning of the redemption into question. Luther felt, however, that this connection between the dogma (such as Trinity) and soteriology is even closer."

70   See Schwarzwäller, *Theologia crucis,* p. 209; Elert, *The Structure of Lutheranism,* pp. 216-217.

71   See *LW* 34, 218, where Luther speaks of being satisfied with a limited knowledge of a certain distinction of the three Persons in the Godhead, until the eschaton when we will clearly see and apprehend it. Loeschen, in his *The Divine Community,* p.21, compares Luther and Calvin: "...On the one hand, Luther was less interested and less well-trained in classical thought than Calvin, and so was less habituated to classical thought than Calvin, and so was less habituated to a classical ontological or metaphysical approach to theology. On the other hand, and more importantly, however, Luther was increasingly influenced by the Hebraic approach to discourse on God, not only as it appeared in the Old Testament narratives but also as it was manifested in the Hebrew language itself. The Hebraic influences showed itself especially in two interrelated ways: in its consistent preoccupation with Yahweh's will and in its almost equally consistent understanding of Yahweh's will, in fact all God's 'attributes,' only in terms of God's relation to his people." Whether Luther was less well-trained than Calvin in classical though or not remains debatable. But Loeschen was right to say that Luther speaks of God as he acts in relation to man, and his evangelical discoveries were profoundly influenced by the Hebrew language and its relational thinking.

72   See *LW* 34, 208. Cf. Kelly, *Early Christian Traditions,* pp. 119-123; Erickson, *Christian Theology,* vol. 1., pp. 334 - 345; Athanasius, *Four Discourses Against the Arians* 2.23.4, and Tertullian, *Adversus Praxeam* 29 as quoted in Erickson, *ibid.*

73   See Kelly, *Early Christian Traditions,* pp. 83, 85, 100, 112, 119-123 as cited

in Sarot, "Patripassianism, Theopaschitism and the Suffering of God," p.370. Tertullian means by "*Pater*" the first person of the Trinity, whereas the modalists use "*Pater*" in the more original sense of "God *simpliciter*."

74   Tertullian, *Adversus Praxean* 15.402 ff. Also cited in Grant, "Possibilities for Divine Passibility," p.5.

75   For a contrary view, cf. Erickson, *Christian Theology*, p.335, who argues that the key reason for the repudiation of partipassianism was its conflict with the hellenistic conception of divine impassibility. Cf. Sarot, "Patripassianism, Theopaschitism and the Suffering of God," p.370.

76   Sarot, "Patripassianism, Theopaschitism and the Suffering of God," p.370. See Mozley, *The Impassibility of God*, pp. 33ff.

77   See Moltmann, *The Future of Creation*, trans. Margaret Kohl (Philadelphia: Fortress Press, 1979), p.73. Moltmann coins this new term "patricompassianism" to indicate the theological position which advocates a trinitarian understanding of the suffering of God, according to which "the Son suffers dying, the Father suffers the death of the Son."

78   Sarot, "Patripassianism, Theopaschitism and the Suffering of God," p.372. See also Jung Young Lee, *God Suffers for Us*, p.74, where he, by rejecting patripassianism, rejects "the unity of Godhead without distinction," not divine passibility. Kazoh Kitamori, *Theology of the Pain of God*, trans. Shinkyo Suppanskha (Virginia: John Knox Press, 1965), p.15, also rejects patripassianism: "My theology, however, cannot be identified with patripassianism unless the critics can prove that I made reference to God the Father as the One who suffered on the cross." See McWilliams, *The Passion of God*, p.21, who labels many theologians as "patripassianists," including Moltmann, James Cone, Geddes MacGregor, Kitamori, Daniel Day Williams, and Jung Young Lee. McWilliams calls them "the new patripassianists" because they insist on stronger trinitarian distinctions than "the old patripassianists." Baron von Hügel, *Essays and Addresses on the Philosophy of Religion*, Series II (London: J.M. Dent & Sons, 1926), pp.205 & 363. Hügel used the *passio/compassio* distinction to support divine impassibility, while Tertullian rejected such a distinction in his attack on the patripassianists. See also Douglas John Hall, *God and Human Suffering. An Exercise in Theology of the Cross* (Minneapolis: Fortress Press, 1986), pp. 213-216.

79   *LW* 15, 303; *WA* 54, 58 (Last words of David).

80   *LW* 15, 311; *WA* 54, 64.

81   *Ibid.*

82   *Ibid.*

83   See WA 39², 287, 21-22. See also LW 11, 226; WA 4, 76 (Psalm); LW 15, 305-306; WA 54, 60-61; Lienhard, *Witness to Jesus*, p.322. Cf. Moltmann, *The Crucified God*, p.235, who claims Luther uses the name "God" generically and promiscuously for the following: (i) the nature of God; (ii) the second Person of the Trinity; (iii) the persons of the Father and the Spirit.

84   See WA 39², 110, 5-17: "For we also say that God is one and not more; but that unity of substance and essence has three distinct persons, just as Christ's nature is united in one person. Therefore, when it is said: Divinity is dead, it then implies that even the Father and the Holy Spirit are dead. But this is not true since only one person of the divinity, the Son was born, died, and suffered, etc. Therefore, divine nature, when it is understood as the person, was born, suffered, died, etc.; it is true. Therefore a distinction must be made. If you understand divine nature as the whole divinity or unity, then the argument is false; for Christ is not whole Trinity, but only one person of the Trinity. Therefore, there is only one God. Let us proclaim here how it can be that those three persons are one God and one being, But we believe that these things are incomprehensible; if they could be understood, there would be no need to believe."

85   See Lienhard, *Witness to Jesus*, pp. 163ff.

86   See Siggins, *Luther's Doctrine of Christ*, p. 226. Cf. LW 24, 98; WA 4, 76; LW 15, 305-306; WA 54, 60-61.

87   See WA 39², 287, 24.

88   See WA 39², 287, 17-18.

89   See WA 39², 303, 24.

90   WA 39², 287, 15-16.

91   LW 38, 266; WA 39², 21, 26-28. See also White, "Luther's view on Language," p.205 (White's translation).

92   *Ibid.*

93   *LW* 38, 275; *WA* 39^2, 22, 4-10 (Translation is White's).

94   See *WA* 39^2, 303, 18ff.

95   See *WA* 39^2, 110, 5ff (On the Divinity and Humanity of Christ).

96   *LW* 37, 361.

97   *LW* 15, 307; *WA* 54, 61.

98   See Braaten, "The Question of God and the Trinity,"in *Festschrift: A Tribute to Dr. William Horden*, ed. Walter Freitag (Saskatoon: University of Saskatchewan Press, 1985), p.15.

99   *LW* 24, 99-100; *WA* 45, 550-551 (John, 1538).

100   *Ibid.*

101   See Sarot, "Patripassianism, Theopaschitism and the Suffering of God," pp.372-373.

102   *Ibid.* See also Adrio König, "The Idea of 'The Crucified God.' Some Systematic Questions," *Journal of Theology for Southern Africa* 39 (June, 1982): 55-61. Eberhard Jüngel, *The Doctrine of the Trinity: God's Being is in Becoming*, trans. Scottish Academic Press (Grand Rapids: William B. Eerdmans, 1976), p.xiv: "And it cannot be chance that it is precisely the event of the death of Jesus Christ upon the cross which calls the being of God in question and compels a Trinitärian statement of the problem."

103   See *LW* 41, 103.

104   See *LW* 41, 103. See also chapter three of this book.

105   See Jansen, *Studien Zu Luthers Trinitätslehre*, p.119. Cf. Moltmann, *The Crucified God*, p.235, says: "Luther's Christology of the crucified God remains within the framework of the early church's doctrine of two natures, represents an important further development of the doctrine of the *communicatio idiomatum* and radicalizes the doctrine of the incarnation on the cross. By presupposing the concept of God gained from his general distinction between God and the world, God and man in his Christology, in the theology of the cross he came later to change his concept of God, but he never arrived at a developed Christological doctrine of the Trinity." Jansen commented: "*Daran ist sicher zutreffend, daß Luther die Linien von der Christologie und von seiner theopaschitischen Tendenz nicht direkt zur Trinitätslehre durchgezogen hat, auch wenn Ansätz dazu da sind.*

Auffallend ist jedoch, daß Luthers ökonomische Trinitätslehre bei Moltmann gar nicht recht in den Blick zu kommen scheint" (See his Studien zu Luthers Trinitätslehre, pp. 119-120, footnote 130).

106   See Jansen, *Studien zu Luthers Trinitätslehre,* p.120: "For in his opinion, becoming human and Jesus Christ's suffering, death and resurrection are grounded in God's being itself. The theory of the Trinity as a differentiation in God's being makes it possible for the reformer to teach God's Incarnation and Passion in Jesus Christ. Precisely in this, Luther is far from metaphysical Monotheism, which teaches the intransitoriness, immutability, indivisibility, incapability of suffering and immortality of God."

107   See *LW* 15, 307; *WA* 54, 61-62, where Luther considers the theme of Phil. 2:7—the incarnate Christ takes "the form of a servant".

108   *LW* 24, 98; *WA* 45, 549.

109   See *LW* 24, 98; *WA* 45, 549. See also LaCugna, *God for Us,* pp. 270-278 for a historical discussion of the concept of *perichoresis* which originates with John Damascene.

110   See *LW* 37, 361.

111   *LW* 17, 165; *WA* 31^2, 391 (Isaiah, 1529).

112   *Ibid.*

113   See Congar, "Christology of Luther," p.377. Luther treats of the hypostatic union solely in terms of the act of salvation. He follows Paul's declaration that "Christ redeemed us from the curse of the law, having become a curse for us" (Gal. 3:13). "For God to take on human nature will amount to the assumption by him (incarnate Son) of our sin, his entry into the drama of sin, the drama of condemnation and death" (pp. 367-377). For a study of Luther's understanding of the Holy Spirit, see Prenter, *Spiritus Creator;* Herms, *Luthers Auslegung des Dritten Artikels;* Arnold E. Carlson, "Luther and the Doctrine of the Holy Spirit." *Lutheran Quarterly* 11 (May, 1959): 135-148; E.L. Towns, "Martin Luther on Sanctification," *Bibliotheca Sacra* CXXVI (April - June, 1969): 115-122; Philip Watson, "Luther and Sanctification," *Concordia Theological Monthly* 30 (April, 1959): 243-259; Lorenz Wunderlich, "The Holy Spirit and the Christian Life," *Concordia Theological Monthly* XXVII (Oct., 1956): 753-764.

114   See Hordern, *Experience and Faith,* p. 96; Strelan, " Theologia Crucis,

Theologia Gloriae," pp. 106ff.

115   See Lindberg, *The Third Reformation*, pp. 113ff. Prenter, in his *Spiritus Creator*, observes that Luther's conception of the person and work of the Spirit occurred in the context of his polemical works against Karlstadt and others (p.206). Luther's polemical works include "Letter to the Princes of Saxony and Concerning the Rebellious Spirit, 1524," in which he urges the princes to act against Müntzer before Müntzer instigated an open rebellion (see *LW* 40, 45-49; *WA* 15, 210-221); cf. "Against the Heavenly Prophets in the Matter of Images and Sacraments, 1525," in which Luther responds to Karstadt's writings against him following their debate in Jena (See *LW* 40, 73-223; *WA* 18, 62-125, 134-214).

116   See *LW* 40, 67 (Letter to the Christians at Strasbourg in Opposition to the Fanatic Spirit, 1524).

117   See *LW* 31, 34ff (The Freedom of a Christian, 1520): "It is evident that no external thing has any influence in producing Christian righteousness or freedom...."

118   *LW* 40, 253 (On the Uncertainty of Faith).

119   *LW* 40, 149 (Against the Heavenly Prophets, 1525). This forms the thrust of article V of the Augsburg Confession, in *The Book of Concord*, p.31; cf. Prenter, *Spiritus Creator*, pp.257ff; Jansen, *Studien zu Luthers Trinitätslehre*, p.124, speaks of the Spirit's work as appropriating the charity of Christ.

120   *LW* 40, 83. See also Hordern, *Faith and Experience*, p.96.

121   See *LW* 40, 146: "God has determined to give the inward to no one except through the outward."

122   *LW* 40, 146(Against the Heavenly Prophets). Also quoted in Lindberg, *The Third Reformation*, p.117.

123   See *LW* 25, 413 (Romans, 1515-16). Cf. *LW* 40, 81, 128ff.

124   *Ibid*.

125   See *LW* 24, 172; *WA* 45, 618 (John). See also Lienhard, *Witness to Jesus*, p.186.

126   Jansen, *Studien zu Luthers Trinitätslehre*, p.123: "Augustine emphasized the following: The Spirit, who is none other than God himself, is given to us as grace, awakens in us love for God. Luther took over the basic

structure of this Augustinian thought but filled it out differently. Faith
as the effect of the Holy Spirit appears in Luther instead of love." Cf.
Margerie, *The Christian Trinity in History*, p.202: "The Spirit of prayer (Cf.
Rom. 8:26) draws us to Christ in faith, the Spirit of grace places us in the
reality of Christ as his instruments in the works of love." See also *LW* 25,
296; *WA* 46, 308-309 (Rom. 5:5).

127   See "The Large Catechism", in *The Book of Concord*, p.419.

128   See "Gospel Sermon, Pentecost Sunday", in *Luther's Church Postil:
        Pentecost or Missionary Sermons*, ed. John Nicholas Lenker (Minneapolis:
        Lutherans in All Lands Co., 1907), vol, 12 p. 279, no: 16.

129   The "Large Catechism", p.415; See also Elert, *The Structure of
        Lutheranism*, pp. 72-73; Thomas McDonough, *The Law and the Gospel. A
        Study of Martin Luther's Confessional Writings* (Oxford Uni. Press, 1963),
        pp. 120ff.

130   "The Large Catechism", p. 415. Cf. "Confession Concerning Christ's
        Supper", in *LW* 37, 366: "... the Holy Spirit ... teaches us to understand
        this deed of Christ which has been manifested to us, helps us receive and
        preserve it, use it to our advantage and impart it to others, increase and
        extend it...."

131   Prenter, *Spiritus Creator*, p.52.

132   Margerie, *The Christian Trinity in History*, p.199.

133   See *WA* 30^1, 192 as cited in Clebsch, "Luther's Conception of God," p.39.

134   "The Large Catechism", p. 419; cf. *LW* 33, 286.

135   Margerie, *The Christian Trinity in History*, p. 203. See also Loeschen, *The
        Divine Community*, pp. 25-26; Congar, "Christology of Luther," p.397;
        Herms, *Luthers Auslegung des Dritten Artikels*, p.53.

136   See the third part of the "Confession Concerning Christ's Supper", in *LW*
        37, 365.

137   *Ibid*. Also quoted in Mühlen, "Luther II: Theologie," p.549.

138   *LW* 51, 198; *WA* 32, 28, 9-15.

139   *LW* 51, 202; *WA* 32, 18-31.

140   *LW* 51, 198; *WA* 32, 28, 22-25.

141   See Sasse, *We Confess Jesus Christ*, p.52. See also Robert Kelly, "The
        Suffering Church: A Study of Luther's *Theologia Crucis*," *Concordia
        Theological Quarterly* 50 (1986), pp. 5-8, where he mentioned of "the sev-
        enth mark of the church," as Luther calls it: suffering.

142   Carlson, "Luther and the Doctrine of the Holy Spirit," pp. 136-137. See
        LW 51, 199; *WA* 32, 28, 25-28.

143   "The Large Catechism", p. 416.

144   *Ibid.* See Herms, *Luthers Auslegung des Dritten Artikels*, p.98, where he
        quotes the third article of "The Large Catechism".

145   Herms, *Luthers Auslegung des Dritten Artikels*, pp. 97-98: "From early on
        Luther designated that transforming process of human existence, under
        the work of the Spirit through Word and sacrament, as the real transfor-
        mation of humanity to conformity with Christ, as a participation or cru-
        cifixion with Christ, or 'a mortification of the flesh'. From the aforemen-
        tioned it is now clear, how these formulations -- in totally traditional
        words—have to be understood: not as the description of an ascetic exer-
        cise of following and of imitation, which the human being seeks to
        achieve through straining his own powers and not even as the renunci-
        ation of the body." See also Prenter, *Spiritus Creator*, pp. 26ff; Loewenich,
        Luther's Theology of The Cross, pp.117ff.

146   See Tinder, "Luther's Theology of Christian Suffering," p.110.

147   See Jüngel, *The Freedom of A Christian*, p.79.

148   Tinder, "Luther's Theology of Christian Sufering," p.110. See *LW* 42, 13
        (A Meditation on Christ's Passion) as cited in Tinder, *ibid.* See also Sasse,
        We Confess Jesus Christ, p.52.

149   See *LW* 11, 318 as cited in Walter Altmann, *Luther and Liberation. A Latin
        American Perspective.*, trans. Mary M. Solberg (Minneapolis: Fortress
        Press, 1992), p.21.

150   Altmann, *Luther and Liberation*, p.21.

151   *LW* 31, 362 (The Freedom of A Christian).

152   *LW* 31, 364-365. See also "The Small Catechism," p.345, where Luther
        clearly states the purpose of all that Jesus does in freeing us, "a lost and

condemned creature," from captivity: service in "everlasting righteousness, innocence, and blessedness."

153   *LW* 37, 366.

154   Luther's Confession presupposes the theology of Nicea. See Torrance, *The Trinitarian Faith*, p.115, where the soteriological thrust of the Nicean Creed is stressed.

155   See Prenter, *Luther's Theology of The Cross*, p.18, who recognizes a trinitarian thought pattern in Luther's Theology :" God is the trinitarian God. He is the God of life, the Creator; he is the God of the world, the Savior; he is the God of faith, the Holy Spirit. This trinity as Father, in our common experience of life, as Son, in the preached word, and as the Holy Spirit, in our personal convictions, teaches us in the last analysis what these words (of Luther) mean: *Omnia bona in cruce et sub cruce abscondita sunt* ("All good things are hidden in and under the cross"). Therefore they cannot be understood anywhere else except under the cross; 'under the cross' means under the cross on which Jesus, our redeemer, bore our punishment, and under the cross which my Creator has laid upon me in my suffering and in my death."

156   See WA 39[2], 101, 24, as cited in Siggins, *Luther's Doctrine of Christ*, p.236. See also chapter three of this book.

157   See *LW* 38, 254. See also chapter three of this book.

158   *LW* 15, 308; *WA* 54, 62-63.

159   See *LW* 51, 192; *WA* 10[3], 49 (5th Sermon at Wittenberg, 1522), where Luther says Christ continues to bear our sin, that Christ is "the eternal satisfaction for our sin."

160   *LW* 42, 107; *WA* 2, 691, 18-19.

161   *LW* 12, 131-132; *WA* 45, 244-245 (Ps. 8).

162   *LW* 42, 107; *WA* 2, 691, 18-19.

163   See *LW* 12, 127, 131-132, where Luther distinguishes between Christ's being Lord over creatures from eternity on the one hand and Christ's being made Lord in time, and as such was and is therefore crowned with glory and power.

164   See Davis Perkins, "The Problem of Suffering: Atheistic Protest and

Trinitarian Response," *St. Luke Journal of Theology* 23:1 (1979): 14-32. Perkins maintains a radical distinction between God in himself or the immanent Trinity and God for us or the economic Trinity, driving a wedge between God *ad extra* and *ad intra*.

165   See *LW* 34, 218-219; Schwarzwäller, *Theologia Crucis*, p.207.

166   See Gordon Kaufmann, *Systematic Theology: A Historicist Perspective* (New York: Charles Scribner's Sons, 1968), p.101: "Thus all we can say— and this is all we need to say—is that the understanding of God given in his revelation (i.e. in the actual relationship of him in which we stand) is his true essence to us." See also Timothy Lull, "The Trinity in Recent Theological Literature," *Word & World* 2 (1982): 61-68.

167   Lienhard, *Witness to Jesus*, p.319.

168   *Ibid.*

169   *LW* 42, 13; *WA* 2, 140, 30. See also Fiddes, *The Creative Suffering of God*, pp. 121-122.

170   *LW*15, 291-292; *WA* 54, 48-49.

171   *LW* 15, 293; *WA* 54, 49-50.

172   See Section Three of this chapter, where the Holy Spirit as a common gift of the Father and the Son "eternally" (*sempiterne*) is discussed.

173   See *LW* 12, 55 (Ps. 2:8).

174   *WA* 1, 362, 18-19; Atkinson, *ibid*, pp.290-291.

175   Cf. Bauckham, " 'Only the Suffering God can Help'," pp. 7-8; Fiddes, *The Creative Suffering of God*, pp. 121-122.

176   *LW* 22, 495.

177   *LW* 22, 355.

178   *LW* 42, 107; *WA* 2, 691 (Preparing to Die).

179   *LW* 42, 13; *WA* 2, 140, 30 (Meditation on Christ's Passion).

180   *LW* 22, 255.

181 See *LW* 37, 366. See also *LW* 51, 46 (Sermon on the Raising of Lazarus, John 11:1-45, 1518) where Luther ascribed "goodness" (or love) to the person of the Holy Spirit: "For to the Father is ascribed power, to the Son, wisdom, and to the Holy Spirit, goodness, which we can never attain and of which we must despair." This pattern of ascription is recognized by Loeschen in his *The Divine Community*, pp. 24ff.

182 Fortmann, *The Triune God*, pp. 143-146.

183 See Augustine, *De trinitate*, 15, 17, 27 as cited in David Coffey, "The Holy Spirit as the Mutual Love of the Father and the Son," *Theological Studies* 51 (1990), p.199.

184 See Augustine, *De trinitate*, 15, 19, 37 as cited in Janesn, *Studien zu Luthers Trinitätslehre*, p.122.

185 See Coffey, "The Holy Spirit as the Mutual Love," p.199.

186 Ibid., p.200. Luther stood in the Augustinian-Western tradition, as Jansen notes, when he designated the Holy Spirit as Person and as Grace eternally. See his *Studien zu Luthers Trinitätslehre*, p.123.

187 *LW* 37, 366 (Confession on the Last Supper). Cf. *LW* 23, 273 (John, 1538): the Holy Spirit came forth not as one born but as one "given"—that is, the Spirit is the bond of the Father and the Son, their common gift. Augustine's view of the Holy Spirit is also assumed by Luther in his exposition of John's Gospel (Cf. John 7:37-39).

188 Cf. "The Large Catechism", p. 419, where Luther's interpretation of the Trinity in soteriological terms as revelatory of God's love is confessed.

189 Here Luther differs radically from modern theologians, especially Karl Rahner and Jürgen Moltmann who tend to collapse the distinction between the immanent Trinity and economic Trinity. This, according to Molnar's observation, compromises God's freedom. For a criticism of Rahner and Moltmann, see Molnar, "The Function of the Trinity in Moltmann's Ecological Doctrine of Creation," *Theological Studies* 51 (1990), pp.673ff.

Conclusion

1 Jüngel, "The Christian Understanding of Suffering," p.10.

Bibliography

Primary Sources: Martin Luther

D. Martin Luthers Werke: *Kritische Gesamtausgabe.* 100 vols. Weimar: Herman Böhlaus Nachfolger, 1883-.

D. Martin Luthers Werke. Kritische Gesamtausgabe. Briefwechsel. 11 vols. Weimar: Hermann Böhlau Nachfolger, 1906-61.

D. Martin Luthers Werke. Kritische Gesamtausgabe. Tischreden. Weimar: Hermann Böhlau Nachfolger, 1912-21.

Luther's Works. 55 vols. Edited by Jaroslav Pelikan and Helmut T. Lehmann. St. Louis: Concordia Publishing House; Philadelphia: Fortress Press, 1955-.

Early Theological Writings in *The Library of Christian Classics.* Vol. 16. Translated and edited by James Atkinson. Philadelphia: Westminster Press, 1962.

Lectures on Romans in *The Library of Christian Classics.* Vol. 15. Translated by Wilhelm Pauck. Philadelphia: Westminster Press, 1961.

Letters of Spiritual Counsel in *The Library of Christian Classics.* Vol. 18. Edited by Theodore G. Tappert. Philadelphia: Westminster Press, 1955.

Luther and Erasmus on Free Will in *The Library of Christian Classics.* Vol. 17. Edited by E.G. Rupp. Philadelphia: Westminster Press, 1969.

The Bondage of the Will. Translated by J.I. Packer and O.R. Johnson. London: Clarke, 1957.

Commentary on Genesis. 2 vols. Translated and edited by J. Theodore Mueller. Grand Rapids: Zondervan Publishing House, 1968.

Luther's Church Postil. 2 vols. Translated and edited by J. Theodore Mueller. Grand Rapids: Zondervan Publishing House, 1968.

Sermons on The Passion of Christ. Translated from German. Rock Island: Lutheran Augustana Book Concern, 1871.

Secondary Sources

Althaus, Paul. *The Theology of Martin Luther.* Translated by Robert C. Schultz. Philadelphia: Fortress Press, 1966.

Aquinas, Thomas. *Summa Theologica.* 2 volumes. Translated by Father of the English Dominican Province and revised by Daniel J. Sullivan. New York: Encyclopedia Britannica, Inc., 1952.

Atmann, Walter. *Luther and Liberation. A Latin American Perspective.* Translated by Mary M. Solberg. Minneapolis: Fortress Press, 1992.

Atkinson, James. *Martin Luther and the Birth of Protestantism.* Atlanta: John Knox Press, 1968.

Augustine, Saint. *The Trinity.* Translated by Stephen McKenna. Washington: The Catholic University of America Press, 1963.

Augustine, Saint. *The City of God.* Translated by Marcus Dods. New York: Random House, 1950.

Aulen, Gustaf. *Christus Victor.* Translated by A.G. Herbert. New York: The MacMillan Co., 1969.

Bägglund, Bengt. *The Background of Luther's Doctrine of Justification in Late Medieval Theology.* Philadelphia: Fortress Press, 1971.

Bainton, Roland. *Here I Stand: A Life of Martin Luther.* New York: Mentor Book, 1950.

Barth, Karl. *Church Dogmatics.* Edited by G.W. Bromiley and translated by T.E. Torrance. Vol. 1-4. Edinburgh: T. & T. Clark, 1962-75.

Bertram, Robert. "Luther on the Unique Mediatorship of Christ," in *The One Mediator, The Saints, and Mary. Lutherans and Catholics in Dialogue VIII.* Edited by H. George Anderson, J. Francis Stafford and Joseph A. Burgess. Minneapolis: Augsburg Publishing House, 1992.

Bettenson, Henry, ed. *Documents of the Christian Church.* London: Oxford University Press, 1981.

Boehmer, Heinrich. *Luther in the Light of Recent Research.* New York: The Christian Herald, 1916.

Boehner, Paul, ed. and trans. *Summa Totius Logicae* in *Ockham: Philosophical Writings*: London: Thomas Nelson & Sons, 1957.

Bornkamm, Heinrich. *Luther's World of Thought.* Translated by Martin H. Bertram. St. Louis: Concordia Publishing House, 1958.

Bornkamm, Heinrich. *Luther and the Old Testament.* Translated by Eric W. and Ruth C. Gritsch. Philadelphia: Fortress Press, 1969.

Braaten, Carl. E. and Jenson, Robert W., eds. *Christian Dogmatics.* 2 vols. Philadelphia: Fortress Press, 1984.

Braaten, Carl E. *Shadow of the Cross.* Toronto: Regis College, 1984.

Braaten, Carl E., ed. *Our Naming of God. Problems and Prospects of God-Talk Today.* Minneapolis: Fortress Press, 1989.

Brasnett, Bertrand R. *The Suffering of the Impassible God.* London: S.P.C.K., 1928.

Brosché, Fredrik. *Luther on Predestination.* Sweden: Uppsala University, 1978.

Brunner, Emil. *The Christian Doctrine of God.* Translated by Olive Wyon. London: Lutterworth Press, 1949.

Brunner, Frederick Dale and Hordern, William. *The Holy Spirit - Shy Member of the Trinity.* Minneapolis: Augsburg Publishing House, 1984.

Büehler, Paul. *Die Anfechtungen bei Martin Luther.* Zürich: Zwingli Verlag, 1942.

Calvin, John. *Institutes of the Christian Religion.* 2 vols. in *The Library of the Christian Classic,* vol.20. Edited by J.T. McNeill and translated by F.L. Battles. Philadelphia: Westminster Press, 1960.

Cameron, Nigel M. de S., ed. *The Power and Weakness of God: Impassibility and Orthodoxy.* Edinburgh: Rutherford House Books, 1990.

Carlson, Edgar M. *Reinterpretation of Luther.* Philadelphia: Westminster Press, 1948.

Chemnitz, Martin. *The Two Natures in Christ.* Translated by J.A.O.

Preus. Saint Louis: Concordia Publishing House, 1971.

Cone, James. *A Black Theology of Liberation*. Philadelphia: J.B. Lippincott, 1970.

Congar, Yves, "Considerations and Reflections on the Christology of Luther," in *Dialogue Between Christians*. London: Geoffrey Chapman, 1966.

Cousar, Charles B. *A Theology of the Cross: The Death of Jesus in the Pauline Letters*. Minneapolis: Fortress Press, 1990.

Creel, Richard E. *Divine Impassibility: An Essay in Philosophical Theology*. Cambridge: University Press, 1986.

Cross, F. L. and Livingstone, E.A., eds. *The Oxford Dictionary of the Christian Church*, 2nd ed. London: Oxford University Press, 1974.

Cuncliffe-Jones, Hubert, ed. *A History of Christian Doctrine*. Philadelphia: Fortress Press, 1978.

Dillenberger, John. *God Hidden and Revealed: The Reinterpretation of Luther's Deus Absconditus for Religious Thought*. Mühlenberg Press: Philadelphia, 1953.

Dillenberger, John, ed. *Martin Luther: Selection from His Writings*. New York: Doubleday & Co., Inc., 1961.

Dinsmore, Charles Allen. *Atonement in Literature and Life*. Boston and London: Houghton, Mifflin, 1906.

Dorner, J. A. *History of the Development of the Doctrine of the Person of Christ*. Vol. 2. Edinburgh: T. & T. Clark, 1839.

Douglas, J.D., ed. *The New International Dictionary of the Christian Church*. Grand Rapids: Zondervan Publishing House, 1978.

Ebeling, Gerhard. *Luther: An Introduction to His Thought*. Translated by R.A. Wilson. London: Collins, 1970.

Egan, John P. "God-forsaken: The Crucified Christ or Suffering Humanity? Current Evaluation of Jürgen Moltmann's and Gregory Nazianzen's Comments on the Crucified Christ's Cry of Abandonment," in *Tradition and Innovation*. Edited by Jos. B. Gavin. Regis: Campion College Press, 1983.

Elert, Werner. *The Structure of Lutheranism*. Vol. 1. Translated by Walter A. Hansen. St. Louis: Concordia Publishing House, 1962.

Erickson, Millard J. *Christian Theology*. Vol. 2. Grand Rapids: Baker Book House, 1984.

Fairweather, Eugene R., ed. *A Scholastic Miscellany: Anselm to Ockham*. New York: The MacMillan, Co., 1970.

Fiddes, Paul. *The Creative Suffering of God*. Oxford: Oxford University Press, 1988.

Forde, Gerhard O. *Theology is for Proclamation*. Minneapolis: Fortress Press, 1990.

Forde, Gerhard O. *Where God Meets Man: Luther's Down-to-Earth Approach to the Gospel*. Minneapolis: Augsburg Publishing House, 1972.

Fortman, Edmund J. *The Triune God: A Historical Study of the Doctrine of the Trinity*. Phildelphia: Westminster Press, 1972.

Frank, R.S., "Passibility and Impassibility," in *Encyclopaedia of Religion and Ethics* 9. Edited by James Hastings. New York: Charles Scribner's Sons, 1928.

Fretheim, Terence E. *The Suffering of God: An Old Testament Perspective.* Philadelphia: Fortress Press, 1984.

Freitag, Walter, ed. *Festschrift: A Tribute to Dr. William Hordern.* Saskatoon: University of Saskatchewan Press, 1985.

George, Timothy. *Theology of the Reformers.* Nashville: Broadman Press, 1988.

Gerrish, Brian. *Grace and Reason: A Study in The Theology of Luther.* Chicago: University Press, 1979.

Gonzàlez, Justo L. *A History of Christian Thought.* 3 vols. Nashville: Abingdon Press, 1970-1975.

Grant, Robert M. *The Early Christian Doctrine of God.* Charlottesville: University Press of Virginia, 1966.

Grillmeier, Aloys. *Christ in Christian Tradition.* Vol. 1. Atlanta: John Knox Press, 1975.

Gritsch, Eric W. *Martin - God's Court Jester.* Philadelphia: Fortress Press, 1983.

Hagen, Kenneth. *A Theology of Testament in the Young Luther. The Lectures on Hebrews.* Leiden: E. J. Brill, 1974.

Hägglund, Bengt. *The Background of Luther's Doctrine of Justification in Late Medieval Theology.* Philadelphia: Fortress Press, 1971.

Hall, Douglas John. *God and Human Suffering. An Exercise in the Theology of the Cross.* Minneapolis: Augsburg Publishing House, 1986.

Hall, Douglas John. *Lighten Our Darkness: Toward An Indigenous Theology of the Cross.* Philadelphia: Westminster Press, 1976.

Hallman, Joseph M. *The Descent of God: Divine Suffering in History and Theology.* Minneapolis: Fortress Press, 1991.

Harran, M. J. *Luther on Conversion: The Early Years.* London: Cornell University Press, 1983.

Hartshorne, Charles, and Reese, William L. *Philosophers Speak of God.* Chicago: University of Chicago Press, 1953.

Hatch, Edwin. *The Influence of Greek Ideas and Usages Upon the Christian Church.* Edited by A.M. Fairbairn. London: William and Norgate, 1892.

Herms, Eilert. *Luthers Auslegung des Dritten Artikels.* Tübingen: J. C. B. Mohr, 1987.

Heschel, Abraham J. *The Prophets.* New York: Harper and Row, 1962.

Hippolytus of Rome. *Contra Noetum.* Edited by and translated by Robert Butterworth, S.J. London: Heythrop Monograph, 1977.

Hordern, William. *Experience and Faith. The Significance of Luther for Understanding Today's Experiential Religion.* Minneapolis: Augsburg Publishing House, 1983.

Hovland, C. Warren. "*Anfechtung* in Luther's Biblical Exegesis," in *Reformation Studies. Essays in Honor of Roland H. Bainton.* Edited by Franklin H. Littell, pp.46-60. Richmond: Virginia: John Knox Press, 1962.

Hügel, Baron von. *Essays and Addresses on the Philosophy of Religion, Series II.* London: J.M. Dent & Sons, 1926.

Iserloh, Erwin. "Luther und die Mystik," in *Kirche, Mystik, Heiligung und das Natürliche bei Luther.* Göttingen: Asheim, 1967.

Jaggar, William Leslie. *The Possibility of God as Atonement Motif in the Theology of Martin Luther.* PhD dissertation, Southwestern Baptist Theological Seminary, 1989.

Jansen, Reiner. *Studien zu Luthers Trinitätslehre.* Frankfurt: Peter Lang, 1976.

Jenson, Robert W. *The Triune Identity.* Phildelphia: Fortress Press, 1982.

Jenson, Robert W. *The Unbaptized God. The Basic Flaw in Ecumenical Theology.* Minneapolis: Fortress Press, 1992.

Johnson, Elizabeth A. *She Who Is: The Mystery of God in Feminist Theological Discourse.* New York: The Crossroad Publishing Co., 1992.

Jüngel, Eberhard. *"Quae supra nos, nihil ad nos,"* in *Entsprechungen: Gott-Wahrheit-Mensch.* München: Kaiser, 1980.

Jüngel, Eberhard. *God as the Mystery of the World. On the Foundation of the Theology of the Crucified One in the Dispute between Theism and Atheism.* Translated by Darrel L. Guder. Grand Rapids, Michigan: William E. Eerdmans, 1977.

Jüngel, Eberhard. *The Doctrine of the Trinity: God's Being is in Becoming.* Translated by H. Harris. Edinburgh: Scottish Academic Press, 1976.

Jüngel, Eberhard. *The Freedom of A Christian.* Minneapolis: Augsburg Publishing House, 1988.

Kadai, Heino O. ed. *Accents in Luther's Theology.* St. Louis: Concordia Publishing House, 1967.

Kasper, Walter. *Jesus the Christ.* Translated by V. Green. London: Routledge & Kegan Paul, 1979.

Kaufmann, Gordon. *Systematic Theology: A Historicist Perspective.* New York: Charles Scribner's Sons, 1968.

Kelly, John N.D. *Early Christian Doctrines.* London: Harper & Row, 1968.

Kitamori, Kazoh. *Theology of the Pain of God.* Translated by Shinkyo Suppanskha. Richmond, Virginia: John Knox Press, 1965.

Kittelson, James M. *Luther the Reformer.* The *Story of the Man and His Career.* Minneapolis: Augsburg Publishing House, 1986.

Knight, George A.F. *Theology as Narration: A Commentary on the Book of Exodus.* Grand Rapids: William B. Eerdmans, 1976.

Knight, Harold. *The Hebrew Prophetic Consciousness.* London: Lutterworth Press, 1947.

Knowles, David. *The Evolution of Medieval Thought.* New York: Vintage Books, 1962.

Köstlin, Julius. *The Theology of Luther in its Historical Development and Inner Harmony.* 2 vols. Translated by Charles E. Hay. Philadelphia: Lutheran Publication Society, 1897.

LaCugna, Catherine Mowry. *God For Us. The Trinity and Christian Life.* San Francisco: Harper & Row, 1991.

Lage, Dietmar. *Martin Luther's Christology and Ethics.* Queenston: The Edwin Mellen Press, 1990.

Lee, Jung Young. *God Suffers for Us: A Systematic Inquiry into a Concept of Divine Passibility.* The Hague: Martinus Nihhoff, 1974.

Leff, Gordon. *Gregory of Rimini: Tradition and Innovation in Fourteenth Century Thought.* Manchester: Manchester University Press, 1961.

Liderbach, Daniel. *Martin Luther's Theology of Suffering in Modern Translation: A comparative study in the Roots of Dietrich Bonhoeffer's Theology of Suffering.* PhD dissertation, University of St. Michael's College, 1979.

Lienhard, Marc. *Luther: Witness to Jesus Christ.* Translated by J.A. Bouman. Minneapolis: Augsburg Publishing House, 1982.

Lindberg, Carter. *The Third Reformation? Charismatic Movements and the Lutheran Tradition.* Georgia: Mercer University Press, 1983.

Lindberg, Carter, "The Mask of God and Prince of Lies: Luther's Theology of the Demonic," in *Disguises of the Demonic.* Edited by Alan M. Olson. New York: Association Press, 1975.

Loeschen, John R. *Wrestling with Luther: An Introduction to the Study of his Thought.* St. Louis: Concordia Publishing House, 1976.

Loeschen, John R. *The Divine Community. Trinity, Church and Ethics in Reformation Theologies.* Missouri: Northeast Missouri State University, 1981.

Loewenich, Walter von. *Luther's Theology of the Cross.* Translated by Herbert Bouman. Augsburg Publishing House, 1982.

Loewenich, Walther von. *Martin Luther. The Man and His Work.* Translated by Lawrence W. Denef. Minneapolis: Augsburg Publishing House, 1982.

Lohse, Bernhard. *Martin Luther: An Introduction to His Life and His*

Thought. Translated by Robert C. Schultz. Philadelphia: Fortress Press, 1986.

Lortz, Joseph. *The Reformation in Germany.* 2 vols. Translated by Ronald Walls. New York: Herder & Herder, 1968.

Luce, A.A. *Monophysitism Past and Present: A Study in Christology.* New York: The MacMillan Company, 1920.

MacDonald, H.D. *The Atonement of the Death of Christ.* Grand Rapids, Michigan: Baker Book House, 1985.

MacKinnon, James. *Luther and the Reformation.* 4 vols. New York: Russell & Russell, 1962.

Margerie, Bertrand de. *The Christian Trinity in History.* Translated by Edmund J. Fortman. Studies in Historical Theology, vol. 1. Still River, Mass.: St. Bede's Publications, 1982.

McDonough, Thomas M. *The Law and the Gospel. A Study of Martin Luther's Confessional Writings.* Oxford: Oxford University Press, 1963.

McGrath, Alister. *The Intellectual Origins of the European Reformation.* Oxford: Basil Blackwell, 1987.

McGrath, Alister. *Luther's Theology of the Cross.* Oxford: Basil Blackwell, Inc., 1985.

McLelland, Joseph C. *God the Anonymous: A Study in Alexandrian Theology.* Patristic Monograph Series, No.4. Massachusetts: The Philadelphia Patristic Foundation, Ltd., 1976.

McSorley, Harry J. *Luther: Right or Wrong: An Ecumenical-Theological Study of Luther's Major Work. "The Bondage of the Will."* New York: Newman Press, 1969.

McWilliams, Warren. *The Passion of God: Divine Suffering in Contemporary Theology*. Atlanta: Mercer University Press, 1985.

Melanchthon, Philip and Bucer, Martin. *Library of Christian Classics*, Vol. 19. Edited by Wilhelm Pauck. Philadelphia: Westminster Press, 1969.

Meyer, Carl S. ed. *Luther for an Ecumenical Age*. St. Louis: Concordia Publishing House, 1967.

Migne, J. P., ed. *Patrologia Graeca*. 162 vols. Paris, 1857-1866.

Migne, J. P., ed. *Patrologia Latina*. 221 vols. Paris, 1844-1864.

Mildenberger, Friedrich. *Theology of the Lutheran Confessions*. Translated by Erwin L. Lueker. Edited by Robert C. Schultz. Philadelphia: Fortress Press, 1986.

Moltmann Jürgen. *The Future of Creation*. Translated by Margaret Kohl. Philadelphia: Fortress, 1979.

Moltmann Jürgen. *The Trinity and the Kingdom of God: The Doctrine of God*, Translated by Margaret Kohl. London: SCM Press, 1981.

Moltmann, Jürgen. *The Crucified God: The Cross of Christ as the Foundation and Criticism of Christian Theology*. Translated by Margaret Kohl. New York: Harper & Row, 1977.

Mozley, J.K. *The Impassibility of God: A Survey of Christian Thought*. Cambridge: University Press, 1926.

Mühlen, Karl-Heinz zur. "*Luther II. Theologie*," in *Theologische Realenzyklopädie* Vol. 21:530-561. Edited by Leonardo da vine-Malachias von Armagh. Berlin: Walter de Gruyter, 1991.

Nagel, Norman E. "Martinus: Heresy, Doctor Luther, Heresy! The Person and Work of Christ," in *Seven-Headed Luther, Essays in Commemoration of a Quincentenary 1483-1983*. Edited by Peter Newman Brooks. Oxford: Clarendon Press, 1983.

Norris, R.A. *The Christological Controversy*. Philadelphia: Fortress Press, 1980.

Nygren, Anders. *Agape and Eros*. Translated by P.S. Watson. Chicago: University Press, 1953.

Oberman, Heiko A. *Forerunners of the Reformation*. Philadelphia: Fortress Press, 1981.

Oberman, Heiko A. *The Harvest of Medieval Theology. Gabriel Biel and Late Medieval Nominalism*. Grand Rapids: William B. Eerdmans Publishing Co., 1967.

Oberman, Heiko A., ed. *Luther and the Dawn of the Modern Era*. Leiden: E. J. Brill, 1974.

Oberman, Heiko A. *Luther. Man Between God and the Devil*. Translated by Eileen Walliser-Schwarzbart. New Haven: Yale University Press, 1989.

Ockham, William. *Summa Logicae*. St. Bonaventure, New York: The Franciscan Institute, 1957.

Ozment, Steven E., ed. *The Reformation in Medieval Perspective*. Chicago: Quadrangle Books, 1971.

Pannenberg, Wolfhart. *Basic Questions in Theology*. Vol. 2. Translated by G.H. Kehm. London: SCM Press, 1971.

Pannenberg, Wolfhart. *Systematic Theology*. Vol.1. Translated by Geoffrey Bromiley. Grand Rapids, Michigan: William B. Eerdmans, 1991.

Park, Andrew Sung. *The Wounded Heart of God. The Asian Concept of Han and the Christian Doctrine of Sin.* Nashville: Abingdon Press, 1993.

Pelikan, Jaroslav. *The Christian Tradition: A History of the Development of Doctrine.* Vols. 1, 4. Chicago: University Press, 1971-84.

Pelikan, Jaroslav. *Luther the Expositor. Introduction to the Reformer's Exegetical Writings.* Luther's Works, companion volume. St. Louis: Concordia Publishing House, 1958.

Peters, Albrecht. "Vergorgener Gott-Dreieiniger Gott. Beobachtungen Und Überlegungen Zum Gottes-Verständnis Martin Luthers," in *Martin Luther Reformator 'und Vater im Glauben',* ed. Peter Manns. Stuttgart: Franz Steiner Verlag Wiesbaden GMBH, 1985.

Peters, Ted. *God as Trinity. Relationality and Temporality in Divine Life.* Louisville: Westminster/John Knox Press, 1993.

Peters, Ted. *God - the World's Future. Systematic Theology for a Postmodern Era.* Minneapolis: Fortress Press, 1992.

Prenter, Regin. *Spiritus Creator.* Translated by John M. Jensen. Philadelphia: Mühlenberg Press, 1953.

Prenter, Regin. *Luther's Theology of the Cross.* Philadelphia: Fortress Press, 1971.

Prestige, Leslie. *God in Patristic Thought.* London: S.P.C.K., 1952.

Preus, James. *From Shadow to Promise: Old Testament Interpretation from Augustine to the Young Luther.* Cambridge: Harvard University Press, 1969.

Quick, Oliver C. *Doctrines of the Creed.* Digswell Place: James Nisbet & Co., Ltd., 1938.

Rahner, Karl. *The Trinity.* New York: Herder & Herder, 1970.

Rahner, Karl. "Why Does God Allow Us to Suffer? in *Theological Investigations* XIX. New York: Crossroads Publishing House, 1983.

Randles, Marshall. *The Blessed God. Impassibility.* London: MacMillan Co., 1900.

Rawlinson, A.E.J., ed. *Essays on the Trinity and the Incarnation.* London: Longmans and Green, 1928.

Relton, H.M. *Studies in Christian Doctrine.* London: MacMillan, 1960.

Richard, Lucien. *What Are They Saying About the Theology of Suffering?* New York: Paulist Press, 1992.

Richardson, Cyril C., ed. *Early Christian Fathers,* in *The Library of Christian Classics,* Vol.1. Philadelphia: Westminster Press, 1953.

Robbins, Jerry K. ed. *The Essential Luther. A Reader On Scripture, Redemption, and Society.* Michigan: Baker Book House, 1991.

Robinson, H. Wheeler. *Suffering Human and Divine.* London: SCM Press, 1952.

Rogers, Jack and McKim, Donald. *The Authority and Interpretation of the Bible.* New York: Harper & Row, 1979.

Reu, M. *Luther's German Bible.* Columbus: The Lutheran Book Concern, 1934.

Rupp, E. Gordon. *The Righteousness of God: Luther Studies.* New York: Philosophical Library, 1953.

Rupp, E. Gordon. *Luther's Progress to the Diet of Worms.* New York: Harper & Row, 1964.

Rusch, William G, trans. & ed. *The Trinitarian Controversy.* Phildelphia: Fortress Press, 1980.

Saarnivaara, Uuras. *Luther Discovers the Gospel.* St. Louis: Concordia Publishing House, 1951.

Sasse, Hermann. *We Confess Jesus Christ.* Translated by Norman Nagel. St. Louis: Concordia Pubilshing House, 1984.

Sayers, Dorothy L. *"The Shattering Dogmas of the Christian Tradition,"* in *Christian Letters to a Post-Christian World.* Grand Rapids: William B. Eerdmans, 1969.

Schaff, Philip, ed. *The Nicene and Post-Nicene Fathers of the Christian Church.* Fourteen Volumes. Grand Rapids: William B. Eerdmans, 1980.

Schilling, Paul S. *God and Human Anguish.* Nashville: Abingdon Press, 1977.

Schleiermacher, Friedrich. *The Christian Faith.* Edited by H.R. Mackintosh and J.S. Stewart. Philadelphia: Fortress Press, 1976.

Schwarzwäller, Klaus. *Theologia Crucis: Luther Lehre von Prädestination nach De servo arbitrio, 1525.* München: Chr. Kaiser Verlag, 1970.

Siggins, Ian D. *Martin Luther's Doctrine of Christ.* New Haven: Yale University Press, 1970.

Siirala, Aarne. *Divine Humanness.* Translated by T.A. Kantonen. Philadelphia: Fortress Press, 1970.

Sittler, Joseph. *The Doctrine of the Word in the Structure of Lutheranism.* Philadelphia: Fortress Press, 1948.

Sölle, Dorothee. *Suffering.* Translated by E.R. Kalin. London: Darton, Longman & Todd, 1975.

Sölle, Dorothee. *Christ the Representative:* An Essay in Theology after the 'Death of God'. Translated by D. Lewis. London: SCM Press, 1967.

Song, Choan Seng. *Third-eye Theology: Theology in Formation in Asian Settings.* New York: Orbis Books, 1979.

Steinmetz, David C. *Luther and Staupitz, An Essay in the Intellectual Origins of the Protestant Reformation,* Duke Monographs in Medieval and Renaissance Studies 4. Durham: Duke University Press, 1980.

Steinmetz, David C. *Luther in Context.* Bloomington: Indiana University Press, 1986.

Steinmetz, David C. *Misericordia Dei: The Theology of Johannes von Stuapitz in Its Late Medieval Setting,* Studies in Medieval and Reformation, Vol. 4. Edited by H. Oberman. Leiden: E.J. Brill, 1968.

Stevens, G. B. *The Christian Doctrine of Salvation.* Edinburgh: T. & T. Clark, 1905.

Stevenson, J., ed. *Creeds, Councils and Controversies.* London: SPCK, 1966.

Surin, Kenneth. *Theology and the Problem of Evil.* Oxford: Basil Blackwell, 1986.

Tappert, Theodore, trans. & ed. *The Book of Concord: The Confessions of Evangelical Lutheran Church.* Philadelphia:

Fortress press, 1959.

Terry, David Jonathan. *Martin Luther on the Suffering of the Christian.* PhD dissertation, Boston University, 1990.

Tertullian, Quintus Septimus Florens. *Against Praxeas.* Translated by A. Souter. London: The MacMillan Company, 1920.

Torrance, Thomas A. *The Trinitarian Faith: The Evangelical Theology of the Ancient Catholic Church.* Edinburgh: T. & T. Clark, 1988.

Trinkhaus, Charles and Oberman, Heiko A., eds. *The Pursuit of Holiness in Late Medieval and Renaissance Religion.* Papers from the University of Michigan Conference, Vol. X. Studies in Medieval and Reformation Thought. Leiden: E. J. Brill, 1974.

Turner, H. E. W. *The Patristic Doctrine of Redemption.* London: Mowbray, 1952.

Vogel, Heinrich J. Vogel's *Cross Reference and Index to the Contents of Luther's Works. A Cross Reference between the American Edition and St. Louis, Weimar and Erlangen Editions of Luther's Works.* Milwaukee: Northwestern Publishing House, 1983.

Watson, Philip. *Let God Be God: An Interpretation of the Theology of Martin Luther.* Philadelphia: Mühlenberg Press, 1948.

Weber, Hans-Ruedi. *The Cross: Tradition and Interpretation.* Translated by Elke Jessette. Grand Rapids: William B. Eerdmans, 1975.

Weber, Otto. *Foundations of Dogmatics.* 2 Vols. Translated by Darrell L. Gruder. Grand Rapids: William B. Eerdmans, 1981.

Weinandy, Thomas G. *Does God Change? The Word's Becoming in the Incarnation.* Still River, Massachusetts: St. Bede's

Publications, 1985.

Welch, Claude. *In This Name: The Doctrine of the Trinity in Contemporary Theology.* New York: Charles Scribner's Sons, 1952.

Westermann, Claus. *Elements of Old Testament Theology.* Translated by Douglas W. Stott. Atlanta: John Knox, 1982.

White, Douglas. *Forgiveness and Suffering: A Study of Christian Belief.* Cambridge: Cambridge University Press, 1913.

Wicks, Jared, ed. *Man Yearning for Grace: Luther's Early Spiritual Teaching.* Cleveland, Ohio: Corpus Books, 1968.

Wicks, Jared, ed. *Catholic Scholars Dialogue with Luther.* Chicago: Loyola University Press, 1970.

Wiles, Maurice. *The Christian Fathers.* London: Hodder & Stoughton, 1966.

Williams, Daniel Day. *The Spirit and the Forms of Love.* Library of Constructive Theology. James Nisbet, Welwyn, 1968.

Williams, Rowan. *Christian Spirituality: A Theological History from the New Testament to Luther and St. John of the Cross.* Atlanta: John Knox Press, 1980.

Willis, David E. *Calvin's Catholic Christology. The Function of the So-called Extra Calvinisticum in Calvin's Theology.* Leiden: E. J. Brill, 1966.

Willis, W. Waite, Jr. *Theism, Atheism and the Doctrine of the Trinity,* in American Academic Religion Academic Series no. 53. Edited by Carl A. Raschke. Atlanta: Scholars Press, 1987.

Wolfson, Harry A. *The Philosophy of the Church Fathers,* vol. 1, *Faith,*

Trinity and the Incarnation. Cambridge, Ma.: Harvard University Press, 1964.

Wood, A. Skevington. *Captive to the Word.* Grand Rapids: William B. Eerdmans, 1969.

Young, Frances. "God Suffered and Died," in *Incarnation and Myth: The Debate Continued.* Edited by M. Goulder. London: SCM Press, 1979.

Young, Frances. *Sacrifice and the Death of Christ.* London: SPCK., 1975.

Periodical Literature

Anderson, Charles. "Will the Real Luther Please Stand Up?" *Dialog* 6 (Aug., 1967): 254.

Attfield, D.G. "Can God Be Crucified? A Discussion of Jürgen Moltmann." *Scottish Journal of Theology* 30 (1977): 47-57.

Bauckham, Richard. "'Only the Suffering of God can Help': Divine Passibility in Modern Theology." *Themelios* 9 (April, 1984): 6-12.

Beglke, M. Vernon. "Luther's *Anfechtungen*: An Important Clue to his Pastoral Theology." *Consensus* 9:3 (1983): 3-17

Bertram, Robert. "Again on the Trinity: Bertram Responds." *Dialog* 29 (1990): 60-61.

Bertram, Robert. "When is God Triune?" *Dialog* 27 (1988): 133.

Braaten, Carl. "A Trinitarian Theology of the Cross." *Journal of Religion* LVI:I (Jan., 1976): 113-121.

Braaten, Carl E. "Let's Talk about the 'Death of God'." *Dialog* 26 (1987): 209-214.

Brown, Colin. "Trinity and Incarnation: In Search of Contemporary Orthodoxy." *Ex Auditu* 7 (1991): 82-104.

Burnley, Edward. "The Impassibility of God." *The Expository Times* 67 (1955/56): 90-91.

Carlson, Arnold E. "Luther and the Doctrine of the Holy Spirit." *Lutheran Quarterly* 11 (May, 1959): 135-146.

Clebscii, William A. "Luther's Conception of God." *Anglican Theological Review* 37 (1955): 25-41.

Coffey, David. "The Holy Spirit as the Mutual Love of the Father and the Son." *Theological Studies* 51 (1990): 193-229.

Dodds, Michael. "Aquinas, Human Suffering and the Unchanging God of Love." *Theological Studies* 52 (1991): 330-344.

Ebeling, Gerhard. "The New Hermaneutics and the Early Luther." *Theology Today* 21.1 (1964): 34-46.

Eckardt, Burnell F. "Luther and Moltmann: The Theology of the Cross." *Concordia Theological Quarterly* 49 (January, 1985): 19-28.

Edwards, R.B. "The Pagan Doctrine of the Absolute Unchangeableness of God." *Religious Studies* 14 (1978): 305-313.

Elert, Werner. "Die Theopaschite Formel." *Theologische Literaturzeitung* 75 (1950): 195-206.

Ellingsen, Mark. "Luther as a Narrative Exegete." *Journal of Religion* 63 (1983): 394-413.

Forde, Gerhard O. "Caught in the Act: Reflections on the Work of Christ." *Word and World* 3:1 (1983): 22-31.

Fretheim, Terence E. "The Repentance of God. A Key to Evaluating God-Talk." *Horizons in Biblical Theology* 10 (1988): 47-70.

Gerrish, B.A. " 'To the Unknown God': Luther and Calvin on the Hiddenness of God." *Journal of Religion* 53 (1973): 263-292.

Goetz, Ronald. "The Suffering of God: The Rise of a New Orthodoxy." *The Christian Century* 103:13 (April, 1986): 385-389.

Grant, Colin. "Possiblities for Divine Passibility." *Toronto Journal of Theology* 4 (1988): 3-18.

Green, Lowell C. "Luther on Revelation: Foundation for Proclamation and Worship." *Consensus* 9:3 (1983): 3-11.

Grislis, Egil. "Martin Luther's View of the Hidden God." *McCormick* Quarterly 21 (1967-68): 81-94.

Grislis, Egil. "Luther's Understanding of the Wrath of God." *Journal of Religion* 41 (1961): 277-292.

Gunton, Colin. "Augustine, Trinity and the Theological Crisis of the West." *Scottish Journal of Theology* 44 (1991): 33-58.

Hagen, Kenneth. "The Testament of a Worm: Luther on Testament and Covenant." *Consensus* 8:1 (1982): 12-20.

Hagen, Kenneth. "Changes in the Understanding of Luther: The Development of the Young Luther." *Theological Studies* 29:3 (1968): 472-496.

Haight, Roger. "The Point of Trinitarian Theology." *Toronto Journal of Theology* 4 (1988): 191-204.

Hinlicky, Paul R. "Some Questions to Bertram on the Trinity."

Dialog 28 (1989): 307-308.

House, Francis H. "The Barrier of Impassibility." *Theology* 83 (1980): 409-15.

Hunsinger, George. "The Crucified God and the Political Theology of Violence: A Critical Survey of Jürgen Moltmann's Recent Thought." *Heythrop Thought* XXIV (1973): 266-279(part I); 379-395(part II).

Irish, Jerry A. "Theology of Contradiction." *Theology Today* 32 (1975): 21-31.

Jüngel, Eberhard. "The relationship between 'economic' and 'immanent' Trinity." *Theology Digest* 24 (1976): 179-184.

Jüngel, Eberhard. "The Christian Understanding of Suffering." *Journal of Theology for Southern Africa* 65 (1988): 3-13.

Kelly, Robert A. "The Suffering Church: A Study of Luther's *Theologia Crucis.*" *Concordia Theological Quarterly* 50 (Jan., 1986): 3-17.

König, Adrio. "The Idea of the 'The crucified God': Some Systematic Questions." *Journal of Theology for Southern Africa* 39 (1982): 55-61.

Kuramatsu, Isao. "Die gegenwärtige Kreuzestheologie und Luther, besonders in Rüecksiche auf die theologie des Schmerzes Gottes von Kazo Kitamori." *Kerygma and Dogma* 36 (1990): 273-283.

Kuyper, Lester J. "The Repentance of God." *The Reformed Review* 18 (Dec., 1964): 3-16.

Kuyper, Lester J. "The Suffering and the Repentance of God." *Scottish Journal of Theology* 22 (Sept., 1969): 3-16.

Lehman, Helmut T. "Luther on the Study of Luther." *Word and*

World 3 (Fall, 1983): 398-404.

Loeschen, John. "Promise and Necessity in Luther's *De Servo arbitrio.*" *The Lutheran Quarterly* 23 (1971): 257-267.

Lotz, David W. "The Proclamation of the Word in Luther's Thought." *Word and World* 3:4 (1983): 344-354.

Lull, Timothy F. "God and Suffering: A Fragment." *Dialog* 25:2 (1986): 9396.

Lull, Timothy F. "The Trinity in Recent Theological Literature." *Word and World* 2 (1982): 61-68.

Luz, Ulrich. "Theologia crucis als Mitte der Theologie im Neuen Testament." *Evangelische Theologie* 34 (1974): 116-141.

McCabe, Herbert. "The Involvement of God." *New Blackfriads* 66 (1985): 464-476.

McGrath, Alister. "The Anti-Pelagian Structure of 'Nominalist' Doctrine of Justification." *Ephemerides Theologicae Lovanienses* 57 (1981): 107-119.

McGuckin, J.A. "The 'Theopaschite Confession(Text and Historical Context)': A Study in the Cyrilline Reinterpretation of Chalcedon." *Journal of Ecclesiastical History* 35:2 (April, 1984): 239-255.

McWilliams, Warren. "The Passion of God and Moltmann's Christology." *Encounter* XL (Fall, 1979): 313-326.

Molnar, Paul D. "The Function of the Trinity in Moltmann's Ecological Doctrine of Creation." *Theological Studies* 51 (1990): 673-697.

Muller, Richard A. "Incarnation, Immutability and the case for Classical Theism." *Westminster Theological Journal* 45 (1983): 22-40.

Neuhaus, John Richard. "Moltmann vs. Monotheism." *Dialog* 20 (Fall, 1982): 239-343.

Oberman, Heiko A. "Notes on the Theology of Nominalism." *Harvard Theological Review* 53 (1976): 47-76.

Orlinsky, H.M. "The Treatment of Anthropomorphisms and Anthropopathism in the Septuagint of Isaiah." *Hebrew Union College Annual* 27 (1956): 193-200.

Pannenberg, Wolfhart. "A Theology of the Cross." *Word and World* 8:2 (1988): 162-172.

Pederson, Ann. "A Question to Bertram and Luther on the Trinity." *Dialog* 28 (1989): 308-309.

Perkins, Davis. "The Problem of Suffering: Atheistic Protest and Trinitarian Response." *St. Luke Journal of Theology* 23:1 (1979): 14-32.

Peters, Ted. "Trinity Talk: Part I." *Dialog* 26 (1987): 44-48.

Peters, Ted. "Trinity Talk: Part II." *Dialog* 26 (1987): 133-138.

Pfitzner, Victor C. "Luther as Interpreter of John's Gospel with special reference to his Sermons on the Gospel of John." *Lutheran Theological Journal* 18 (1984): 65-73.

Pless, John T. "Martin Luther: Preacher of the Cross." *Concordia Theological Quarterly* 51 (1987): 83-101.

Pollard, T.E. "The Impassibility of God." *Scottish Journal of Theology* 8 (Dec., 1955): 353-364.

Russell, John M. "Impassibility and Pathos in Barth's Idea of God." *Anglican Theological Review* LXX:3 (1988): 221-233.

Sarot, Marcel. "Auschwitz, Morality and the Suffering of God." *Modern Theology* 7:2 (1991): 135-152.

Sarot, Marcel. "Patripassianism, Theopaschitism and the Suffering of God: Some Systematic and Historical Considerations." *Religious Studies* 26 (1990): 363-375.

Sasse, Hermann. "Theologia Crucis." *Lutheran Theological Journal* 11 (1968): 115-127.

Scaer, David R. "The Concept of *Anfechtung* in Luther's Thought." *Concordia Theological Quarterly* 47 (Jan., 1983): 15-30.

Schwarz, Hans. Review of *The Crucified God*. *The Lutheran Quarterly* 27 (May, 1975): 183-186.

Shofner, Robert. "Luther on '*The Bondage of the Will*': An Analytical-Critical Essay." *Scottish Journal of Theology* 26 (1973): 24-39.

Snook, Lee E. "A Primer on the Trinity: Keeping our Theology Christian." *Word & World* 2:1 (1982): 5-16.

Streeter, B.H. "The Suffering of God." *The Hibbert Journal* (April, 1914): 603-611.

Strelan, John G. "*Theologia Crucis, Theologia Gloriae*: A Study in Opposing Theologies." *Lutheran Theological Journal* 23 (1989): 99-113.

Surin, Kenneth. "The Impassibility of God and the Problem of Evil." *Scottish Journal of Theology* 35 (1982): 97-115.

Thomas, Terry. "Luther's Canon: Christ Against Scripture." *Word and World* 8:2 (1988): 141-149.

Thompson, John. "Modern Trinitarian Perspectives." *Scottish Journal of Theology* 44 (1991): 349-365.

Tinder, Galen. "Luther's Theology of Christian Suffering And Its Implications for Pastoral Care." *Dialog* 25:2 (1986): 108-113.

Towns, E.L. "Martin Luther on Sanctification." *Bibliotheca Sacra* CXXVI (April-June, 1969): 115-122.

Vercruysse, Joseph E. "Luther's Theology of the Cross at the time of *Heidelberg Disputation.*" *Gregorianum* 57 (1976): 523-548.

Visser, 'T Hooft, W.A. "Triumphalism in the Gospels." *Scottish Journal of Theology* 28 (1985): 491-501.

Vogelsang, Eric. "Luther und die Mystik." *Luther-Jahrbuch* XIX (1937): 32-54.

Watson, Philip. "How Luther Speaks of God." *Dialog* 6 (Aug., 1967): 279.

Watson, Philip. "Luther and Sanctification." *Concordia Theological Monthly* 30 (April, 1959): 243-259.

Wells, Harold. "The Holy Spirit and Theology of the Cross: Significance for Dialogue." *Theological Studies* 53:3 (1992): 476-492.

White, Graham. "Luther's View on Language." *Literature and Theology* 3 (1989): 188-218.

Wilch, John R. "Luther as Interpreter: Christ and the Old Testament." *Consensus* 9:4 (1983): 11-20.

Williams, Daniel Day. "The Vulnerable and the Invulnerable God." *Christianity and Crisis* 22:3 (Mar. 5, 1962): 27-30.

Wondra, Gerald. "The Pathos of God." *The Reformed Review* 18 (Dec., 1964): 28-35.

Woollcombe, Kenneth J. "The Pain of God." *Scottish Journal of Theology* 20 (June, 1967): 129-148.

Wunderlich, Lorenz. "The Holy Spirit and the Christian Life."

Concordia Theological Monthly XXVII (Oct., 1956): 753-764.

Zimany, Roland. "Views and Counterviews: Moltmann's *The Crucified God.*" *Dialog* 15 (Winter, 1977): 49-56.

Index

Index of Names

Index of Subjects